Annotated Teacher's Edition

Be A Better Reader

Level C/Seventh Edition

Contents

Copyright © 1997 by Globe Fearon Educational Publisher, a division of Simon & Schuster, One Lake Street, Upper Saddle River, New Jersey 07458. All rights reserved. No part of this book may be reproduced or transmitted in any form or by any means electrical or mechanical, including photocopying, recording, or by any information storage and retrieval system, without permission in writing from the publisher.

Permission is given for individual classroom teachers to reproduce pages AT1-AT16 for classroom use. Reproduction of these materials for an entire school system is strictly forbidden.

Printed in the United States of America

   6 7 8 9 10   00 01

ISBN 0-8359-1925-0

C12

Globe Fearon Educational Publishers
A Division of Simon & Schuster
Upper Saddle River, New Jersey

Be A Better Reader

By Nila Banton Smith

NEW! *The Seventh Edition of Nila Banton Smith's Classic Program*

■ Teaches the reading, comprehension, and study skills that students in grades 4-12 need

■ Applies these skills to the content areas:
- Literature
- Social Studies
- Science
- Mathematics

■ **Lessons always begin with instruction** so that students learn successfully (and independently) before they apply a skill.

■ **Focuses on one important skill in each Lesson** so that students concentrate on a skill and master it—independently.

- **Reading, comprehension, and study skills include:**

  literal comprehension

  interpretive and inferential comprehension

  critical and creative reading

  main idea

  cause and effect

  fact and opinion

  sequencing

  details

  literary concepts (such as plot and theme)

  following directions

  graphic and pictorial aids

  locating information

  reading symbols

  previewing

  outlining

  classifying

  problem solving

  reading rate

  and much more

- **Student independence** Instruction is in the student's book, so that students work and learn *independently*.

- **Each unit follows the same structure** so that students know what to expect and can work independently:

  A Lesson with a literature selection

  A Lesson with a social studies selection

  A Lesson with a science selection

  A Lesson with a mathematics selection

  Several brief "worksheet" Lessons that reinforce important phonics (in levels A–C), comprehension, and study skills

- **Vocabulary Instruction** Students learn vocabulary words *before* they read. Students also learn to use different types of *context clues* to increase vocabulary power: definitions, synonyms, antonyms, appositives, details, comparisons and contrasts, examples, and similes.

- **Easy to manage in your classroom** Use with individual students, small groups, or the entire class. *Be A Better Reader* is used successfully with students working below level, on level, and above level. (Level A— grade 4 reading level, Level B—grade 5, and so on to Level F—grade 9.)

- **Lessons may be used in any order** Correlate Lessons to your curriculum. Use them for reinforcement of specific skills or as a complete program.

- **Each Lesson ends with a Real Life Connection** that applies what students have learned to their own lives, communities, or interests.

- **Each unit ends with a brief Lesson on a practical life or school-to-work skill,** such as how to fill out a job application and order form; how to read a bus schedule, floor plan, map, and help wanted ads; and how to follow directions.

- **Assessment tests are free** in the *Annotated Teacher's Edition* (Level A—F).

First, a sample

Be A Better Reader

Lesson with

Instruction first on one comprehension or study skill, then on vocabulary

A content area reading selection

Written comprehension activities

A written activity on the Lesson skill

(See Level A, Lesson 44)

Sample Lessons

Lessons begin with instruction.

Lesson 44

1 Primary Source

___ Reading a Social Studies Selection _____

2 ▶ Background Information

The Nez Percé lived in the plateau country, an area that is now where the states of Washington, Oregon, and Idaho meet. The Nez Percé originally called themselves Nee Me Poo, which means "the Real People." French-Canadian fur trappers called them Nez Percé and the people adopted the name, pronouncing it *nez purse.*

The most famous chief of the Nez Percé was Chief Joseph, whose Indian name was Thunder Traveling to Loftier Mountain Heights. Joseph was 31 years old when he became chief after the death of his father.

In this lesson, you will read about Chief Joseph. You will also read the stirring speech that he delivered to President Hayes in Washington, D.C.

3 ▶ Skill Focus

Using a **primary source** will help you learn about past events. A primary source is a firsthand account. It is usually written by a person who took part in the event being described. Primary sources give facts about events. They also give insight into the thoughts and feelings of the

people in the events. Letters, speeches, and newspaper articles, are primary sources.

Often textbooks, magazines, encyclopedias, and so on, will contain excerpts, or pieces, of primary source materials. These excerpts are usually set apart in some way from the rest of the text.

When reading a primary source, use the following two steps.

1. **Find out all you can about the primary source.** Ask yourself the following questions.
   a. What type of document is it? Is it a letter, a report, an article, or a speech?
   b. Who wrote it? Was the author part of the event?
   c. When was it written?

2. **Study the primary source to learn about a past event.** Try to distinguish facts from opinions. A fact can be proven. An opinion is a judgment that reflects a person's feelings or beliefs.
   a. What facts can I learn from this document?
   b. What was the author's opinion about what was reported?

4 ▶ Word Clues

Read the sentences below. Look for context clues that explain the underlined word.

> As the early <u>settlers</u> moved west, they came into conflict with the Indians who lived there. The settlers had left their homes to find new land. They wanted land for farming and for raising cattle.

If you do not know the word *settlers* in the first sentence, read the next two sentences. They give details about the settlers. The details tell more about the word so that you understand it.

Use **detail** context clues to find the meaning of the three underlined words in the selection.

5 ▶ Strategy Tip

As you read Chief Joseph's words, keep in mind the two steps for using a primary source. Reading this speech will give you insight into the thoughts and feelings of Chief Joseph and his people.

Lesson 44 *Using a primary source* **123**

1
Lessons and skills are easy to find—Lessons are numbered and give the skill in the title.

2
Background Information—provides students with important content, cultural, and historical information and tells students what the selection is about.

3
Skill Focus—Instruction comes first—so that students are successful later.

4
Word Clues—Vocabulary instruction—before students read and need help.

5
Strategy Tip—gives students background and reminds them to use the Lesson skill.

A Great and Honorable Leader

The Gold Rush

The Nez Percé lived peacefully in their country for hundreds of years. They had experienced good relations with the white trappers and explorers. But in 1860, white prospectors illegally entered Nez Percé territory and found gold. During the gold rush, thousands of miners settled on Nez Percé reservation lands, disobeying an earlier treaty. For the first time, friction developed between whites and the Nez Percé.

In 1863, under pressure from the gold miners to remove the Nez Percé from valuable mineral sources, the U.S. government demanded that the Nez Percé cede, or give up, about 6 million acres of reservation land. The majority of Nez Percé refused. A government commissioner bribed several chiefs who sold the land and signed the treaty. The government official reported to the U.S. government that he had secured all lands demanded "at a cost not exceeding 8 cents per acre."

As a result of the land sale, the Nez Percé divided into "treaty" and "nontreaty" bands. Among those who were angry about the selling of Indian land was Tuekakas, also known as Old Joseph. By 1871, thousands of settlers had moved onto reservation land, as was allowed by the new treaty. Near his death, Old Joseph spoke to his son Young Joseph about their homeland:

> *My son, my body is returning to my mother earth, and my spirit is going very soon to see the Great Spirit Chief. When I am gone, think of your country. You are the chief of these people. They look to you to guide them. Always remember that your father never sold his country. You must stop your ears whenever you are asked to sign a treaty selling your home.*
>
> *. . . My son, never forget my dying words. This country holds your father's body. Never sell the bones of your father and your mother.*

Chief of Peace

Upon his father's death, Joseph became the civil, or peace, chief of his father's band. Joseph held many councils, or meetings, with civil and military officials. In 1873, Joseph convinced the government that it had not legally secured title to the reservation lands. The government ordered the whites to move out of the territory. However, the government then reversed its decision under pressure from Oregon politicians and settlers.

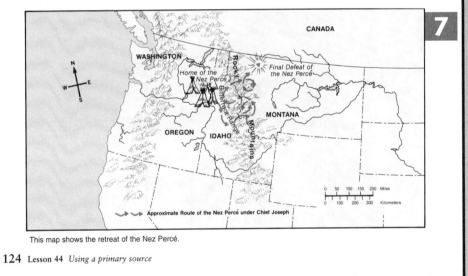

This map shows the retreat of the Nez Percé.

124 Lesson 44 *Using a primary source*

6

Primary Sources—In social studies selections, primary source materials aid comprehension, as well as provide valuable first-hand accounts of events and people.

7

Illustrations, photos, and captions increase interest and aid comprehension.

Understanding the dilemma of the U.S. government, Joseph continued to strive for a peaceful solution to the land problem. In 1877, General Oliver O. Howard concluded that the only solution was to force all the Nez Percé off their land and onto a reservation in Washington.

Many of the "nontreaty" Nez Percé wanted to fight for their land. Chief Joseph didn't want to fight. He knew that fighting would only bring death and sadness to his people. Joseph believed that he had no other choice but to lead his people to the reservation. So in the spring of 1877, Joseph agreed to the demands of the U.S. government. Several other nontreaty bands joined Joseph's for one last gathering on their land. While there, several men decided to seek revenge on white settlers for the death of one's father and for other grievances. They killed four white settlers.

8 Knowing that General Howard would send troops after them, the bands withdrew to Whitebird Canyon. Thus began a remarkable <u>retreat</u>, in which the Nez Percé fought, alluded, and outwitted one military force after another for four months. With about 750 people, including sick and elderly people, women, and children, the Nez Percé circled over a thousand miles trying to reach safety in Canada.

The soldiers who fought Chief Joseph thought that he was a great and honorable man. The soldiers knew that the Nez Percé never killed without reason. They could have burned and destroyed the property of many settlers, but they did not. Joseph and his people fought only to defend themselves and their land. The white soldiers were also impressed with their ability to allude the army for so many months and over so many miles.

"I Will Fight No More, Forever"
But the end finally came. Unaware that the army under Colonel Nelson A. Miles was in close <u>pursuit</u>, the Nez Percé camped less than 40 miles south of the Canadian border. At the end of a five-day siege, Chief Joseph decided to <u>surrender</u> to Miles on October 5, 1877. He rode into the army camp alone and handed his rifle to the soldiers. He said:

I am tired of fighting. My people ask me for food and I have none to give. It is cold and we have no blankets, no wood. My people are starving. . . . Hear me, my chiefs. I have fought, but from where the sun now stands, Joseph will fight no more, forever.

After Joseph's surrender, the U.S. government ordered them onto a reservation in Kansas, then to a disease-ridden reservation in Oklahoma. Many of the Nez Percé died of malaria and other sicknesses.

Chief Joseph pleaded on behalf of his people to gain permission to return to a reservation in the Northwest. In 1879, Chief Joseph traveled to Washington to plead his case to President Hayes.

Chief Joseph's Speech
If the white man wants to live in peace with the Indian, he can live in peace. There need be no trouble. Treat all men alike. Give them the same laws. Give them all an even chance to live and grow.

All men are made by the same Great Spirit Chief. They are all brothers. The earth is the mother of all people, and all people should have equal rights upon it. You might as well expect all rivers to run backward as that any man born a free man should be contented penned up and denied liberty to go where he pleases. If you tie a horse to a stake, do you expect he will grow fat? If you pen an Indian

Chief Joseph of the Nez Percé Indians.

...wars. We shall all be alike—brothers of ...ther and mother, with one sky above us ...one country around us and one ...ment for all. Then the Great Spirit ...who rules above will smile upon this ...and send rain to wash out the bloody ...made by brothers' hands upon the face ...earth. For this time, the Indian race are ...g and praying. I hope no more groans ...unded men and women will ever go to ...r of the Great Spirit Chief above, and ...ll people may be one people.

...1885, after eight years of campaigning ...half of his people, Joseph and the other ...Percé were allowed to return to the ...west. Unable to join the treaty bands on ...aho reservation, Joseph and the others ...escorted to the Colville Reservation in ...ngton Territory. It was there that ...died in 1904, reportedly from a ...heart.

...ACTS

...ring and contrasting
9 ...y did the soldiers think that Chief ...eph was a great leader?
...ople never killed without a reason, did not burn

...roy the property of settlers, and fought only to

...themselves and their land.

...g details
10 ...er living on a reservation, where did ...ief Joseph say he wanted to take his ...ople? Why?
...oseph wanted to take his people to Canada,

...hey would not have to live on a reservation.

...ontext clues
11 ...te the letter of the correct meaning in ...t of each word.

...retreat   a. following in
                order to capture

...pursuit   b. to give up

...surrender c. to go to a safe place

8

Word clues—Unfamiliar words are defined using context clues, such as synonyms, appositive phrases, comparisons, and details, to aid reading and comprehension.

9

After reading, students complete written activities.

10

Recalling Facts—checks students' literal comprehension of the selection. (In the *Annotated Teacher's Edition*, each question has a skill label and answer for the teacher's benefit.)

11

Vocabulary Skills—The last item in "Recalling Facts" is a vocabulary check.

T6

The lesson ends with a skills check.

12

Identifying point of view

1. For each pair of sentences, circle t[...]
   Joseph's thoughts and opinions in [...]

   (a.) The white man can live in peace [...]
   same law.

   b. Because so many promises have [...]
   man and the Indian.

   a. There will be no more wars wh[...]
   (b.) There will be no more wars wh[...]

Drawing conclusions

2. Decide whether Chief Joseph is a g[...]
   must look carefully at Chief Josep[...]
   are listed in order below. For each [...]

   a. Chief Joseph first agrees to lead [...]
   He knows that the small number of Nez Pe[...]

   b. Chief Joseph decides to lead his [...]
   He wants to escape the army's punishmen[...]
   put on reservations.

   c. Chief Joseph will fight the army [...]
   He knows that the battle will end only in de[...]

   d. Chief Joseph leads his people o[...]
   He is trying to avoid battle and being captu[...]

   e. During this time, Chief Joseph t[...]
   He knows that the skills of his warriors will [...]

   f. Chief Joseph says that he will "f[...]
   reservation.
   The army has trapped them. His people hav[...]
   They must either surrender or die.

   g. Two years later, Chief Joseph sp[...]
   even though he led his people th[...]
   He believes that taking away a people's fre[...]
   live "penned up." Yet, he has given his word[...]

Now answer this question: Do you think that Chief Joseph was a great and honorable leader? In your answer, first tell what you mean by the words *great* and by *honorable*. Then tell why you think Chief Joseph was or was not a great and honorable leader.

Conclusions will vary, but all answers should include the following: (a) Student's definition of *great* and *honorable* and

(b) student's conclusion about Chief Joseph should be consistent with their definitions of *great* and *honorable* and

should cite facts in the selection and speech that led to the conclusion.

13

Reread Chief Joseph's speech. Pay special attention to what it tells you about Chief Joseph's feelings and motives. Then answer the questions below.

1. *Find out all you can about the primary source.*

   What type of document is this? __a speech__

   Who wrote it? __Chief Joseph__

   Was the author involved in the event? __yes__

   When was it written? __1879__

2. *Study the primary source to learn about a past event.*

   What facts can you learn from this document? Indian lands were being overrun by white men; many Indians were dying and being treated as outlaws.

   What was the author's opinion about what was reported? Chief Joseph believed that the Indians and white men could live in peace if all were subject to the same laws. He thought that his people would prosper if they could be moved back to the Pacific Northwest (Oregon).

 Real Life Connections Write an interesting fact or story about the history of your community. List your primary sources.

14

128 Lesson 44 *Using a primary source*

12

Interpreting Facts—checks students' comprehension on *inferential* and *critical* levels.

13

Skill Focus—checks students' understanding of the Lesson skill. In the "Skill Focus" at the beginning of the Lesson, students learned about the Lesson skill. Now students

complete a written activity that applies the skill to the reading selection.

14

Real Life Connections— asks students to apply what they have read or learned to their own lives, communities, or interests.

Lesson 40

Main Idea and Suppo...

Many times in reading, you will l...
details. Details give more informati...
supporting details because they sup...

Below is a paragraph about how the brakes ...
the supporting details are listed.

Braking a car is an interesting process. ...
most cars, a liquid called brake fluid begi...
the steps that stop the moving automobil...
When the brakes are not being used, the flu...
rests in the master cylinder and the brak...

Main Idea Braking a car is an interesti...
Supporting Details

a. In most cars, a liquid called brake flui...
automobile.
b. When the brakes are not being used, t...
tubes.
c. When the driver steps on the brake pe...
d. The brake shoe presses against the bra...
e. Each wheel has its own braking system...

On the next page, write the main idea and th...

1. In the United States, almost everyone...
life is linked to the auto industry. Most peopl...
depend on a car, bus, or truck fo...
transportation. More than 12 million peopl...
earn their living in some part of the ca...
industry by building, shipping, servicing, ...
selling cars, buses, or trucks. These peopl...
account for about one tenth of the labor forc...
In fact, there are 500,000 automobile-relat...
businesses in the United States.

2. Several steps go into designing a ne...
car model. Automobile designers crea...
hundreds of sketches on computers. Final idea...
for the new model come from these sketche...
Then a full-sized clay model is made. Furthe...
improvements are made in the design. ...
fiberglass model is made. Finally, when eve...
part has been approved, blueprints of the ca...
are drawn so that the car can be cut out of ste...
and built.

3. Most of the early automobile builder...
were mechanics or knew about machine...

112 Lesson 40 *Identifying the main idea and supporti...*

Lesson 42

Comparing Car Ads

If you are interested in buying a new car, reading ads in newspapers and magazines should start you in the right direction. The details in ads can help you decide what kind of car will suit your needs and your budget. After you decide on the best car for your needs, you shop around for the best price.

Carefully read the following ads to compare the two cars.

PASHUBI: WE DESIGNED OUR CAR FOR ▪ *YOU* ▪ *THE* DRIVER

At Pashubi, we think you are very important. So we created the 630-X, a fully equipped luxury sports car. The 630-X surrounds the driver with more window than other sports cars. The 630-X has a steering wheel and instrument panel that can be moved up or down.

The roomy bucket seats can be easily moved and can tilt back as far as you like. And the large storage area in back lifts up to become two additional seats.

There are 30 standard equipment features, including power disc brakes, power windows, electrically heated outside rearview mirror, two-tone paint, and CD player.

At $20,025, the 630-X offers more than other imported cars. And you'll save on gas—an exceptional 43 EST HWY MPG, 28 EST MPG. Use MPG for comparison. Mileage may differ depending on conditions. Highway mileage may be less.

The 630-X. By Pashubi. It's *not* for everyone—but it is for *you*.

TILTON:
The American way to get more for your money.

You get more for your money with our cars. Take the Star, for example. This compact car uses 3,000 computer-assisted robot welds, more than any other car. This helps to create an easy-to-maintain car which will give you more for your money for years to come.

The Star gives you more for your money because it's sensibly priced. It starts as low as

$16,999*. The Star gives you more for your money with front-wheel drive. With the engine pulling in front and rack-and-pinion steering, you get the real feel of the road.

The six-passenger Star gives you more for your money with comfort.

And the Star gives you more for your money when you study the mileage figures:

41 EST HWY, 26 EST MPG.+

The Star's standard equipment includes power disc brakes, CD player, and 5-speed transmission (3-speed automatic is extra). Among the other extras are two-tone paint, luggage rack, leather steering wheel, power windows, and more.

Last year's Star was the best-selling compact car. See the Star today—and learn how to get more for your money the American way.

* $19,698 as shown in photograph

+ Use EST MPG for comparison. Mileage may vary depending on speed, trip length, and weather. Actual highway mileage lower.

116 Lesson 42 *Comparing car ads*

15
Each brief Lesson focuses on one important skill and begins with instruction.

16
Students benefit from skills practice and reinforcement without full-length reading selections. (In Levels A, B, and C, phonic skills are reviewed in the Lessons.)

17
The last Lesson in each unit is on a practical skill—such as reading a bus schedule, filling out a job application, or following directions.

(See Level A, Lessons 40 and 42)

Basic Reading Skills

Whether students are reading a story for pleasure, skimming newspapers or magazines for information, or studying a chapter in a textbook, they need the following basic reading skills.

Word Recognition: the ability to recognize words.

Comprehension: the ability to derive stated and implied meanings from printed symbols.

Reading Rate: the ability to adjust reading rate to content and purpose.

Study Skills: the ability to apply what is already understood in a new context.

Word Recognition

In *Be A Better Reader*, specific skills instruction in word recognition is designed to provide students with a variety of word attack strategies needed to read an unfamiliar word.

Phonetic Analysis: recognizing and identifying the sounds of consonants, consonant blends, and digraphs; recognizing and identifying vowel sounds and their variant spellings.

Structural Analysis: recognition of root words, prefixes and suffixes, compound words, multisyllabic words, accent marks, and syllabication.

Context Clues: determining word meaning from a particular context clue.

Respellings, Footnotes, and Other Word Helps: using vocabulary aids typical of content-area textbooks.

Comprehension

Reading comprehension is a process that begins with word recognition, but does not end until students have derived meaning from the ideas both stated and implied in the text and have been able to evaluate these ideas. In *Be A Better Reader*, each lesson focuses on a specific reading skill that helps students recognize and understand a text pattern that is typical of a content area, as well as a variety of other reading materials that students encounter in their daily lives.

Literal Comprehension

Literal questions are included to help students process information that is stated explicitly in the text. These questions require students to recall from memory or to select from the text specific answers; in other words, to reproduce what has been stated in the text.

The literal comprehension activities and questions in the Understanding Facts and Skill Focus activities sections require students to do the following.

1. Identify stated main idea
2. Identify stated main idea and details
3. Recall details
4. Identify stated cause and effect
5. Recognize sequence of events
6. Recognize fact and opinion
7. Recognize elements of a short story (plot, character, setting, theme, etc.)
8. Recognize variety of literary types or genres (fiction, play, nonfiction, biography, primary sources, etc.)

Inferential and Critical Comprehension

Numerous activities and questions are included to encourage students to probe for deeper meanings that are implied but not explicitly stated in the text. These questions require students to think about the meanings that can be derived from their reading, not just reproduce what the text has stated. Inferential and critical comprehension begins with literal meanings, but advances to higher-level thinking and reasoning skills that require students to go beyond the printed symbol.

The inferential and critical comprehension questions in the Interpreting Facts and Skill Focus activities sections require students to do the following.

1. Infer unstated main idea
2. Infer cause and effect
3. Infer details
4. Infer conclusions
5. Infer comparisons and contrasts
6. Distinguish fact from opinion
7. Infer information about elements of a short story (plot, character, setting, theme, etc.)
8. Draw conclusions and make generalizations
9. Evaluate validity of ideas
10. Predict outcomes

Reading Rate

Studies indicate that students are ready for a variety of reading rates by the latter part of fifth grade or by sixth grade. Students who have acquired reading skills through reading fiction only need to learn that there are different rates at which they should read different content. Practice in adjusting reading rate is introduced in Level C of *Be A Better Reader*. Emphasis is placed on adjusting the rate of reading to the content and the purpose of the material.

Study Skills

An analysis of questions, exercises, explanations, visuals, and directions in the various content area textbooks reveals that certain basic study skills are called for again and again in all subject areas. Most of these skills involve using comprehension skills to study and understand information in the content area. As students work with materials in literature, social studies, science, and mathematics, *Be A Better Reader* provides instruction and practice in the following study skills.

Selecting and Evaluating Information: the ability to select items from context and evaluate them in terms of conditions or specifications.

Organizing Information: the ability to put together or organize similar ideas.

Locating Information: the ability to find information in reference books and periodicals.

Reading Visuals: the ability to understand information presented in visuals, such as diagrams, maps, and graphs.

Following Directions: the ability to follow a specific sequence of steps.

Previewing: the ability to use previewing skills to understand the meaning and organization of a selection before reading it.

Reading Special Materials: the ability to read materials other than classroom textbooks.

Selecting and Evaluating Information

Just as word recognition skills are basic to reading, selection and evaluation are basic to study skills. Textbooks in the content areas contain many questions and directions that call for selection and evaluation skills. The skill of selecting and evaluating information requires students to select a piece of information and judge its worth in meeting the specifications of an activity or question. The answers to most literal comprehension questions need only to be selected from the text. However, inferential questions require students to go beyond the selection process to evaluation, the highest level of critical comprehension. In *Be A Better Reader*, lessons on fact and opinion, primary sources, and propaganda teach students selection and evaluation skills.

Organizing Information

The skill of organizing information is important because of the frequency with which students must apply it in studying textbooks, listening in class, and writing papers and tests. This skill provides opportunity for applying comprehension of content to a different format. Organizing information calls for putting together systematically items or ideas that belong to a whole. *Be A Better Reader* includes lessons on the procedures most often used in organizing information: (1) classifying items that belong to one group or that occur in a certain order; (2) outlining to show the relationship among ideas; (3) summarizing important ideas.

Locating Information

The skill of locating information includes activities that range from using a table of contents and an index to using a dictionary, an encyclopedia, and the library database system. Skill in locating information begins with recognizing alphabetical order and advances to finding information in complex reference books. In *Be A Better Reader*, lessons on locational skills are self-contained and include representative examples of typical dictionary and encyclopedia entries, indexes, and tables of contents.

Reading Visuals

Most content-area textbooks require students to read a variety of visuals, such as maps, timelines, diagrams, and graphs. Throughout *Be A Better Reader*, in all content areas, students are taught how to extract specific information from visuals and how to compress textual information into a brief visual presentation.

Following Directions

Reading to follow directions is a fundamental skill needed in studying all content areas. In *Be A Better Reader*, students are given directions for carrying out the activities that follow the reading selections. Thus, in addition to specific lessons in following directions, students acquire abundant experience in reading and following directions throughout each level of the program.

Previewing

Previewing a selection is another organizational skill. Previewing results in an organized "picture" or understanding of the structure of the selection. In *Be A Better Reader*, students learn to preview a selection by noting headings of sections, main ideas, and visuals.

Reading Special Materials

Students must be able to read special materials that they encounter outside the classroom. The last lesson in each unit of *Be A Better Reader* provides specific directions on how to read the yellow pages, a recipe, a floor plan, a travel brochure, and so on. Practice with these materials helps students make the transition from relatively controlled classroom reading situations to everyday reading situations.

Reading research has shown that different types of content require specialized reading skills. In preparing **Be A Better Reader**, textbooks in four different content areas were analyzed.

Literature

Social Studies

Science

Mathematics

Books were analyzed for text patterns, visual programs, and study aids typical of each content area. The specific skills situations that occurred most often in each content area were selected for inclusion in **Be A Better Reader**. The situations in which the skills were used were more abstract and higher levels of thinking were required in the books intended for the higher grades, but the skills situations are basically the same at all grade levels at which each subject is taught.

Literature

The literature selections in **Be A Better Reader** were carefully selected to appeal to student interest and are written at appropriate reading levels. The basic goal of the lessons with literature selections is threefold: (1) to acquaint students with various literary genres; (2) to increase students' awareness of the literary elements; and (3) to provide practice in applying comprehension skills to reading literature. A variety of genres is included in each level of **Be A Better Reader**. In the instructional section of each lesson, an important literary concept is stressed in terms appropriate to the particular level.

Each level of **Be A Better Reader** provides a lesson that develops one of the following special skills required in understanding and appreciating literature.

Recognizing plot

Recognizing character

Recognizing conflict

Recognizing setting

Recognizing theme

Plot
Most short stories have a plot, or sequence of events. They have a beginning, a middle, and an end, and events are arranged to build to a climax. As students read stories, it is important for them to keep the events in order, to notice how one event leads to the next, and to be able to identify the climax, or turning point of the story.

Character
The characters in a story are as important as the plot. Students need to be able to identify the main character, or protagonist, in a story. They should think about what motivates characters to act as they do. They should also notice how characters develop and change by contrasting how the characters behave at the beginning of a story with how they behave at the end.

Conflict
Students should be able to recognize a story's central conflict, or problem. Most stories are built around one of three common conflicts.
1. The main character is in conflict with himself or herself.
2. The main character is in a conflict with other characters.
3. The main character is in conflict with nature, society, or some outside force over which he or she may not have any control.

Setting
Setting is the time and place of the events in a story. Awareness of setting is essential to understanding the characters and their conflicts. Students must be shown how to interpret setting and its impact on the story's characters and events.

Theme
The theme, or idea, of a story is usually the most difficult concept for students to formulate by themselves. Students need to use higher-level comprehension skills to infer the author's underlying message.

Social Studies

Social studies texts have their own characteristic text patterns that require special reading skills. For example, social studies texts include frequent references to visuals, such as maps, graphs, and pictures. These references may require students to find information in a specific visual and then combine that information with information in the text.

Students need to become familiar with the text patterns typical of social studies textbooks. **Be A Better Reader** teaches some of the skills that are necessary to aid in comprehension of the patterns.

Reading visuals, such as pictures, maps, and graphs

Recognizing cause-and-effect relationships

Understanding sequence of events

Making comparisons and contrasts
Understanding detailed statements of fact
Thinking and reading critically

Visuals

Pictures in social studies textbooks are selected to depict historical concepts and events. The ability to read pictures and captions that accompany them results in students gaining information and implied meanings that go beyond the text. Reading pictures requires close attention to detail.

Reading maps and graphs is a highly specialized kind of reading skill. Map reading requires recognition and interpretation of symbols for rivers, mountains, lakes, towns and cities, boundary lines, and such features as scales of miles, color keys, and meridians. When reading graphs, students need to know how to extrapolate data and use it to make generalizations, thereby supplementing information in the text.

Cause and Effect

While the cause-and-effect text pattern occurs to some extent in most content areas, it occurs with the highest frequency in social studies, especially history. Every major event in history comes about as the result of some cause or set of causes, and when the event happens its effect or effects are felt. Sometimes the effect of one event becomes the cause of another event. Thus, the student often encounters a chain of causes and effects. Students who are adept at recognizing cause-and-effect patterns will find this to be a valuable asset in studying social studies textbooks.

Sequence of Events

Another text pattern encountered in social studies presents events in specific time sequences accompanied by dates. Students should read this pattern for two purposes: (1) to grasp the chronological order of large periods or whole blocks of events and (2) to grasp times of important happenings within each period or block—stopping long enough to associate events with dates and to think about how each event led to others.

Social studies textbooks include several kinds of visual aids designed to help students understand time relationships. These aids include charts of events and dates, chronological summaries, timelines, outline maps with dates and events, and so on. Each of these visual aids requires special reading skills.

Comparison and Contrast

A text pattern calling for the comparison of likenesses and/or contrast of differences is common in social studies textbooks. This pattern occurs most frequently in discussions of such topics as the theories of government or policies of different leaders; physical features, products, or industries of different countries; and so on. Students who recognize a comparison and contrast chapter or section of a text can approach it with the foremost purpose of noting likenesses and differences.

Detailed Statements of Fact

Much social studies text contains many details and facts. Facts, however, are usually included within one of the characteristic text patterns already discussed. The facts in social studies textbooks are not as dense as they usually are in science textbooks, nor are they as technical. Because they are often associated with sequential events or with causes and effects, they are more easily grasped.

Critical Thinking

Many social studies texts require students to interpret material critically. Students are expected to make inferences from facts, to distinguish fact from opinion, to analyze propaganda, to interpret primary sources, to draw conclusions and make generalizations, and to answer open-ended questions. Students need specific instruction and practice in these skills if they are to probe for deeper meanings and respond to higher-level questions.

Combination of Patterns

A single chapter in social studies may contain several text patterns. For example, a chapter may contain biographical material similar to the narrative pattern, a chronology of events during a certain time period, maps and charts depicting those events, and cause-and-effect relationships. If students who start to study such a chapter have not acquired the skills necessary to recognize and process each of these text patterns and instead use the same approach in reading all of them, the resulting understandings of the concepts presented will be extremely limited.

Science

Science text, like all other types of text, calls for the use of such comprehension skills as identifying main ideas and making inferences. However, an analysis of science textbooks reveals text patterns unique to science text that call for other approaches and special reading skills.

As in social studies textbooks, science texts include frequent references to such visuals as diagrams and pictures. Students need continued practice in combining text reading with visual reading in order to process all the information that is available on a science text page.

Be A Better Reader provides lessons on the following special reading skills that are needed for science textbooks.

Understanding classification

Reading an explanation of a technical process

Recognizing cause and effect relationships

Following directions for an experiment

Understanding detailed statements of fact

Recognizing descriptive problem-solving situations

Understanding abbreviations, symbols, and equations

Reading text with diagrams

Classification

The classification pattern is characteristic of science text. In this pattern, living things, objects, liquids, gases, forces, and so on are first classified in a general grouping that has one or more elements in common. This group is further classified into smaller groups, each of which varies in certain respects from every other group in the general grouping. Students who recognize the classification text pattern will concentrate on understanding the basis of the groupings and the chief characteristics of each one.

Explanation of a Technical Process

Another text pattern particularly characteristic of science is the explanation of a technical process. Explanation is usually accompanied by diagrams, necessitating very careful reading of text with continuous references to diagrams. The diagrams themselves require students to use special reading skills in addition to those needed to grasp the text explanations.

Cause and Effect

A text pattern sometimes encountered in science textbooks, but not unique to science, is the cause-and-effect pattern. In this pattern the text gives information that explains why certain things happen. In reading this type of pattern, students first read to find the causes and effects. A careful rereading is usually necessary to determine how and why the causes had the effects that they did.

Following Directions for an Experiment

This text pattern consists of explicit directions or instructions that must be carried out exactly. The common study skill of following directions is essential in reading this science pattern, but experiments also call for the mental activities of making discriminating observations, understanding complex explanations, and drawing considered conclusions.

Detailed Statements of Fact

Another pattern frequently encountered in science textbooks is detailed statements of fact. This pattern in science differs from factual text in the other content areas in two respects: (1) the facts are more dense; and (2) they frequently lead to or embody a definition or a statement of a principle.

In reading this text pattern, students can make use of the reading skill of finding the main ideas and supporting details. Students first locate the most important thought or main idea in each paragraph, then proceed to find details that reinforce the main idea— noting particularly any definitions or statements of principles.

Descriptive Problem Solving

This text pattern describes problem-solving situations by taking the reader through a series of scientific experiments conducted by one or by many people. Students should approach this pattern with the idea of finding out what each successive problem was and how it was solved.

Abbreviations, Symbols, and Equations

Another science text pattern that requires a special kind of reading makes liberal use of abbreviations, formulas, and equations. For example, grasping the meaning of the symbol $°$ (degree) and the formula $CaCO_3$ (calcium carbonate) when they are integrated with words in the text, calls for special recognition skills in addition to the usual recognition of word symbols. This pattern is still further complicated when symbols and abbreviations are involved in equations or number sentences.

Diagrams

Science textbooks usually contain many diagrams. Students need to learn how to go from the text to the diagrams and back to the text if they are to understand the meaning of scientific concepts. Reading diagrams requires an understanding of the purpose of diagrams, ability to interpret color and other visual devices used to highlight parts of a diagram, and comprehension of labels.

Combination of Patterns

As in social studies textbooks, a single chapter of a science text at the higher levels may contain several text patterns. If students who start to study such a chapter have not acquired the skills necessary to recognize and process each of these patterns and instead use the same approach in reading all of them, then the resulting understandings of the concepts presented will be extremely limited.

Mathematics

The reading skills needed for reading mathematics are sharply different from the skills needed in other content areas. Many students who read narrative with relative ease have great difficulty in reading mathematics, especially word problems and abstract mathematical symbols. The mathematics selections in *Be A Better Reader* are not included for the purpose of teaching mathematics. Their function is threefold: (1) to develop in students an awareness of the difference between reading mathematics texts and reading other texts; (2) to give students practice in reading the different types of text and symbols used in mathematics textbooks; and (3) to apply basic reading skills to mathematics text.

One of the special characteristics of mathematics text is compactness. Every word and every symbol is important. Unlike reading in other content areas, skipping an unfamiliar word or guessing its meaning from context will impair students' progress in mathematics. Students should be aware of this difference.

Another adjustment students have to make in reading mathematics is a change in basic left-to-right eye movement habits. Mathematics text often requires vertical or left-directed eye movements for rereading portions of the text for better understanding or for selecting certain numbers or symbols. While some students read mathematics more rapidly than others, text patterns in mathematics are not appropriate for speed reading.

Reading in mathematics makes heavy demands on the comprehension skills that call for interpretation, critical reading, and creative reading. Many mathematical situations call for a careful weighing of relationships. Of great importance is the ability to discover principles as a result of studying pictures and diagrams.

The inferential reading skills and the study skills of reading pictures and diagrams emphasized throughout **Be A Better Reader** should transfer to the following skills and attitudes specifically needed in working with mathematics.

Reading word problems

Reading mathematical terms, symbols, and equations

Reading graphs and other mathematical visuals

Reading explanation for processes or principles, such as fractions, decimals, and percents

Word Problems

Because problem solving is a priority in mathematics and closely related to basic reading skills, the Seventh Edition of **Be A Better Reader** includes in each level two lessons on problem solving. A five-step strategy is introduced in the first problem-solving lesson and used throughout the series. The steps in the strategy closely parallel the steps used in most mathematics textbooks. However, **Be A Better Reader** emphasizes the reading and reasoning skills necessary to solve word problems.

While the problem-solving strategy remains the same throughout the series, each succeeding lesson focuses on slightly more sophisticated problems. For example, the first problem-solving lesson focuses on problems that involve one mathematical operation. At a later level, problems are introduced in which two operations are necessary.

Terms, Symbols, and Equations

In mathematics, students must read sentences composed of word symbols and number symbols, such as equations. Recognizing and understanding symbols of various types is reading and should be taught as such in mathematics.

In reading equations, students have to recognize the meaning of the entire mathematical sentence, as well as the symbols $+$, $-$, $\times$, $\div$, and $=$. They also have to recognize and understand the symbols x and n, just as they have to learn to recognize and grasp the meaning of a new word in reading.

Students have to learn to recognize and understand the properties of geometric figures, such as the octagon, pentagon, prism, cube, cylinder, and pyramid. Parentheses, $>$, $<$, and other symbols are used frequently.

Graphs and Charts

Other distinctive text patterns in mathematics are graphs, such as bar graphs and circle graphs. While these visual aids are used in social studies, science, and other subjects, they almost always represent mathematical concepts.

To get the most information from a graph, students should: (1) read the title to determine exactly what is being compared; (2) read the numbers or labels to determine what the figures or labels stand for; (3) study the graph to compare the different items illustrated; and (4) interpret the significance of the graph as a whole. Due to the prevalence of graphs and similar mathematical visuals in most content area textbooks, most students profit from instruction in reading these types of text patterns.

Explanation

The explanation text pattern in mathematics texts is similar to the explanation text pattern in science textbooks, except that in mathematics text explanations describe a mathematical principle or process rather than a scientific process. Mathematical explanations are comparatively short and often contain symbols other than words. They are usually accompanied by or are preceded by a series of exercises or questions designed to guide students in discovering the principle or process. This text pattern calls for very careful reading and rereading until the process is understood.

Administering Level Assessment Tests

Assessment tests for Level C are designed to measure students' level of achievement in each of the important comprehension and study skills that receive emphasis in *all* levels of **Be A Better Reader**. The tests may be used as pre-tests and/or post-tests, depending on students' needs and your particular classroom management style. Combined with an overview of student performance on each lesson, the tests should enable you to refine your assessment of students' performance and determine students' readiness to advance to the next level.

The four tests in Level C can be administered separately or at one time, depending on time available. Because directions are provided for each test, students should be able to take the tests independently. However, enough time should be allowed for each student to complete the tests.

The skill for each test item is identified in the answer key below. Following the skill is the number of the lesson or the lessons in Level C where that skill is treated as a Skill Focus. To simplify the scoring process, you can use the answer key to make a scoring mask, which when placed over the answer sheet reveals only those items that are correct. The total score is equal to the number of correct items. Criterion scores are not specified, as the individual class or group situation should determine the appropriate criterion.

Answer Key and Skills Correlation

Test 1

1. c   Identifying conflict and resolution (41)
2. a   Identifying conflict and resolution (41)
3. a   Identifying conflict and resolution (41)
4. b   Identifying conflict and resolution (41)
5. a   Identifying plot (1)
6. b   Identifying plot (1)
7. a   Identifying plot (1)
8. c   Identifying plot (1)
9. a   Identifying setting (33)
10. c   Identifying setting (33)
11. a   Identifying setting (33)
12. b   Identifying setting (33)
13. a   Inferring theme (11)
14. a   Inferring theme (11)
15. b   Inferring theme (11)
16. c   Inferring theme (11)
17. c   Inferring the unstated main idea (8, 18)
18. b   Inferring the unstated main idea (8, 18)
19. b   Inferring the unstated main idea (8, 18)
20. c   Identifying point of view (48)
21. a   Identifying point of view (48)
22. b   Identifying point of view (48)
23. b   Identifying point of view (48)
24. c   Recognizing multiple meanings of words (45)
25. c   Using detail context clues (2, 12, 34)
26. b   Using synonym context clues (3, 22)

Test 2

27. b   Identifying the main idea (8, 18, 27)
28. a   Identifying the main idea (8, 18, 27)
29. a   Identifying the main idea (8, 18, 27)
30. a   Inferring the unstated main idea (8, 18)
31. c   Inferring the unstated main idea (8, 18)
32. c   Inferring the unstated main idea (8, 18)
33. b   Identifying the main idea and supporting details (27)
34. a   Identifying the main idea and supporting details (27)
35. b   Identifying cause and effect (12, 22, 35)
36. a   Identifying cause and effect (12, 22, 35)
37. c   Identifying cause and effect (12, 22, 35)
38. b   Comparing and contrasting (2)
39. b   Comparing and contrasting (2)
40. a   Comparing and contrasting (2)
41. a   Making inferences (28, 50)
42. c   Distinguishing fact from opinion (37)

43. b Making inferences (28, 50)
44. b Making inferences (28, 50)
45. c Making inferences (28, 50)
46. b Making inferences (28, 50)
47. c Making inferences (28, 50)
48. a Recognizing multiple meanings of words (45)
49. a Recognizing multiple meanings of words (45)
50. c Using detail context clues (2, 12, 34)
51. b Using synonym context clues (3, 22)
52. c Using detail context clues (2, 12, 34)
53. a Reading a map (34)
54. c Reading a map (34)
55. b Reading a map (34)
56. c Reading a map (34)

Test 3

57. a Identifying the main idea (8, 18, 27)
58. c Identifying the main idea (8, 18, 27)
59. b Identifying the main idea and supporting details (27)
60. c Identifying the main idea and supporting details (27)
61. a Identifying cause and effect (12, 22, 35)
62. a Identifying cause and effect (12, 22, 35)
63. c Identifying cause and effect (12, 22, 35)
64. b Comparing and contrasting (2)
65. b Comparing and contrasting(2)
66. c Classifying (3)
67. a Classifying (3)
68. c Classifying (3)
69. a Classifying (3)

70. b Making inferences (28, 50)
71. b Making inferences (28, 50)
72. c Recognizing multiple meanings of words (45)
73. a Recognizing multiple meanings of words (45)
74. a Using appositive context clues (13, 42)
75. b Using detail context clues (2, 12, 34)
76. c Reading text with diagrams (13)
77. c Reading text with diagrams (13)
78. b Reading text with diagrams (13)
79. a Reading text with diagrams (13)
80. b Solving word problems (23)
81. a Solving word problems (23)
82. b Solving word problems (23)
83. c Solving word problems (23)

Test 4

84. c Using a dictionary (9)
85. b Using a dictionary (9)
86. a Using a dictionary (9)
87. a Using a dictionary (9)
88. c Using a dictionary (9)
89. b Using an index (46)
90. a Using an index (46)
91. c Using an index (46)
92. c Using an index (46)
93. c Using an index (46)
94. a Using an index (46)
95. c Adding prefixes to words (17)
96. b Adding suffixes to words (29)
97. a Dividing words into syllables (24)
98. a Dividing words into syllables (24)
99. c Locating the accented syllable (25)
100. b Locating the schwa sound (26)

T16

Be A Better Reader

Level C

Seventh Edition

Nila Banton Smith

Upper Saddle River,
New Jersey

Pronunciation Key

Symbol	Key Word	Respelling
a	act	(akt)
ah	star	(stahr)
ai	dare	(dair)
aw	also	(awl soh)
ay	flavor	(flay vər)
e	end	(end)
ee	eat	(eet)
er	learn	(lern)
	sir	(ser)
	fur	(fer)
i	hit	(hit)
eye	idea	(eye dee ə)
y	like	(lyk)
ir	deer	(dir)
	fear	(fir)
oh	open	(oh pen)
oi	foil	(foil)
	boy	(boi)
or	horn	(horn)
ou	out	(out)
	flower	(flou ər)
oo	hoot	(hoot)
	rule	(rool)
yoo	few	(fyoo)
	use	(yooz)

Symbol	Key Word	Respelling
u	book	(buk)
	put	(put)
uh	cup	(kuhp)
ə	a as in	
	along	(ə lawng)
	e as in	
	moment	(moh mənt)
	i as in	
	modify	(mahd ə fy)
	o as in	
	protect	(prə tekt)
	u as in	
	circus	(ser kəs)
ch	chill	(chil)
g	go	(goh)
j	joke	(johk)
	bridge	(brij)
k	kite	(kyt)
	cart	(kahrt)
ng	bring	(bring)
s	sum	(suhm)
	cent	(sent)
sh	sharp	(shahrp)
th	thin	(thin)
z	zebra	(zee brə)
	pose	(pohz)
zh	treasure	(treszh ər)

Be A Better Reader, Level C, Seventh Edition
Nila Banton Smith

Copyright © 1988 by Globe Fearon Inc., One Lake Street, Upper Saddle River, New Jersey, 07458, www.globefearon.com. All rights reserved. No part of this book may be kept in any information storage or retrieval system, transmitted or reproduced in any form or by any means without the prior written permission of the publisher.

Printed in the United States of America
10 11 12 13 14 04 03 02 01 00

C12
ISBN 0-8359-1922-6

Acknowledgments
We wish to express our appreciation for permission to use and adapt copyrighted materials.

The dictionary definitions in this book are reprinted with permission of Macmillan Reference USA, a Division of Simon & Schuster, from WEBSTER'S NEW WORLD DICTIONARY, Basic School Edition. Copyright © 1983 by Simon & Schuster Inc.

A & W Publishers for the almanac entry. Reprinted by permission of A & W Publishers, Inc., from INFORMATION PLEASE ALMANAC 1982. Copyright © 1981 by Simon & Schuster, a Viacom Company.

Photo Credits
p. 12: UPI/Bettmann, **p. 13:** (*left*) NASA/The Image Works, (*right*) AP/Wide World; **p. 18:** Neg. No. 126941, Courtesy of American Museum of Natural History (Photo: AMNH–Sinclair Aerial Survey); **p. 28:** UPI/Bettmann; **p. 40:** Archive Photos; **p. 42:** AP/Wide World; **p. 68:** The Granger Collection; **p. 73:** Alexander Farnsworth/The Image Works; **p. 74:** Margot Granitsas/Photo Researchers Inc.; **p. 97:** UPI/Bettmann; **p. 98:** The Bettmann Archive; **p. 133:** David Madison/DUOMO; **p. 139:** Ken Karp; **p. 159:** (*left*) Ken Karp, (*right*) IBM Archives; **p. 160:** IBM Archives; **p. 161:** (*top*) UPI/Bettmann (*bottom left*) Don Smetzer/Tony Stone Images, (*bottom right*) Superstock.

Contents

4

For more than thirty years, **Be A Better Reader** has helped students improve their reading skills. **Be A Better Reader** teaches the comprehension and study skills that you need to read and enjoy all types of materials—from library books to the different textbooks that you will encounter in school.

To get the most from **Be A Better Reader**, you should know how the lessons are organized. As you read the following explanations, it will be helpful to look at some of the lessons.

In each of the first four lessons of a unit, you will apply an important skill to a reading selection in literature, social studies, science, or mathematics. Each of these lessons includes the following seven sections.

Skill Focus

This section teaches you a specific skill. You should read the Skill Focus carefully, paying special attention to words that are printed in boldface type. The Skill Focus tells you about a skill that you will use when you read the selection.

Word Clues

This section teaches you how to recognize and use different types of context clues. These clues will help you with the meanings of the underlined words in the selection.

Reading a Literature, Social Studies, Science, or Mathematics Selection

This section introduces the selection that you will read and gives you suggestions about what to look for as you read. The suggestions will help you understand the selection.

Selection

The selections in the literature lessons are similar to those in a literature anthology, library book, newspaper, or magazine. The social studies selec-tions are like chapters in a social studies textbook or encyclopedia. They often include maps and tables. The science selections, like a science textbook, include special words in boldface type and sometimes diagrams. The mathematics selections will help you acquire skill in reading mathematics textbooks.

Recalling Facts

Answers to the questions in this section—the first of three activity sections—can be found in the selection. You will sometimes have to reread parts of the selection to do this activity.

Interpreting Facts

The second activity includes questions whose answers are not directly stated in the selection. For these questions, you must combine the information in the selection with what you already know in order to *infer* the answers.

Skill Focus Activity

In the last activity, you will use the skill that you learned in the Skill Focus section at the beginning of the lesson to answer questions about the selection. If you have difficulty completing this activity, reread the Skill Focus section.

The remaining lessons in each unit give you practice with such skills as using a dictionary, an encyclopedia, and other reference materials; using phonics and syllabication aids in recognizing new words; locating and organizing information; and adjusting reading rate. Other reading skills that are necessary in everyday experience are also covered, such as reading a bus schedule and a menu.

Each time that you learn a new skill in **Be A Better Reader**, look for opportunities to use the skill in your other reading at school and at home. Your reading ability will improve the more you practice reading!

Lesson 1

Plot

Reading a Literature Selection

▶ **Background Information**

A myth is a story created to dramatize the central conflicts of human life. Myths are handed down through the centuries. The story that you will read is a Greek myth that is over five thousand years old.

▶ **Skill Focus**

The plan of action or series of events in a story is called the **plot**. In most stories, the plot follows a basic pattern.

1. **Beginning:** The beginning introduces the main character and the conflict and establishes the setting.
2. **Rising Action:** The plot begins to build as the conflict develops. The main character struggles to achieve a goal or to solve a problem.
3. **Climax:** The climax marks the story's turning point. After the climax, you are often able to predict how the story will end.
4. **Falling Action:** The events after the climax focus on how the main character resolves the story's conflict.

5. **Conclusion:** A final event ties together all loose ends. If you drew the plot of a story, it would look like this.

Use the diagram above and the following questions to help you follow the plot of a story.

1. What do you know about the story's setting and characters at the beginning?
2. What conflict develops as the story's action rises?
3. What is the climax?
4. How is the conflict resolved as the action falls?
5. Is the story's conclusion appropriate?

▶ **Word Clues**

When you read, you may come across a word that names a special person, place, or thing. If the

paragraph has no context clues to explain the word, there may be a clue elsewhere. Read the sentence below.

> With a fist of iron, he ruled the kingdom of Crete.[1]

Notice that there is a raised number after the word *Crete.* This is a signal to look at the bottom of the page for a footnote with the same number. A footnote gives a brief definition or explanation.

[1] Crete (KREET) an island southeast of Greece.

Use **footnote** information to find the meaning of the three other numbered words in the selection.

▶ **Strategy Tip**

As you read "The Flight of Daedalus," use the diagram and the five questions in the Skill Focus to help you follow the plot. When you think the story has reached its climax, try to predict the conclusion. Doing this exercise will help you understand the story better.

The Flight of Daedalus

Long, long ago lived a proud and terrible king. His name was Minos. With a fist of iron, he ruled the kingdom of Crete.[1]

Daedalus, another proud man, also lived on the island of Crete. He was a sculptor and a builder. He may have been the finest builder of his time. Daedalus built many fine buildings for King Minos.

The most famous structure that Daedalus built for Minos was the Labyrinth.[2] It was designed as a prison and a trap. No one could find a way out of its passageways without knowing the design. Minos imprisoned his enemies there.

One day Minos became very angry with Daedalus. The builder had given away the secret of the Labyrinth. In anger, Minos imprisoned Daedalus in the Labyrinth. Within a short time, however, Daedalus managed to escape. Minos had been foolish to imagine that Daedalus could not escape from his own trap.

The sculptor found his son, Icarus, and planned to flee from Crete. But Minos was determined to recapture Daedalus. The king's soldiers searched all the ships before they left the island.

Minos knew that Daedalus and Icarus were hiding in the countryside, but he didn't care. He was sure that Daedalus and Icarus could not escape from Crete. So Minos decided to let Daedalus wander free for a while. "Soon the master builder will realize that he is trapped here. He will have to admit that he is in my power and will give himself up. Then I will give him many difficult tasks to perform."

Daedalus tried many times to find a way to escape from the island. He stood on the rocky hills of Crete and stared out to sea. Above him, the sea gulls and other sea birds wheeled and dipped in the sky. Below, the sun glistened on the water in the harbor and on the helmets of Minos' soldiers. Daedalus could see the trap that Minos had set.

[1] Crete (KREET): an island southeast of Greece.

[2] Labyrinth (LAB ǝ rinth): a building on ancient Crete with many winding passages and blind alleys; a maze.

"I cannot let Minos get the better of me," he thought. "I must escape with my son. There must be a way off the island."

At times, Daedalus feared that he and his son would be captives on Crete forever. But his quick mind kept searching for a way out. As he pondered, he watched the many birds that soared high in the blue sky. Suddenly, Daedalus was struck by a thought. "Minos may rule the land and sea, but he cannot control the air!" Daedalus said, as he watched feathers drop from the wings of the sea gulls.

He quickly sent his son Icarus in search of stray sea-gull feathers. Icarus found tiny, soft feathers. He picked up long, strong feathers. He gathered black plumes and white ones. He found blue feathers and brown feathers. Soon, Icarus had made a great mound of feathers of all kinds.

Then Daedalus set to work. He built a large wooden frame shaped like a bird's wing. He fastened feathers to it. Some he sewed on; others he stuck on with wax. Finally, he used wax to mold all the feathers into shape. Once

he had finished this frame, he made another one and covered it with feathers, too. Now, he had two huge wings, like those of a giant bird.

Daedalus fastened the wings to his shoulders. Would they work? He flapped the wings and tried to fly. After some minutes, the wings lifted him from the ground.

He could fly! But Daedalus soon learned that there was more to flying than flapping his wings. He had to learn to swoop, to soar on the winds, to turn and gather speed.

With all haste, Daedalus made wings for Icarus. Icarus watched gleefully as his father sewed and glued the feathers in place. Icarus could scarcely wait to put on the wonderful wings.

At last, the wings were finished. Daedalus fastened them to his son's shoulders. Icarus looked very handsome. The beautiful wings covered his entire body. His golden hair shone in the sunlight, and his eyes sparkled with excitement.

Icarus learned to fly in no time. He seemed to have been born to it. His father, knowing how daring Icarus could be, warned him often to be careful. "Don't fly too close to the water," he would say. "The fog will weigh you down. And don't fly close to the sun. Its warmth will melt the wax on your wings."

Icarus listened impatiently to his father's warnings. He thought, "I can take care of myself!"

One fair morning, Daedalus said, "The wind is just right today. We shall fly to Sicily."[3]

Strapping on their wings, Daedalus and Icarus walked to the top of a rocky hill. Daedalus flapped his huge wings, rose in the air, and flew out over the sea. Icarus lifted himself with his wings and followed. Minos could never catch them now!

Daedalus headed out over the ocean, beating the air strongly and surely. Icarus swooped and turned as he followed his father. Flying free in the air, Icarus knew the joy of being a bird. He looked down at the white-capped waves. How wonderful to be soaring above them! Then he looked at the clouds above. How exciting it would be to fly above them!

Icarus forgot his father's warnings. Beating his wings faster and faster, he rose up and up. As he flew higher, the sun flickered and gleamed on his feathers. On and on he flew, higher and higher. The sun grew brighter.

The air became very warm, but Icarus flew on. As he flew, it became more and more difficult to climb higher. His wings drooped. Feathers began to fall like snowflakes. The sun's heat was melting the wax! Furiously, Icarus beat his wings, but they could no longer support him. As he fell toward the glittering ocean far below, Icarus cried out to his father.

Daedalus heard the cry and turned. He caught only a glimpse of his son as Icarus plunged into the white-capped waves. Nothing

> *Flying free in the air, Icarus knew the joy of being a bird.*

---

[3] Sicily (SIS ə lee): an island south of Italy.

remained except a few feathers floating on the surface.

In deep grief, Daedalus flew on to Sicily. He went to the temple of the sun god Apollo.[4]

4 Apollo (ə POL oh): a Greek god; the son of Zeus, king of the gods.

There he hung up his wings as an offering to the god.

Daedalus had beaten his enemy, Minos, but at the terrible cost of the life of his son. Perhaps the gods were punishing Daedalus for daring to do something mere mortals were not meant to do: fly with the wings of a bird.

RECALLING FACTS

Write the answers to the following questions on the lines provided. You may go back to the selection to find an answer.

Recalling details

1. Identify the three story characters.

_____Minos_____, King of Crete

_____Daedalus_____, a master builder

_____Icarus_____, his son

Recalling details

2. What did the builder make for the king that pleased the king very much?

Daedalus made the Labyrinth.

Identifying cause and effect

3. Why was Daedalus imprisoned?

He gave away the secret of the Labyrinth.

Recalling details

4. How did Daedalus attach feathers to the wings?

He used wax to attach some feathers to the wooden

frames, and others he sewed onto them.

Identifying cause and effect

5. What caused the feathers to drop from Icarus' wings?

When Icarus flew too close to the sun, the heat

melted the wax and the feathers fell off.

Using context clues

6. Complete each statement with the correct word.

Apollo   Sicily   Labyrinth

a. Archaeologists think they have discovered the original

_____Labyrinth_____ on a mountainside in Crete.

b. In Greek mythology, _____Apollo_____ is the god of light and the sun.

c. The Strait of Messina separates

_____Sicily_____ from the mainland of Italy.

INTERPRETING FACTS

Not all the questions about a story are answered directly in the story. For the following questions, you will have to figure out answers not stated directly in the story. Write questions on the lines provided.

Drawing conclusions

1. Below are two proverbs. Circle the one that fits the story. Explain your answer.

   a. Haste makes waste.

   (b.) Pride goes before a fall.

Icarus forgot to be cautious because of his pride in his ability to fly.

Making inferences

2. For all the three characters in the story, state how pride caused their downfall, or defeat.

Minos' pride made him careless about letting Daedalus wander freely; Daedalus' pride in his craftsmanship and in

beating Minos lost him his son; Icarus' pride cost him his life.

Making inferences

3. Why did Icarus ignore his father's warnings?

He was proud and daring; he was too involved in the joy of flight.

Inferring comparisons and contrasts

4. Why didn't Daedalus, like Icarus, forget himself and fly too close to the sun?

Daedalus was wiser; he concentrated on reaching safety.

Drawing conclusions

5. Do you think that Daedalus ever flew again? Explain your answer. Use an event from the story to support your answer.

Answers may vary. No. He hung up his wings as an offering to Apollo.

SKILL FOCUS

Below are some of the events in the myth of Daedalus. Write the letter of the appropriate event on the lines provided in the plot diagram. It may help if you first decide which event is the climax.

a. Daedalus escapes from the Labyrinth.

b. Daedalus sees Icarus fall into the sea.

c. Daedalus builds two pairs of wings to help him and Icarus escape from Crete.

d. Daedalus hangs up his wings as an offering to the sun god Apollo.

e. With their wings, Daedalus and Icarus head for Sicily.

f. Icarus, ignoring Daedalus' warnings, flies too close to the sun.

g. Alone, Daedalus flies to Sicily.

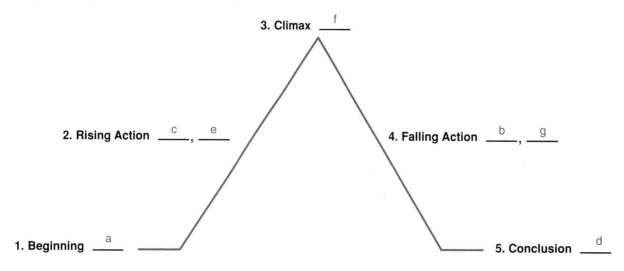

3. Climax __f__

2. Rising Action __c__ , __e__

4. Falling Action __b__ , __g__

1. Beginning __a__

5. Conclusion __d__

▶ **Real Life Connections** Describe one way in which pride hurt someone you know.

Lesson 2

Comparing and Contrasting

___ Reading a Social Studies Selection ___

▶ **Background Information**

The history of flight was made by brave and daring individuals. The selection that you are about to read discusses Amelia Earhart and Sally Ride, both pioneers of flying. In 1932, Amelia Earhart became the first woman to fly solo across the Atlantic Ocean. During her life, Earhart set many other flight records as well. As an astronaut, Sally Ride made history in our time. She was the first American woman to fly in space. She now teaches physics. As you read "Flying to Fame," draw comparisons and contrasts between the two women.

▶ **Skill Focus**

To **compare** is to find what is alike between two or more things. To **contrast** is to find what is different between two or more things. Comparing and contrasting is something that you do every day.

When you wake up, you look outside or turn on the television to find out if the weather is either the same as or different from yesterday's weather. When you shop, you compare and contrast items: are these two sweaters that cost the same really the same, or is one of them better?

When reading a social studies selection, you will often need to compare or contrast two or more people, places, or events. Remember that when you compare, you look for what is similar. When you contrast, you look for differences.

A writer sometimes presents material about two topics separately. The writer may discuss two people one at a time, each in a separate paragraph. The writer might describe the childhood, education, and achievements of one person first. Then the writer would give the same information for the other person.

When you read material organized in this way, keep in mind the similarities and differences between the two people being discussed. Because information about each person is given in a separate section, you must draw the comparisons and contrasts.

▶ **Word Clues**

When you read a word that you do not know, look for context clues to help you understand it.

Context clues are words near the unknown word that make its meaning clearer. Read the sentence below.

> Sally Ride <u>donned</u> her space suit and her bubble helmet with the ease that you slip on a coat and hat.

If you do not know the meaning of the word *donned,* the phrase *with the ease that you slip on a coat and hat* can help you. You can figure out the meaning of *donned* from the details in the phrase that follows it. You can tell that *donned* means "to put on."

Use **detail** context clues to find the meaning of the three underlined words in the selection.

▶ **Strategy Tip**

When reading textbooks, you may find words that are difficult to say. These words are usually respelled to help you pronounce them. The pronunciation key on page 2 will help you learn how to pronounce these difficult words.

FLYING TO FAME

Amelia Earhart and Sally Ride, pioneers of flight, have pushed back the boundaries of the world and the universe. These two women are also pioneers for their gender. They have proven that women, as well as men, have the courage and determination to make history.

✗ In 1932, a young woman named Amelia Earhart set off on a dangerous flight. She pulled on her leather flying gear, adjusted her goggles, and climbed into her propeller plane. Alone, she took off from Newfoundland, Canada, to cross the Atlantic Ocean. The world cheered when Earhart landed safely in Ireland. Amelia Earhart had become the first woman to fly solo across the Atlantic.

✗ Half a century later, on June 18, 1983, another woman set out to make history. Sally Ride donned her space suit and her bubble helmet with the ease that you slip on a coat and hat. She climbed aboard the *Challenger* space shuttle with three other astronauts and blasted off into outer space. Sally Ride became the first American woman in space.

Amelia Earhart

Amelia Earhart was born on July 24, 1898, in Atchison, Kansas. While growing up, she liked to experiment with daring stunts. Once, Earhart jumped off her father's barn using an umbrella for a parachute. Another time, she built a roller coaster on the roof of her father's tool shed. Even as a child, Earhart's imagination knew no bounds.

At the age of nineteen, Amelia Earhart discovered flying. She was working as a nurse's aide in a Canadian military hospital. One of her friends was a pilot in the Royal Flying Corps. She spent her free time at a nearby airfield watching him fly. But for Earhart, being only a spectator made her feel like a young athlete left on the bench to watch.

In her early twenties, Earhart began her thrilling and dangerous career as a pilot. The engines of early airplanes were not much bigger than a modern motorcycle engine. In her first two months of flying, Earhart made two crash landings. She was a natural pilot, however. She worked hard to save enough money to buy her own plane in 1922.

When Amelia Earhart took to the air, flying was an endeavor, an effort that was still new and risky. But she pushed herself and the world's flying records to the limit. She set her first record by flying at 14,000 feet (4,200 meters), breaking the women's altitude record.

✔ In 1927, history was made in flying when Charles Lindbergh made the first flight across the Atlantic Ocean. By 1932, Amelia Earhart became the first woman to fly solo across the Atlantic. Her flight brought her international fame. It also inspired her to set one new record after another.

✔ ✔ In 1935, Earhart became the first person to fly nonstop alone from Honolulu, Hawaii, to the United States mainland. Later, she became the first person to fly nonstop from Los Angeles to Mexico City and from Mexico City to Newark, New Jersey.

Amelia Earhart's daring flights made her a hero to Americans. She was admired and cheered wherever she went. At the time, her accomplishments seemed especially remarkable because of her gender. But Earhart herself deeply believed in gender equality. She believed that women "must earn true respect and equal rights from men by accepting responsibility."

Amelia Earhart's greatest challenge came on May 17, 1937. She had decided to attempt another record-breaking flight—a 27,000-mile (43,200 kilometers) trip around the world. She asked Fred Noonan, an experienced navigator, to join her. Taking off from Oakland, California, they flew to Florida, then to South America, then across the Atlantic to Africa and on to Asia. Finally, they arrived on the island of New Guinea (GIN ee). From there, they faced the most dangerous leg of their journey. They would have to fly 2,556 miles (4,089.6 kilometers) across the Pacific Ocean and then land on tiny Howland Island. On July 2, Earhart and Noonan took off across the Pacific. Somewhere between New Guinea and Howland Island, the plane disappeared. Amelia Earhart was never heard from again.

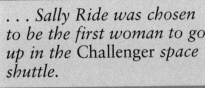

. . . Sally Ride was chosen to be the first woman to go up in the Challenger *space shuttle.*

Sally Ride

Even as a young girl, Sally Ride enjoyed challenges. She competed successfully with neighborhood boys in baseball and football. Once, she threw a ball so hard that it broke the nose of the child next door. At the age of twelve, Ride took up tennis. She was soon winning tournaments. Sally Ride learned early to work hard at everything that she did.

✚ As a young woman, Ride never planned a career in flying. In college, she continued to play tennis. She also gave a great deal of time to serious studying. She spent nine years earning degrees in English, science, and laser physics.

"Then one day in 1977," Ride said, "I read an announcement in the paper that NASA was accepting applications. And all of a sudden, I realized that I wanted to do it. There was no question in my mind." Ride wrote to the National Aeronautics and Space Administration. She expressed her interest in becoming an astronaut. They accepted her immediately, along with five other women.

By the time Sally Ride joined NASA in 1978, an astronaut had already walked on the moon. Training and scientific know-how were most important for space-age pilots. Ride joined a team of astronauts training for space flights. She worked closely with NASA scientists and other crew members.

After her initial training, Sally Ride was chosen to be the first woman to go up in the *Challenger* space shuttle. As one of two mission specialists aboard the shuttle, Ride made use of two communications satellites and conducted special experiments in space. Ride's extensive training for the STS-7 mission was demanding. Many procedures were practiced again and again. Ride and the other astronauts spent intense hours every day in conditions like those they would face in outer space. There, they would have no weight because gravity would not exist.

As one of the first women astronauts, Sally Ride broke barriers for her gender. Treated with respect by fellow crew members, Ride was simply another good astronaut. She had confidence in the experience and technology of NASA and in her own abilities and training.

Amelia Earhart took off across the huge, lonely Pacific Ocean to achieve a dream. Sally Ride was exposed to an even greater vastness as she blasted off into the endless stretch of emptiness known as outer space. Amelia Earhart and Sally Ride will both go down in history as brave women and pioneers of flight.

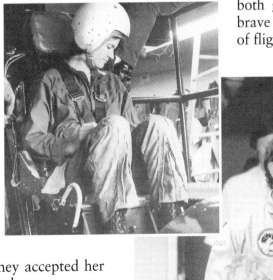

Write the answers to the following questions on the lines provided. You may go back to the selection to find an answer.

Recalling details

1. What was the first flight record that Amelia Earhart set?

She broke the women's altitude record.

Recalling details

2. Why didn't Sally Ride do her flying solo?

Astronauts work in teams.

Identifying the main idea

3. On page 12, reread the two paragraphs that have X's next to them. Underline the sentence that states the main idea in each paragraph.

Using context clues

4. Decide if each statement is true or false. Write *true* or *false* on the lines provided.

    false   **a.** A spectator plays in a football game.

    true   **b.** A lot of furniture is needed to fill the vastness of a large living room.

    true   **c.** Riding a bicycle for the first time is an endeavor most children love.

INTERPRETING FACTS

Not all the questions about a selection are answered directly in the selection. For the following questions, you will have to figure out answers not directly stated in the selection. Write the answers to the questions on the lines provided.

Making inferences

1. Why did Earhart ask Noonan to accompany her on her flight around the world?

She needed the help of an experienced navigator.

Inferring cause and effect

2. What effect did Ride's space flight have on future astronaut teams?

There are now more women astronauts.

Inferring details

3. Reread the paragraph with a cross next to it. Which of the following statements can you infer from the paragraph?

    a. Sally Ride hated to fly.

    (b.) Sally Ride is very intelligent.

    c. Sally Ride was a bad student.

Inferring the unstated main idea

4. Reread the paragraph with a check mark next to it. Write a sentence describing its main idea.

Earhart matched Lindbergh's flight and set many new records.

Inferring the unstated main idea

5. Reread the paragraph with two check marks next to it. Write a sentence describing its main idea.

Twice Earhart set a nonstop distance record.

1. Use the following chart to outline similarities between Amelia Earhart and Sally Ride. In the middle of the chart are general topics. Reread the selection for information on how the women's lives compare. For each topic, write one sentence about each woman. The first one is done for you.

COMPARISONS

Amelia Earhart	Topic	Sally Ride
Earhart was active and daring as a child.	Childhood	Ride was active and competitive as a child.
Earhart was the first woman to try many dangerous flights.	Breaking barriers for women	Ride was the first woman astronaut.
Earhart set many flight records during her life.	Record setting	Ride was the first American woman in space.
Earhart risked her life many times and finally lost it.	Taking risks	Ride's space flight involved many dangers.

2. Use the following chart to outline differences between Amelia Earhart and Sally Ride. In the middle of the chart are general topics. Reread the selection to find how the women's lives contrast on these topics. Then write one sentence about each.

CONTRASTS

Amelia Earhart	Topic	Sally Ride
At nineteen, Earhart knew she wanted to fly.	Beginning of flying career	Ride did not fly until she joined NASA several years after college.
Earhart flew propeller planes over record distances.	Frontiers of flying	Ride's frontier was outer space.
Earhart did most of her flying solo.	Teamwork	Ride worked on a team with other astronauts.

3. Look at the photographs of Amelia Earhart and Sally Ride on pages 12 and 13. In one paragraph, describe the similarities and differences that you see.

Answers may vary. The photographs show Amelia Earhart and Sally Ride with their aircrafts. While Amelia Earhart is

in casual clothes, Sally Ride is in her official space uniform.

▶ **Real Life Connections** Which quality in these women do you most admire? Tell why.

Classifying

___ Reading a Science Selection ___

▶ **Background Information**

The following selection describes four classes, or types, of objects in space. Each can be found in our solar system. Look over the selection before you read it. Look at the headings that give the names of the four classes. Also look at the boldfaced words in the paragraphs. Following these words, you will find examples of each class. Use headings and boldfaced words to help you understand how the information is organized.

▶ **Skill Focus**

Sometimes information is organized by **classifying** similar objects or ideas into groups. It is then easier to see similarities and differences among these groups.

You often classify information in your daily life. For example, when you make a budget, you classify expenses. Some costs, such as gasoline, tolls, and parking charges, you classify as transportation expenses. Other costs you classify as housing, food, or medical expenses.

Classifying also helps scientists compare and contrast objects within

groups or among groups.

When scientists classify various kinds of rocks, for example, they do so according to how they were formed and the materials they are made of. Each class or type includes rocks that are similar in an important way.

When reading information that explains classes, or types, of objects, notice the headings. They will help you understand how the objects have been divided into classes. As you read, "Objects in Space," ask yourself questions like the following:

1. What is similar about the objects that scientists classify in the same group?
2. How are the objects in one group different from the objects in another group?

▶ **Word Clues**

When you read a word that you do not know, look for context clues to help you. Context clues are nearby words and phrases that help make the meaning clearer. For example, when you see a word that you do not know in a magazine or newspaper, you often can figure it out by connecting it to words around it that you do know.

Suppose you read:

> The comet flew between other starlike bodies. Its long tail of light shone across the sky.

You can see that a comet is a starlike body with a tail of light that flies across the sky.

Read the sentences below.

> Four classes of objects revolve around the sun. The largest objects that circle the sun are called **planets.**

If you don't know the meaning of the word *revolve*, the word *circle* in the next sentence can help you. The words *revolve* and *circle* are synonyms. To revolve is to circle something.

Use **synonym** context clues to find the meaning of the three underlined words in the selection.

▶ **Strategy Tip**

As you read the selection, notice in what ways the members of each class are alike. Also notice in what ways the members of each class are different.

Objects in Space

Four classes of objects revolve around the sun. The largest objects that circle the sun are called **planets**. Smaller objects include **asteroids, comets,** and **meteoroids.**

Planets

The word *planet* comes from a Greek word meaning "wanderer." A planet is an object in space that revolves around the sun. It produces no light of its own. But sunlight <u>reflects</u> off it. A planet appears to shine in the sky because sunlight bounces off its surface.

Our solar system includes nine planets (*Solar* means "having to do with the sun.") All but two of the planets have moons. Each planet moves around the sun in an oval <u>orbit</u>, or path. The planets that are closer to the sun have shorter orbits than those that are farther away. While each planet moves around the sun, it also <u>rotates</u>, or spins.

The planets are divided into two groups. The planets closest to the sun are called the **inner planets.** These are Mercury, Venus, Earth, and Mars. The planets farthest from the sun are called the outer planets. These are Jupiter, Saturn, Uranus, Neptune, and Pluto.

The Inner Planets The inner planets are similar to Earth in some ways. Like Earth, each is made up of rock and metals. The largest of the inner planets is Earth. It is 12,800 kilometers in diameter. The smallest of the inner planets is Mercury. It is 4,900 kilometers in diameter.

Mercury is a fast-moving planet. It takes tiny Mercury only 88 Earth days to make a trip around the sun. Like Earth's moon, Mercury has many craters. It has no moon of its own, and its atmosphere is extremely thin.

Venus is the brightest of all the planets. In the night sky, it shines even more brightly than a star. Of course, its light is not its own. It is reflected light from the sun.

The atmosphere of Venus is thick. It contains carbon dioxide. This gas keeps heat trapped on Venus. As a result, the temperature on Venus is always over 459°C. The surface of Venus is covered with craters, mountains, and valleys. Venus has no moon.

Earth is often called the "living" planet. This is because Earth is the only planet known to have life. Earth's atmosphere has large amounts of oxygen and clouds of water drops. These gases help make life possible on Earth. Earth has mountains, valleys, craters, and large bodies of water. Earth also has one moon.

Mars is a rocky planet that looks red in space. Large, red, desertlike areas give the planet its color. Mars has a thin atmosphere and icy polar caps. It has two small moons.

The Outer Planets Except for Pluto, the

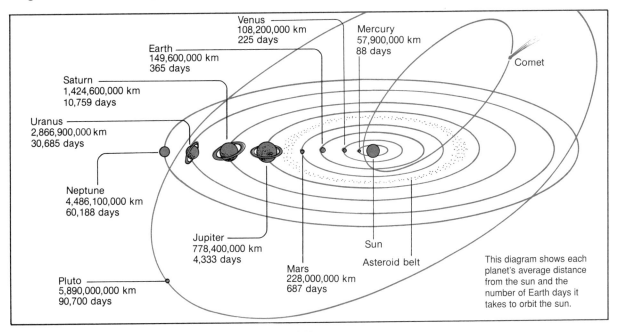

Venus
108,200,000 km
225 days

Mercury
57,900,000 km
88 days

Earth
149,600,000 km
365 days

Comet

Saturn
1,424,600,000 km
10,759 days

Uranus
2,866,900,000 km
30,685 days

Neptune
4,486,100,000 km
60,188 days

Jupiter
778,400,000 km
4,333 days

Sun

Asteroid belt

Mars
228,000,000 km
687 days

Pluto
5,890,000,000 km
90,700 days

This diagram shows each planet's average distance from the sun and the number of Earth days it takes to orbit the sun.

Figure 1. Nine planets plus numerous other bodies orbit the sun.

outer planets are much larger than the inner planets and are made up largely of gases. Most scientists believe that the outer planets have atmospheres that contain large amounts of hydrogen and helium, as well as small amounts of frozen ammonia and methane. The centers of these planets may contain heavy liquids.

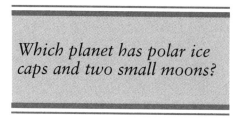

Which planet has polar ice caps and two small moons?

Jupiter is twice the size of all the other planets put together. It is 142,800 kilometers in diameter. Colorful clouds surround this large planet, and 16 moons circle it. Jupiter seems to have a huge red area on its surface. Scientists have named it the Great Red Spot. The spot is so large that three Earths could fit side by side across it. The Great Red Spot seems to be a giant gas storm caused by new gases rising from deep inside the planet.

Saturn is one of the most beautiful planets. It is surrounded by seven rings. Scientists believe these rings are made of billions of rock and ice bits revolving around the planet like tiny moons. Saturn has 17 true moons.

Uranus and **Neptune** are called the twin planets. They look alike and are about the same size. Uranus, however, has many rings and at least 15 moons. Neptune has no rings

and eight known moons. Because Neptune is farther from the sun, it is colder than Uranus.

Pluto is the planet that is farthest from the sun. Sometimes, though, its unusual orbit brings it closer to the sun than Neptune. Pluto is unlike the other outer planets. It is made up of rocky, earthlike materials, not gases. And it is not a large planet. In fact, with a diameter of 2,284 kilometers, Pluto is smaller than Mercury. Pluto has one moon.

Asteroids

Like the inner planets, asteroids are made up of chunks of rock and metal. However, asteroids are smaller than planets. Some are only about one kilometer in diameter. Others are several hundred kilometers in diameter.

Our solar system contains thousands of asteroids. The number now known and named is over 5,000. Most move around the sun in the gap between Mars and Jupiter. This gap is called the **asteroid belt**. A few asteroids move around the sun in oval orbits.

The larger asteroids have been given names. Ceres, the largest, is about 1,030 kilometers in diameter. It is one of the asteroids that moves in an orbit outside the asteroid belt.

Comets

A comet is a spectacular sight. The head, or **coma**, of a comet is made up of frozen gases and bits of rock and dust. As a comet nears the sun, a bright tail develops behind the head.

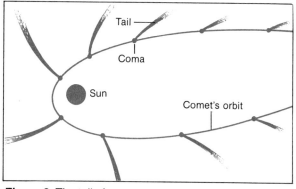

Figure 2. The tail of a comet grows longer as it nears the sun.

Figure 3. Barringer Crater in Arizona is 1.3 kilometers across and 200 meters deep.

Energy given off by the sun pushes material away from the coma to form the tail. The tail grows as the comet nears the sun. Most comas are only a few kilometers across.

Only a few comets are seen regularly. This is because most comets follow extremely long orbits. Some take thousands of years to complete an orbit around the sun. The most famous comet is **Halley's Comet.** It passes Earth every 76 years. It last appeared in 1986.

Meteoroids

Meteoroids are rock and metal objects that speed around the sun. Most are no bigger than a grain of sand. A few are larger and may weigh many tons.

Every now and then, a meteoroid enters Earth's atmosphere. When this happens, it is called a **meteor,** or "shooting star." Earth's atmosphere causes the meteor to burn and glow. Groups of meteors entering Earth's atmosphere together are called meteor showers.

Most meteors burn up completely while passing through Earth's atmosphere. A few are large enough to make it to Earth's surface. The rocky material that hits Earth is called a **meteorite.** A few large meteorites have made craters on Earth. **Barringer Meteorite** made a crater in Arizona 1.3 kilometers wide.

RECALLING FACTS

Write the answers to questions 1 through 8 on the lines provided. You may go back to the selection to find an answer.

Classifying
1. What do a planet and an asteroid have in common?

They both orbit the sun. Like the inner planets, asteroids

are made of rocky material.

Classifying
2. How are planets different from asteroids?

Planets are larger than asteroids.

Recalling details
3. Name two ways in which a planet moves.

It revolves around the sun. It also rotates, or spins.

Recalling details
4. What kinds of objects in space have moons?

Planets may have one or more moons.

Recalling details
5. What is the asteroid belt?

It is a gap between Mars and Jupiter where many

asteroids orbit the sun.

Identifying cause and effect
6. What pushes material away from a comet's head, or coma, to form its tail?

Energy from the sun forms the comet's tail.

Recalling details
7. Why are comets seen so seldom?

Most of them have very long orbits around the sun.

Recalling details
8. What is the difference between a meteoroid and a meteor?

A meteor is a meteoroid that has entered Earth's

atmosphere.

Using context clues
9. Fill in the space next to the word that completes each sentence.

a. A mirror _____ the image of the person looking into it.
|| rotates || revolves   ▌ reflects

b. Wheels, tops, and planets _____.
|| reflect   ▌ rotate || orbit

c. Some human-made satellites can _____ the earth in less than one hour.
▌ orbit || reflect || vapor

d. Many planets have one or more _____ that orbit around them.
|| meteors || comets   ▌ moons

e. The distance through the center of a planet from one side to the other side is called its_____.
|| orbit || atmosphere   ▌ diameter

Not all the questions about a selection are answered directly in the selection. For the following questions, you will have to figure out answers not directly stated in the selection. Write the answers to the questions on the lines provided.

Making inferences

1. Why does the word *wanderer* apply as much to comets, asteroids, and meteoroids as it does to planets?

All move in orbits around the sun.

Making inferences

2. What is the main difference between a planet, an asteroid, and a meteoroid?

The main difference between them is size.

Making inferences

3. Some scientists call Pluto an Earthlike planet and classify it with Mercury, Venus, Earth, and Mars. Explain why.

It is made of earthlike materials and is smaller than

the other outer planets.

Making inferences

4. Ikeya-Seki approached the sun in 1965. Its tail was extremely bright. To what group does this object belong?

It belongs with the comets.

Making inferences

5. In your reading and in the pictures, you can see the planets' oval orbits. How would you describe the meaning of oval?

An egg is oval in shape.

SKILL FOCUS

Use details from the selection about each class of objects in space to complete the chart below. The first part has been done for you.

	Materials	Size	Movement and Other Characteristics
INNER PLANETS Mercury, Venus, Earth, Mars	Rock and metal	4,990–12,800 km in diameter	Move in oval orbit; rotate; all but two have moons; produce no light
OUTER PLANETS Jupiter, Saturn, Uranus, Neptune, Pluto	Most: gasses Pluto: rock	Most: larger than inner planets Pluto: smaller than inner planets Smallest: 2,284 km in diameter Largest: 142,800 km in diameter	Same as inner planets
ASTEROIDS	Rock and metal	From one to several hundred km in diameter	Orbit sun; most in asteroid belt
COMETS	Frozen gases, bits of rock, and dust	Most: only a few km in diameter	Most have extremely long orbits; form tails as they near sun
METEOROIDS	Rock and metal	Most: no bigger than a grain of sand Some: weigh a few tons	Orbit sun at high speeds; called meteors when they enter Earth's atmosphere, where they burn and glow; called meteorites when they hit Earth's surface

▶ Real Life Connections Would you accept an invitation to travel through space? Tell why or why not.

Mathematical Terms and Symbols

Reading a Mathematics Selection

▶ **Background Information**

As you read the following selection, pay close attention to the diagrams. They will help you understand the special meanings of certain words. Also study the symbols that represent some of the ideas. These symbols are shortened ways of writing mathematical concepts.

▶ **Skill Focus**

When reading many types of material, you may come across terms, or words that are used in a special way. The words may have meanings that you know when they are used in an ordinary situation. However, when they are used in a special situation, they may have different meanings.

Look at the following words. Most of them have familiar meanings that you know from using them in your daily life. In mathematics, they have different meanings, though some are similar to meanings that you already know.

• **Point:** We ask people to "get the point," meaning to understand our meaning. We speak of "a point of time," meaning a specific time, such as 3:15 P.M. In mathematics, however, a point is invisible; it has no size and no dimensions.

• **Line:** In life, we talk about a line on a football field, a line on a page, a line of people at the movies or in a store. In mathematics, a line is many points placed next to each other; it goes on forever.

• **Plane:** A plane is a flat space. In life, we usually refer to planes as specific things— a table top, a street, a floor. In mathematics, a plane has length and width but no height; it goes on forever.

• **Intersect:** Many of us use the word "intersection" every day for a place where two or more streets or highways cross each other. In the same way, lines and planes can cross, or intersect.

• **Perpendicular:** When lines or planes intersect and form square corners, they are perpendicular. The doors and walls of rooms are perpendicular to their floors. The walls of buildings are perpendicular to sidewalks and streets.

• **Parallel:** Lines on a plane that do not intersect are parallel to each other. The tracks for trains run parallel, but sometimes intersect when the trains change their direction. In mathematics, parallel lines never intersect.

▶ **Word Clues**

When reading the following selection, look for these important words: *point, line, plane, intersect, perpendicular,* and *parallel.* The diagrams should help you understand these words as they apply to mathematics. Be sure also to pay special attention to the symbols that stand for special words.

▶ **Strategy Tip**

Be sure that you understand each idea before you go on to the next one. If you fail to understand one idea, others that follow it may be confusing. In mathematics, you must pay attention to logical connections at every point.

Reading Mathematical Terms and Symbols

To study geometry, you must understand three important terms. They are *point, line,* and *plane.* A **point** has no dimensions. It cannot be seen. It has no size. A point is shown by a dot and named with a capital letter. This is the symbol for point *A.*

•A

A **line** is many, many points placed next to each other. When a line is drawn, it looks as if it has a beginning and an end. But the arrows show that it goes on forever.

A line can be named with a small letter. This is line *s.* It is written *line s.*

A line can also be named using two points. A capital letter is used to name each of the two points on the line. The two points can be placed anywhere on this line.

This is line *AB.* The symbol for line *AB* is $\overleftrightarrow{AB}$.

Just like a line, a **plane** goes on and on. It never ends. It has length and width but no height. A plane is also named with a capital letter. This is plane *M.* It is written *plane M.* The four-sided figure shows that it is a plane.

Each side goes on forever. When you see this figure, you should remember that the sides do not mean that the plane ends. The capital letter that names the plane is in the lower right corner of the figure.

✔ When two lines cross, they **intersect.** Two lines intersect in a point. This is line *x* and line *y* intersecting in point *O.*

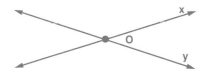

Two lines can intersect and form square corners. The lines are **perpendicular** to each other. Line *l* is perpendicular to line *m.* The symbol for showing that line *l* is perpendicular to line *m* is $l \perp m$.

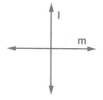

Sometimes two lines never intersect. The distance between them is always the same. When two lines never intersect, they are said to be **parallel** to each other. Line *a* is parallel to line *b.* The symbol to show that line *a* is parallel to line *b* is $a \| b$.

A line can also intersect a plane. A line and a plane intersect in a point. This is $\overset{\frown}{RS}$ intersecting plane P at point L. The dotted line shows the part of the line that is behind the plane.

Two planes can also intersect. When planes intersect, they always intersect in a line. This shows plane S and plane T intersecting along $\overset{\frown}{CD}$.

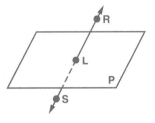

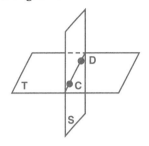

RECALLING FACTS

Complete the following sentences by writing the correct words on the lines provided.

Recalling details
1. What are three important terms in geometry?

____point____, ____line____, ____plane____

Recalling details
2. When two lines cross, they ____intersect____.

Recalling details
3. Two lines that never intersect are

____parallel____ to each other.

Recalling details
4. Two lines that intersect and form square

corners are ____perpendicular____ to

each other.

Identifying the main idea
5. Reread the paragraph with a check mark next to it. Draw a line under the sentence that states the main idea.

Recalling details
6. Write a meaning for each of the following phrases.

intersecting lines _Intersecting lines are_

lines that cross.

parallel lines _Parallel lines are lines_

that never intersect.

perpendicular lines _Perpendicular lines are_

lines that intersect and form square corners.

INTERPRETING FACTS

Not all the questions about a selection are answered directly in the selection. For the following questions, you will have to figure out answers not directly stated in the story. Write the answers to the following questions.

Making inferences
1. Could two planes intersect in a point? Why or why not?

No. They have both length and width.

Making inferences
2. Could two lines intersect in two points?

no

Making inferences
3. Write the words *plane, point,* and *line* in order from the one that takes the least space to the one that takes the most space.

____point____, ____line____, ____plane____

A. Write the name or symbol for each figure.

1.

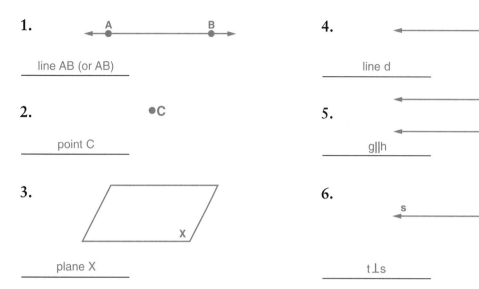

line AB (or AB)

2.

•C

point C

3.

plane X

4.

line d

5.

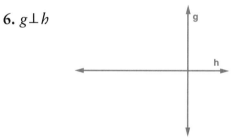

g‖h

6.

t⊥s

B. Draw a diagram for each name or symbol.

1. point X

•X

2. $\overleftrightarrow{AB}$

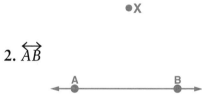

3. line m

m

4. plane D

D

5. $a‖b$

a

b

6. $g \perp h$

g

h

7. line CD and line ST intersecting in point H

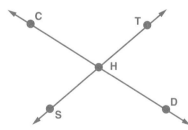

8. line XY intersecting plane M in point C

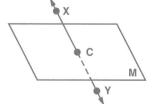

▶ **Real Life Connections** Describe something around you that is perpendicular.

Lesson 5

Vowel Diphthongs

Say the words *oil* and *boy* to yourself. Listen to their vowel sound. The letters *oi* and *oy* have the same vowel sound. When this vowel sound appears at the beginning or in the middle of a word, it is usually spelled *oi*. When this same sound is at the end of a word, it is spelled *oy*. This sound is called a **vowel diphthong.**

Read the sentences below. Choose a word from the list to complete each sentence. Write the word on the line.

coin	annoy	broil
enjoy	coil	noise

1. Some children _____annoy_____ their parents by breaking their toys.

2. This vine will _____coil_____ around the tree.

3. Cars in heavy traffic often make _____noise_____ by honking their horns.

4. Mr. Larsen is planning to _____broil_____ the hamburgers over charcoal.

5. Joe and Ann _____enjoy_____ going to hockey games.

6. Numismatics, or _____coin_____ collecting, is a popular hobby.

Say the words *out* and *cow* to yourself. Listen to their vowel sound. The letters *ou* and *ow* have the same vowel sound. This sound is also called a **vowel diphthong.**

Read the sentences below. Choose a word from the list to complete each sentence. Write the word on the line.

town	cloud	crowd	shout
pouch	blouse	plow	brow

1. The cowhands rode off in a _____cloud_____ of dust.

2. Heather wore her blue _____blouse_____ with her gray skirt.

3. A _____town_____ is larger than a village but smaller than a city.

4. In earlier times, an ox was used to pull a _____plow_____.

5. The female kangaroo carries her young in her _____pouch_____.

6. A large _____crowd_____ gathered at the scene of the fire.

7. Neil wiped the sweat from his _____brow_____.

8. Kerry tried to _____shout_____ to the other players on her team.

Vowel-Consonant Combinations

The vowel-consonant combinations *aw* and *al* and the vowels *au* have the same sound you hear in the words *claw, bald,* and *auto.* The vowel sound in all three words is the same, but the letters that stand for the sound are different.

Read the sentences below. Choose a word from the list to complete each sentence. Write the word on the line.

hawk	thaw	because	caught	fault	salt	ball
yawn	crawl	sauce	dawn	false	paw	gnaw
taught	pause	bald	haul	straw	halt	law

1. Tired people often _____yawn_____.

2. Last year Ms. White _____taught_____ geometry.

3. It is not healthful for people to put too much _____salt_____ on their food.

4. Carol _____caught_____ four fish within a short time.

5. An answer that is not true is _____false_____.

6. The sun rises at _____dawn_____.

7. Mr. Barlaz poured _____sauce_____ over the spaghetti.

8. Most babies _____crawl_____ before they learn to walk.

9. It is Robert's _____fault_____ that we are late for dinner.

10. Althea left the party early _____because_____ she was tired.

11. The hot sun made the ice start to _____thaw_____.

12. My cat hurt its _____paw_____ while running on the gravel driveway.

13. Ruth was told to _____pause_____ before reading the story.

14. My grandfather is _____bald_____.

15. This _____hawk_____ has a very sharp beak.

16. Ming's new truck can _____haul_____ our glass to the recycling plant.

17. My large _____straw_____ hat will protect my face from sunburn.

18. The horse will _____halt_____ if you pull on the reins.

19. The players kicked the _____ball_____.

20. After dinner, our dog would _____gnaw_____ the bones that we gave him.

21. To drive when you are drunk is against the _____law_____.

Lesson 7

Syllables

One way to help you pronounce long words is to divide the words into syllables. Then pronounce each syllable until you can say the whole word. There are several different ways of deciding how a word should be divided.

Guide 1: Compound Words

One of the easiest guides to use in dividing words is the one that is used with a compound word. Because a compound word is made up of two words, it must have at least two syllables. Always divide a compound word into syllables by separating it between the two smaller words first. If one or even both of the smaller words in a compound word have more than one syllable, it may be necessary to use another guide. However, you can pronounce most compound words if you divide them into two words.

sailboat   sail boat

Read each of the following compound words. Divide the word into two syllables by writing each of the two smaller words separately on the line to the right of the compound word.

1. weekday   week day
2. seaweed   sea weed
3. flashlight   flash light
4. driftwood   drift wood
5. grassland   grass land
6. withdraw   with draw

7. bathtub   bath tub
8. baseball   base ball
9. windshield   wind shield
10. drumstick   drum stick
11. highchair   high chair
12. background   back ground

Guide 2: Words with Double Consonants

Another guide that you may use is for words with double consonants. Divide the word into two syllables between the two consonants and read each syllable.

tennis   ten nis

Divide the following two-syllable words into syllables. Write each syllable separately on the line to the right of the word.

1. raccoon   rac coon
2. penny   pen ny
3. lesson   les son
4. slipper   slip per
5. lettuce   let tuce
6. kitten   kit ten
7. sudden   sud den

8. rabbit   rab bit
9. tunnel   tun nel
10. splatter   splat ter
11. muffin   muf fin
12. gossip   gos sip
13. hammer   ham mer
14. traffic   traf fic

Stated or Unstated Main Idea

When you read a textbook or reference book for information, the main idea of each paragraph will often be stated in a sentence. The rest of the paragraph will contain the supporting details that give additional information about the main idea.

Sometimes the main idea of a paragraph is not stated in one of the sentences. The information given in the paragraph will help you to **infer**, or figure out, the main idea yourself. To do this, you need to ask yourself what the paragraph is about. Then think of a sentence that summarizes this idea.

Read the following selection from beginning to end to become familiar with the content. Then reread each paragraph. Think about whether the main idea in each paragraph is stated or unstated.

Shooting for the Moon

1. Dr. Mae Jemison will never forget the day of September 12, 1992. She leads an adventure-filled life, but this was surely one of her most exciting days. "I had this big smile on my face," said Jemison. "I was so excited. This is what I had wanted to do for a very long time." Jemison was aboard shuttle mission STS-47 Spacelab, a cooperative mission to outer space between the United States and Japan.

2. Space travel is exciting, but in some ways it only emphasizes what a small planet Earth is. "The first thing I saw was Chicago. I looked out the window and there it was," she said about seeing her hometown from the shuttle. "I looked over at one point, and there was Somalia.

3. "Space is so meaningful to Earth. The Third World will be the [part of our world to gain the most from] space technology," she said, because old-fashioned telephone lines and electrical generators won't be necessary. She thinks that the "space age" will enable the Third World to skip over the "industrial age."

4. Jemison is a physician, chemical engineer, and former astronaut. When she was in medical school, Jemison studied social medicine in Cuba. Later, she practiced medicine with rural Kenyan villagers and Cambodians who had escaped to Thailand after the fall of Phnom Penh to a communist government. She also worked as a Peace Corps medical officer in Sierra Leone and Liberia. Born in 1957, Jemison is still young, but she has already done much to help people all over the world.

5. Jemison insists, however, that she does not do what she does for the good of other people. "I don't believe in [doing good just to be unselfish]," she said. "I've gotten much more out of what I have done than the people I was supposed to be helping." Jemison was in the camp in Thailand for refugees, people who left their countries to escape war and find freedom. "I learned more about medicine there than I could have in a lifetime somewhere else," she said.

6. Only a handful of women have gone up in space, and Jemison was the first African American woman to do so. However, she does not like her ethnicity to be highlighted in her work. "When I'm asked about the relevance to black people of what I do, I take that as an [insult]. It presupposes that black people have never been involved in exploring

the heavens, but this is not so. Ancient African empires—Mali, Songhay, Egypt—had scientists and astronomers.

7. "The fact is that space and its resources belong to all of us, not to any one group," Jemison emphasizes. "We need more African Americans and Latinos in the field. We need biologists, who can put together parts of experiments; chemists for rocket fuel; and even lawyers, who one day might write the contracts to determine who has mineral rights to mine the moon. If we're not there from the beginning, helping to determine what happens to these resources, we'll have no say in how they are to be used."

8. Jemison chose some very special objects to take with her in the shuttle: "An Alvin Ailey American Dance Theater poster, an Alpha Kappa Alpha banner, a flag that had flown over the Organization of African Unity, and [important writings] from Chicago's DuSable Museum of African American History and the Chicago public-school system." She explained, "I wanted everyone to know that space belongs to all of us. There is science in dance and art in science. It belongs to everyone. I'm not the first or the only African American woman who had the skills and talent to become an astronaut. I had the opportunity. All people have produced scientists and astronomers."

9. When poet Nikki Giovanni interviewed Jemison in 1993 after her shuttle mission, she asked her what her ideal space trip would be. Jemison replied, "Me in a clear bubble floating through the galaxy . . . shooting for the moon." When asked who she would bring with her, she said, "Sneeze, my cat. I think I'd like to have Sneeze. He came with me from Africa, so he's used to flying. Then if some aliens came by and invited me to another galaxy—well, look for me on *Unsolved Mysteries*. I'm gone."

For each paragraph in the selection, if the main idea is stated, write *stated* on the line. If the main idea is unstated, choose a main idea from the sentences below and write the letter on the line.

a. Jemison's cat Sneeze came with her from Africa, so he's used to flying.

b. Space is particularly meaningful to the Third World.

c. Black people have always explored space.

d. Jemison worked as a Peace Corps officer in Sierra Leone and Liberia.

e. Old-fashioned telephone lines and electrical generators won't be necessary in the Third World.

f. On September 12, 1992, Jemison reached her goal of going up in a shuttle.

g. Jemison is always ready for another adventure.

h. Lawyers can one day write contracts to determine who has mineral rights to mine the moon.

i. More African Americans and Latinos are needed in space so that they will have a say in what happens.

Paragraph 1 _____f_____   *Paragraph 6* _____c_____

Paragraph 2 ___stated___   *Paragraph 7* _____i_____

Paragraph 3 _____b_____   *Paragraph 8* ___stated___

Paragraph 4 ___stated___   *Paragraph 9* _____g_____

Paragraph 5 ___stated___

Now go back to each paragraph that has a stated main idea and underline the sentence with the main idea.

Lesson 8 *Identifying the stated or unstated main idea* **29**

The Dictionary

In a dictionary, you may find several pages of words that all begin with the same first three letters. To find a word on these pages, you will need to use the fourth letter of a word. For example, the word *collar* is listed before the word *color* because *l* comes before *o* in the alphabet. When words begin with the same three letters, they are arranged in alphabetical order according to the fourth letter of the words.

On the numbered lines, write each set of words below in alphabetical order according to the first four letters in each word. Cross out each word in the list after you write it.

beam	1. beach	stole	1. stock
beagle	2. bead	stove	2. stodgy
bear	3. beagle	stomach	3. stoke
beauty	4. beak	stoop	4. stole
beat	5. beam	store	5. stomach
beach	6. bean	stodgy	6. stone
beaver	7. bear	stop	7. stoop
bean	8. beat	stoke	8. stop
bead	9. beauty	stone	9. store
beak	10. beaver	stock	10. stove

At the top of each dictionary page are two words in boldfaced type. These words are called **guide words.** Guide words help you find, easily and quickly, the entry words—the words for which the dictionary gives definitions. They tell you the first entry word on the page and the last entry word on the page. All the other entry words on the page come between these two words in alphabetical order.

Below is a pair of guide words that might appear on a dictionary page. Following them is a list of entry words. If the entry would be on the same page as the guide words, write *yes* next to the word. If the entry would appear on an earlier page, write *before.* If the entry would appear on a later page, write *after.*

parboil / parson

1. parrot	yes	7. pastry	after
2. part	after	8. pardon	yes
3. parcel	yes	9. paragraph	before
4. pass	after	10. parlor	yes
5. parasol	before	11. Paris	yes
6. parent	yes	12. part	after

13. parallel ___before___   16. pare ___yes___

14. party ___after___   17. particle ___after___

15. parade ___before___   18. parole ___yes___

In a dictionary, an entry word and all the information about it is called an **entry.** The entry word always appears in boldfaced type. If the entry word has more than one syllable, it is divided into syllables to show where the word can be divided at the end of a line of writing. The entry word is followed by a **respelling** of the word in parentheses. The respelling shows you how to say the word. The part-of-speech label follows the respelling. The labels are usually abbreviated as follows: *adj.* for adjective, *adv.* for adverb, *conj.* for conjunction, *interj.* for interjection, *n.* for noun, *prep.* for preposition, *pron.* for pronoun, and *v.* for verb.

The meanings of an entry word are arranged according to parts of speech. For example, if an entry has noun meanings, all the noun meanings are grouped together and numbered following the *n.* label. Any meanings the word may have for any other part of speech are numbered and placed after the abbreviated part-of-speech label. When an entry has only one meaning for any part of speech, the definition is not numbered. Many words that appear in dictionary entries are synonyms for the entry word.

At the end of some entries are idioms. An **idiom** is a group of words that has a meaning different from the meaning the words have by themselves.

Use the dictionary entry below to answer the following questions.

name (nām) *n.* **1** a word or words by which a person, animal, thing, or place is known: title [Grace, Lopez, Wyoming, and poodle are *names.*] **2** a word or words used instead of the real name, sometimes in order to insult [They were mean and called him *names,* such as "liar" and "cheat."] **3** reputation [Guard your good *name.*] ◆*v.* **named, nam'ing 1** to give a name to [He *named* the child after her mother.] **2** to tell the name or names of [Can you *name* all the Presidents?] **3** to refer to; mention [to *name* an example]. **4** to choose for a certain position; appoint [She was *named* president of the company.] **5** to fix or set, as a date for a meeting, a price, etc. —**in the name of, 1** for the sake of [*in the name of* good sense]. **2** by the authority of [Open *in the name of* the law!] —**to one's name,** belonging to one.

1. What is the entry word? ___name___

2. Write the respelling. ___nām___

3. How many noun meanings follow the part-of-speech label *n*? ___3___

4. How many verb meanings follow the part-of-speech label *v*? ___5___

5. Write the first verb meaning. ___to give a name to___

6. Write the second idiom. ___to one's name___

7. Write the two synonyms given for the entry word as a noun. ___title___, ___reputation___.

8. Write the idiom that has the same meaning as the underlined words in the following sentence.
   I ordered the equipment <u>by the authority of</u> my supervisor. ___in the name of___

Reading Help Wanted Ads

Help wanted ads are found in the classified section of the newspaper. The classified section of the newspaper lists advertisements for all kinds of things arranged by subject. In the help wanted listings, ads for the same kind of job are listed together. Each ad begins with a job title or a descriptive heading that identifies the job. Sometimes a key word in the upper left-hand corner of the advertisement tells the kind of job being offered. Ads are listed in alphabetical order by job title or key word.

Most help wanted ads give the job seeker a variety of information. In addition to the job title, a help wanted ad may describe the skills needed for the job. It may state that previous experience, or former work in the same type of job, is required. An ad tells how to apply for the job. Other information, such as salary, or pay, may be included.

Because help wanted ads must give a lot of information in a small amount of space, abbreviations, or shortened forms of words, are used. For example, *exp* is the abbreviation for the word *experience.* Sometimes the abbreviations contain the first few letters of the word; sometimes the abbreviations use only consonants. If you use context clues, you can usually figure out the abbreviations.

Sometimes an ad may state that the company requires a résumé. A résumé is a sheet of written information about yourself and your work experience that you make available to a company. If the company wants to meet you after reading your résumé, someone at the company will contact you for an interview.

Examine the help wanted ads below.

| AIRLINE
FLIGHT ATTENDANTS
Major airlines looking for college grads. No exp necessary. Must be willing to move to Atlanta or Dallas. Interviews 9–5 Sept 2 at 616 N. Orchard Ave.
See Cheryl Barnes.

AIRLINE
GROUND PERSONNEL
Be a reservation or ticket agent at airport. Weekends or evenings 11 PM–7 AM shift. Sal up to $25,000 dep on exp. Call 555-4597 wkdys. | AIRLINE/TRAVEL
Reservation/
  ticket agents   to $25,000
Secretaries/typists   to $20,000
Baggage handlers   to $17,000
Aircraft mechanics   to $26,000
NEAR & FAR Agency will find the right job for you. 30 E. Orange St. 555-8000. | AIRLINE
PILOTS
wanted
Minimum 5 years exp in commercial flying. Flights to Europe. Send resume and sal requirements to:
OVERSEAS AIRWAYS
105 Park Place
San Jose, CA 95126

AIRLINE Secy–Ludwig Airport
Must type 60 wpm and know DOS. P/T Mon–Thurs 8AM–11AM.
Call Jonathan Chong
for appointment 555-8188. | AIRLINE Station/Operations
Manager
Exp in all phases of airport operations. Excellent salary. Call 555-0433. |

A. Read the abbreviations from the ads. On the line next to each abbreviation, write the word it stands for. If necessary, use context clues from the ads.

1. grads _____ graduates _____

2. sal _____ salary _____

3. dep _____ depending _____

4. wkdys _____ weekdays _____

5. yrs _____ years _____

6. secy _____ secretary _____

7. wpm _____ words per minute _____

8. P/T _____ part-time _____

B. Use the information in the ads to answer each question.

1. Which job requires someone to run an airport? _____ airline station/operations manager _____

2. Which job requires moving to another city? _____ flight attendants _____

3. Which two jobs are for someone who likes to travel by airplane to different places?
Flight attendants work for major airlines, and pilots have flights to Europe.

4. Which job would be for someone who wants to work a few hours a day?
An airline secretary would work "P/T Mon.-Thurs 8 AM–11 AM."

5. Which job pays up to $17,000? _____ baggage handlers _____

6. Which two jobs require previous experience? _____ pilots and station/operations manager _____

7. Which two telephone numbers would you call for information about a job as a secretary?
People looking for jobs as secretaries would call 555-8000 and 555-8188.

8. How would you apply for the job of flight attendant? _____ You would go to an interview between 9:00
and 5:00 on September 2 at 616 N. Orchard Avenue.

9. What is the job title for a reservation or ticket agent at an airport? _____ ground personnel _____

10. What is the location of the part-time job for an airline secretary? _____ Ludwig Airport _____

11. Which ad asks the applicants to tell how much money they would like to make?
The ad for pilots tells applicants to send salary requirements.

12. What skill would you need to apply for the airline secretary job? _____ You must type 60 wpm. _____

13. What are two requirements for people who want to apply for the flight attendant's job?
They must be college graduates and must be willing to move.

14. Why might some people not want to apply for the ground personnel job?
Ground personnel must work weekends or evenings.

15. Where can you go to find out about a job involved with airlines or travel if you're not
certain exactly what you're best suited for? _____ You should go to the Near and Far Agency. _____

16. What do you think an aircraft mechanic does? _____ He or she repairs airplanes. _____

17. The ground personnel job pays up to $25,000. Who do you think could earn that salary—
a person with no experience or a person who has been a ticket agent? _____ A person who has been
a ticket agent would be preferred.

Lesson 11 _____

Theme

Reading a Literature Selection _____

► Background Information

When you start a new class, get a new teacher, or join a club or team, you have to deal with new people and new ways of doing things. On a job, you often face changes—new work, new bosses, new co-workers. As our world grows smaller, more and more people from different countries and races come together and have to get along with each other.

Learning how to get along in a new situation can be one of life's hardest lessons. In this story, a young Japanese American girl tries to find her roots in Japan. She struggles with customs that are difficult for her to learn, such as wearing a kimono, hiding her feelings, and arranging flowers.

► Skill Focus

Theme is the meaning or message in a story. In most stories, the author does not directly state the theme. Instead, the reader must think about the characters and plot to infer, or figure out, the theme. A story's title might also give a clue about the theme.

In a story with a theme, characters often experience a change of attitude that makes us see a truth about life. We put ourselves in their place and learn a lesson by sharing their experiences.

In a similar way, the plots of such stories, by describing the problems that people face, allow us to see how the characters deal with these challenges. Their struggles help us gain a deeper understanding of the values that make life worthwhile. Without telling us directly, the author lets us see behavior that can bring maturity, self-respect, and happiness.

The following questions will help you figure out the theme of a story.

1. What does the main character learn about himself or herself or others by the end of the story?
2. What does the title of the story mean? How is it appropriate?
3. What is the author's message?

► Word Clues

Read the sentence below. Look for context clues that explain the underlined word.

> Keiko was shy, not <u>outspoken</u> like Tomi.

If you don't know the meaning of the word *outspoken*, the word *shy* can help you. *Outspoken* and *shy* are antonyms, or words that are opposite in meaning from one another. *Outspoken* means "not shy."

Look for **antonym** context clues to find the meaning of the three underlined words in the selection.

► Strategy Tip

As you read, think about the customs that Tomi must learn, especially flower arranging. See if you can figure out how the key to arranging flowers helps Tomi adjust to other customs. Use the questions to help you infer the story's theme.

A Simple Arrangement

"I give up!" Tomi cried. She threw the spray of yellow flowers to the floor.

Her cousin Keiko blinked her eyes in amazement. Keiko was shy, not outspoken like Tomi. Tomi had never learned to keep her feelings to herself as Japanese girls are taught to do. Keiko did not know what to say.

"I'm sorry I shouted," Tomi said. She bent to pick up the flowers. "It's just that I'll never learn to arrange flowers."

"Yes you will," Keiko said gently. "It is the Japanese way."

"But that's just it!" Tomi burst out again. "I'm not Japanese. I'm American. I was born in California, and I lived there all my life until now. My parents may be Japanese, and I may look Japanese, but that just makes it harder. Everyone expects me to do things the Japanese way. But I can't!"

All the anger Tomi had felt these last few months came rushing out. She hadn't wanted to come to Japan in the first place. But when her grandparents had invited her to spend a year in Japan, Tomi's father said it was a fine idea. Once Father made up his mind, it was no use arguing. The word of a Japanese father is not questioned—even in America!

Once she was in Japan, Tomi had honestly tried to be the sort of girl her grandparents wanted her to be. She had worked very hard at doing well in school and at becoming <u>adept</u> in flower arranging. But her hands seemed clumsy working with flowers. She felt that she did everything wrong.

"I think you are very lucky to be both Japanese and American," Keiko said. "You have two homes and two languages. That is something special."

"You're the one that's lucky," said Tomi. "You belong here. I don't."

Tomi cut three flowers from the spray and put them in the bowl as she had seen Mr. Tanaka, her teacher, do many times. She had cut the stems in the Japanese way so that they were three different lengths. The flower with the short stem represented earth. The tall flower stood for heaven. The medium length flower stood for human beings, who link heaven and earth.

Once heaven, human beings, and earth were in harmony, the flower arrangement succeeded. An arrangement was supposed to have <u>proportion</u>. But Tomi's flowers looked unbalanced. The design was all wrong. It was supposed to be so simple to achieve a pleasing arrangement of flowers. Why couldn't she learn how to do it? Would Tomi ever be able to please her grandparents?

Tomi sighed. "I hoped I could make a pretty flower arrangement for the party tonight," she said sadly. "It would make Grandmother so happy."

Keiko's eyes danced at the thought of the celebration. "Are you going to wear the kimono that Grandmother and Grandfather gave you when you arrived here?" she asked. "It is so beautiful."

"I know it is," Tomi said. "But I wouldn't feel right wearing it." The long, flowing kimonos that many Japanese women wear on special occasions looked lovely on them. Kimonos were really much prettier than Western clothes, Tomi thought. But she would make a fool of herself in a kimono. Kimonos are narrow, so you have to take short steps with your knees close together. Otherwise, the kimono will flap open. Tomi was sure she would forget about walking properly. She would look clumsy and silly. It was better not even to try.

"It's time for me to go home and help my family get ready for tonight," Keiko said. She got to her feet and crossed the room in quick, graceful steps.

Tomi felt a stab of envy as she watched her cousin. Keiko would wear a kimono to the family gathering tonight. Keiko would know the right things to do and say, too. Manners are much more casual in America, Tomi thought. Here it is important to do everything just right. Tomi always seemed to do everything wrong.

After Keiko had gone, Tomi felt tears in her eyes. She thought about her family back in California. More than anything, she wanted to feel like part of a family again. But she would never be accepted here, not when she couldn't even arrange a few flowers!

Tomi picked up the flowers again. The

words of Mr. Tanaka came back to her: "Arranging flowers is a simple thing, but it cannot be done unless your heart is <u>serene</u>."

"That must be my problem," Tomi thought. "My heart is anything but serene. I feel tense and anxious. My heart is not at peace."

Just then, Grandmother came into the room. Her arms were filled with packages of food for the party.

"I smell rice burning!" Grandmother said.

Oh dear! Tomi suddenly remembered that she had put rice on the stove to cook. She had hoped to please Grandmother by making the evening rice, but she had forgotten it. The water must have boiled away. The rice would be black and burned. Couldn't she do anything right?

Tomi fled from the house. Once she was in the garden, she let the tears fall. She sank into the soft moss and put her face in her hands. She had never felt so lost and alone.

It was very quiet. Her sobbing slowed, and she wiped her eyes. She looked around the garden. How beautiful it was! A pine branch was reflected in the little pond. The cherry tree was a huge ball of white blossoms.

It was a tiny garden, yet every inch of it was a delight. Her grandfather had planned it that way, she knew. It was very Japanese to draw from each thing its special beauty. The Japanese found joy in the smallest things. Things as simple as the moon rising or a bird singing were treated as treasures.

Tomi had been in the garden many times, but she had always been too busy to notice how carefully planned yet simple it was. Few other Americans would have noticed it either, she thought. Americans moved too fast. They didn't have time to watch a flower bud.

Perhaps she had been trying to move too fast, Tomi thought. She had been in such a great hurry to learn everything right away. If she moved a bit more slowly, perhaps she would find the beauty in simple things. The Japanese knew there was comfort in beauty. I'm lucky to be Japanese, Tomi thought. Lucky to be here. Lucky just to be alive!

Tomi hugged that warm feeling to her as she went back inside. Her heart was full of joy as she slipped off her shoes at the door.

"Where is the pot I burned, Grandmother?" she asked. "I want to scrub it clean."

"I've done it for you," said Grandmother.

Tomi waited for her to say more about the burned rice. Tomi had acted like an American again, wasting food! But her grandmother just went on with the preparations for dinner. She knows I can't help being what I am, Tomi thought. I am American, too.

Relieved, she picked up the yellow flowers again. This time her hands moved easily as she placed the stems in the bowl. She arranged the flowers slowly and with love for their beauty.

> *It was very Japanese to draw from each thing its special beauty.*

She stepped back to see the results. It was a very simple arrangement. There were just three stems. But it looked natural, almost as if the spray grew right out of the bowl. It was beautiful and right and Japanese.

That night, Tomi put on the silk kimono that her grandparents had given her. It was as blue as the sky and had peach blossoms scattered across it. The long, flowing sleeves fell almost to the floor.

That evening, Tomi's steps were not always as tiny as they should have been. But most of the time she remembered how to walk, and she knew she looked right. Like Keiko, Tomi helped make the passing moments of the evening beautiful.

Grandmother said nothing about the flowers. Grandfather didn't mention the kimono. But Tomi saw the glow of pride in their eyes. She felt their love reach out and wrap her like a cloak.

In the garden, the wind blew among the cherry trees, scattering the white flowers like confetti against the moon. Tomi watched each petal fall through the air of the peaceful Japanese evening.

RECALLING FACTS

Directions for Recalling Facts and Interpreting Facts are given in Unit One only.

Identifying cause and effect

1. Why did Tomi go to Japan?
Her parents sent her to visit her grandparents.

Recalling details

2. What is the relationship between Tomi and Keiko?
They are cousins.

Comparing and contrasting

3. a. How are Tomi and Keiko alike?
They both have a Japanese heritage.

   b. How are they different?
Tomi also has an American background; she is not as

comfortable or familiar with Japanese customs as her

cousin Keiko.

Recalling details

4. Why did Keiko say Tomi was lucky?
Tomi had the benefit of two cultures.

Recalling details

5. Why did Tomi go to Japan?
Her grandparents asked her and her father made her go.

Identifying cause and effect

6. Why did Tomi run to the garden and cry?
She was angry with herself and did not want to face

her grandmother after another failure.

Recalling details

7. Why didn't Tomi want to wear a kimono?
She knew that she would look clumsy in it.

Recalling details

8. What do the shortest flowers in a Japanese arrangement represent? The tallest? The medium size?
shortest: earth; tallest: heaven; medium: people

Using context clues

9. Draw a line to match each word with its meaning.

proportion — trained
adept — calm and peaceful
serene — balance of parts

INTERPRETING FACTS

Drawing conclusions

1. If Keiko visited the United States, what customs and traits might she have to get used to?
fast pace of life; casual manners; spontaneity of

emotions

Making inferences

2. How is Tomi changing as a result of her time in Japan?
She is growing to like the subtleties of small things;

she is becoming serene.

Making inferences

3. How would you describe the grandparents' attitude toward Tomi at the end?
They feel pride and love and accept her as Japanese.

Distinguishing fact from opinion

4. Mr. Tanaka told Tomi that flower arranging is done with different lengths of stems and a serene heart. Part of this statement is a fact, and part is opinion. Which is which?
Fact: length of stems. Opinion: a serene heart.

Lesson 11 *Inferring theme* 37

5. Is Tomi likely to wear her kimono when she is back in the United States? Will she continue flower arranging? Will she hide her feelings? Give reasons for your answer to each question.

Tomi might wear the kimono for special occasions; it

would have memories for her, as would flower

arranging, her new skill. She probably will continue

to show her feelings.

SKILL FOCUS

The following questions will help you figure out the theme of "A Simple Arrangement." Thinking about the title and the characters will help you infer the message of the story.

1. Think about the title of the story. To what kind of arrangement does it refer?

flower arrangement; also the arrangement of Tomi's visit to Japan

2. Who is having difficulty with this arrangement? Why?

Tomi—she moves too fast and cannot appreciate the simplicity of making flower arrangements.

3. What Japanese customs are difficult for her?

hiding her feelings; wearing a kimono; not wasting food; being gracious; having a serene heart; flower arranging

4. Why is Tomi's visit to her grandparents' garden a turning point for her?

She begins to appreciate simple beauty in a Japanese way; she becomes more serene.

5. What is the author's message or theme? *Possible answers: It is important to look for the beauty*

in every moment, to choose simplicity when possible; the customs and traditions of other countries, while different,

are not necessarily better or worse than those of one's own country; with special effort, one can appreciate and

belong to two cultures at the same time.

6. How does family love help Tomi and her Japanese relatives reach a happy solution to their conflicts? *Keiko and the grandmother are patient with Tomi. They do not criticize her failures. Tomi's love for*

her family makes her want to be accepted by them so that she tries harder.

▶ **Real Life Connections** Describe an experience where you felt—like Tomi did—as though you could do nothing right.

Lesson 12

Cause and Effect

Reading a Social Studies Selection

▶ **Background Information**

After World War II, the Allied forces occupied Germany. Tensions between the Soviet Union and the Western Allies forced the division of this country into two. The Communist government built the Berlin Wall, which divided the city of Berlin. It took twenty-eight years for the wall to come down and unite the two countries once again.

Before you read this selection, preview it. Previewing will help you understand the main ideas in the selection. First, look at the title. Then read the headings in boldfaced type. Read the first and last paragraphs; they often give a summary of what is in the selection. Finally, study the pictures and read the captions.

▶ **Skill Focus**

Many events that you read about in your textbooks are connected by **cause and effect.** A cause is a reason, condition, or situation that makes an event happen. An effect is the result of a cause.

Often, several causes will result in one effect. Read the example in the box. As you read, try to understand how

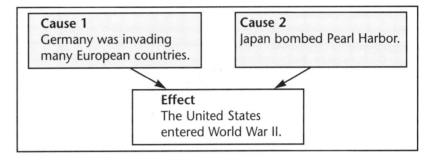

One cause may also have several effects. Read the example below.

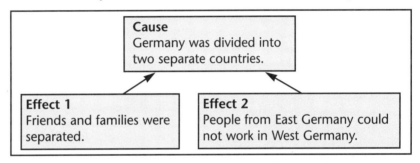

causes and effects are connected.

▶ **Word Clues**

Read the sentences below. Look for context clues that explain the underlined word.

In return, the Soviets brought their currency to the eastern part of the city and blockaded Berlin. They blocked off all roads, railways, and canals, and turned off power lines that supplied power from East Berlin to the western side of the city.

The word *blockaded* in the first sentence is explained in the next sentence, which gives details that help you understand that something

that is blockaded is blocked or difficult to pass through.

Use **detail** context clues to find the meaning of the four underlined words in the selection.

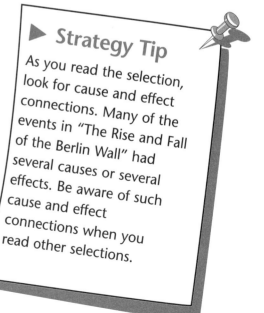

▶ **Strategy Tip**

As you read the selection, look for cause and effect connections. Many of the events in "The Rise and Fall of the Berlin Wall" had several causes or several effects. Be aware of such cause and effect connections when you read other selections.

The Rise and Fall of the Berlin Wall

For 28 years, the Berlin Wall divided Berlin, once the proud and beautiful capital of Germany. The concrete wall stood nine to twelve feet and zigzagged for 28 miles through the center of the city. Another 70 miles of wall separated all of West Berlin from East Germany. The Berlin Wall was like a deadly moat that made West Berlin an island in the middle of East Germany.

To understand how it happened that a wall was built that kept neighbors, friends, and families from getting together or even seeing one another except maybe from apartment windows that were higher than the wall, it is important to know about the history of Germany and the rest of Europe.

Germany Struggles After World War I

✘ Germany was defeated in World War I in 1918 by the Allied forces, which included the United States, Britain, and France. <u>The war was devastating for Germany.</u> The country lost about two million soldiers, and millions more had been wounded. Under the Treaty of Versailles, Germany was forced to give up much of its territory to the Allies and pay $33 billion in <u>reparations</u> for war damage.

The new German government faced an enormous economic challenge, and it failed. Inflation skyrocketed. At one point, German workers were taking their pay home in wheelbarrows because the German money was nearly worthless. The 1929 depression that spanned the globe hit Germany particularly hard. There were no jobs and little food. Germans were very bitter and believed that they were still being unjustly punished for the war they had lost. People were looking for a leader to solve their problems and make Germany a wealthy country again.

Adolph Hitler, the leader of the National Socialist German Workers Party (also called the Nazi Party), promised Germans that he could make Germany successful again. He said that Communists were trying to destroy Germany, and he blamed Jews for the economic depression. By 1933, he had become the head of the German government.

World War II Changes Germany Forever

Hitler was able to convince many Germans that they were a "super race" of people who deserved to rule the world. After so much bitter frustration, many were ready to take up arms and claim that power. Germany had already taken over Austria and Czechoslovakia before World War II began in 1939, with Hitler's invasion of Poland. Denmark, Norway, Belgium, Luxembourg, and France all fell to Hitler even before Germany and Italy joined forces. In 1941, Germany broke an alliance it had with the Soviet Union and instead attacked that country. Also in 1941, Japan, as an ally of Germany, attacked Pearl Harbor, a U.S. military base in the Pacific Ocean. Afterward, the United States declared war on Japan, and Hitler declared war on the United States.

✘ <u>By the time the war ended in 1945, the devastation and suffering all over Europe were enormous.</u> About 55 million people died. About six million Jews were killed by the Nazis just

An armed soldier patrols the east side of the Berlin Wall to prevent people from escaping to West Berlin.

because they were Jewish. Germany itself lost about six million people. Germany was left to <u>reconstruct</u> itself once again.

✗ <u>This time, the rest of the world was going to have a say in how Germany built its power.</u> The United States, Britain, and the Soviet Union formed the European Advisory Commission and divided Germany into four zones. Each country, including France, was supposed to occupy one zone to be sure that Germany could not build up a military force again. The occupation was supposed to be temporary. The city of Berlin was in the Soviet zone, but because Berlin was the capital of Germany, the countries divided Berlin into four zones of occupation.

The division of Germany wasn't easy, however. The United States, Britain, and France agreed to stop <u>dismantling</u> Germany and to begin to help its economy recover. This made the Soviets angry and relations between the Western countries and the Soviet Union grew more tense. The nations that had been friends in World War II were becoming enemies.

Tensions Grow Between East and West

✗ <u>Meanwhile, the Soviets were committed to spreading Communism, and Western leaders were concerned.</u> In the years that followed, the rivalry between the United States and the Soviet Union grew. In 1948, the Soviets tried to force the Allies to leave Berlin and limited entry to West Berlin, but the Allies refused to leave. France, Britain, and the United States united their three zones into a single zone, and much to the anger of the Soviets, they used West German money in this new zone.

In return, the Soviets brought their money to the eastern part of the city and blockaded Berlin. They blocked off all roads, railways, and canals, and turned off power lines that supplied power from East Berlin to the western side of the city. It is estimated that the people of West Berlin could have survived only six weeks with all 80 entry spots to the city sealed off. Some people thought that all American, British, and French troops would have to leave Berlin to the Soviet Union. Instead, on June 26, 1948, planes came from all over the world to deliver supplies to West Berlin. By the next year, the Soviets turned the electrical power on again.

The Cold War Begins

The Berlin blockade signaled the start of the Cold War. People in the West began to think of Soviets as enemies who would be willing to go to war for the sake of spreading Communism. Germans began to think of the Allied forces more as their protectors than as occupying troops.

The Cold War continued, and East Germany and West Germany officially became separate countries in 1949. The Western countries offered financial assistance to help West Germany get back on its feet, and the economy gradually grew stronger. In East Germany, however, the Soviets were gaining more control and increasingly limiting the freedom of the citizens. Soon, literature, newspapers, theater, art, and radio were only mouthpieces for the government. In addition, the economy was terrible. The Soviet economy was completely controlled by the state and did not create much wealth. Living conditions were poor, food was scarce, and jobs paid very little.

✗ <u>West Berlin was always a problem to the Communists.</u> It sprouted as a prosperous city right in the middle of the poverty of East Germany. East Germans went to Berlin often, and many East Germans even had jobs there. Those who worked in West Berlin were paid much better and could afford to live well. This upset the East German government, but what upset the leaders even more was that many people used West Berlin as an escape route. East Germans would come to the city, and then they would stay there or the West German government would help them to travel to other parts of the West.

As the population in East Germany declined, the people who stayed grew more and more upset at the conditions they faced. In 1953, the dissatisfaction turned into a real uprising in East Berlin's main square. Rioters opened jails and filled the streets in mass demonstrations. The Soviets sent in armed troops, and about 800 East Germans were killed, 240 of them East Berliners. This was the first time that the Soviets used military force to control people in another country, and it further widened the gap between the East and the West.

The Cold War grew worse, and through the 1950s, East Germans continued to flee to the West through Berlin. On August 13, 1961, the East German government made a strong move. Soviet troops ringed Berlin, and 10,000 East German soldiers stood behind them ready to fight. Workmen lined the border between East and West Berlin. They dug in concrete posts that they strung with barbed wire—wire with sharp spikes on it that is used to make fences. Then the workers erected the wall.

✘ The wall that made an island of West Berlin was probably the most guarded wall in all the world. Thirty thousand troops patrolled 193 watchtowers, 208 bunkers, and other watch posts. The guards were ordered to shoot escapees on sight, and shoot they did. Over the 28 years that the wall stood, many people managed to escape over the wall or under the wall in tunnels, but many people were also killed by East German border guards.

Through the 1960s and 1970s, tensions between the Communist and democratic worlds went up and down. With arms control agreements in 1972, the Cold War seemed to be warming up, but the Vietnam conflict and the Soviet invasion of Afghanistan had tensions high again by the end of the 1970s.

Tensions Begin to Ease

The 1980s brought about changes in leadership and changes in the rivalries. Mikhail Gorbachev became the first secretary of the Soviet Communist Party in 1985 and introduced policies of openness and economic restructuring to the Soviet people. Because Eastern European countries took their leads from what the Soviet Union did, East German leaders watched all this nervously, not knowing what it would mean for their country.

✘ What Gorbachev's policies eventually meant for Eastern Europe truly was an opening of possibilities and opportunities for self-government. In 1989, Poland held its first free elections since the 1930s. In mid-1989, Hungary opened its borders with the West. Because East Germans were permitted to travel within Communist-ruled countries, people fled through Hungary and its open borders to Austria and then West Germany, which guaranteed them citizenship.

The East Germans who remained grew more restless as they saw reform come to their neighboring countries. In early November 1989, more than 500,000 people marched in a peaceful demonstration in East Berlin, and other demonstrations went on in other East German cities. The East German government promised changes and tried to keep control. Finally, the government decided that if people were free to go back and forth to West Germany, perhaps they would not feel the need to emigrate, or leave the country.

The Gates Open

✔ On November 9, 1989, the government announced that the border between East and West Germany was finally open. The announcement came in the evening, and by midnight crowds of East Berliners came to the wall to cross by foot, bike, or car into West Germany. West Germans greeted them with applause and cries of joy. After 28 years, the opening of the wall seemed almost incomprehensible! People could go back and forth without any fear of being shot. Even the East German border guards were friendly to the East Germans crossing over.

Celebrations continued over the days and weeks as the wall came down, and the two Germanys got to know one another again. The economic and political situations in

After the Berlin Wall was torn down, people freely entered and left East and West Berlin through large holes that had been cut out of the wall.

the two countries had been so different for so long, that it took much time and debate for the two countries to figure out how to become one again. France, Britain, the United States, and the Soviet Union held talks with the two Germanys. Finally, at midnight on October 3, 1990, East Germany became a part of West Germany, and the two nations were once again one country! Friends and family were reunited in their home country.

RECALLING FACTS

Recognizing sequence of events

1. What happened after Western Allies introduced West German marks in West Berlin?

The Soviets introduced their own money into East Berlin.

Comparing and constrasting

2. a. In the 1950s, what was the economy like in East Berlin?

The economy was bad: food was scarce, and jobs paid

very little.

   b. In the 1950s, what was the economy like in West Berlin?

The economy grew stronger, and West Berlin became

a prosperous city.

Recalling details

3. Why were Germans searching for a strong leader after World War I?

Inflation had skyrocketed, there were no jobs, and there

was very little food. They also hated the reparations.

Identifying the main idea

4. Reread the paragraphs that have **X**'s next to them. Underline the sentence that states the main idea in each paragraph.

Using context clues

5. Circle the correct meaning of the underlined word in each sentence.

   a. If you lose the only copy of my story, you'll have to give me reparations for my loss.

   (payments) repairs

   b. The doctor said that she could reconstruct my broken nose.

   (rebuild) remove

   c. We have been dismantling the furniture in preparation for our move.

   repair (take apart)

   d. To protest the lack of daycare, the working mothers organized several demonstrations at the mayor's office.

   parties (marches)

INTERPRETING FACTS

Drawing conclusions

1. Do you think the World War I Allies made a good decision when they insisted that Germany pay so much in war reparations?

Answers may vary. No. The reparations made Germans

welcome Hitler as a leader.

Making inferences

2. Why did the Allies occupy Germany after World War II?

They wanted to be sure that Germany could never

become such a strong military power again.

Predicting outcomes

3. What would have happened if planes from around the world didn't fly supplies to West Berlin when it was blockaded?

People would have starved to death, or the Soviet

forces would have taken over the entire city.

Inferring comparison and contrast

4. Who suffered more from the Berlin Wall, East Berliners or West Berliners?

East Berliners suffered because they weren't allowed to

go to the West, where the economy was better and

people were free.

5. Reread the paragraph with a check mark next to it. Circle the letter next to the sentence below that states its main idea.

(a.) People from East Germany and West Germany were thrilled and unbelieving that the border was open.

b. In fall of 1989, the border between East and West Germany was open.

c. Border guards were happier than anyone else about the news.

d. East Germans and West Germans were happy, but could not understand each other very well.

6. Study the two photographs and their captions on pages 40 and 42. Then compare and contrast East Berlin as it was in 1961 and 1989.

After the wall was built: East Berlin was closed off. No one was allowed to enter or leave the city; it was closely guarded.

After the border was opened: People could freely travel between East and West Berlin.

SKILL FOCUS

Many cause and effect relationships are described in "The Rise and Fall of the Berlin Wall." In some cases, one cause had several effects. In others, one effect had several causes.

A. Two causes are listed below. On the lines provided, write the effects of each cause.

1. **Cause** Germany was defeated in World War I.

   Effects a. Germany had to pay war reparations.

   b. Germany was forced to give up territory.

2. **Cause** Gorbachev introduced policies of openness.

   Effects a. Poland held free elections.

   b. Hungary opened its borders with the West.

B. Two effects are listed below. On the lines provided, write the causes of each effect.

1. **Causes** a. East Germany blocked all entries to West Berlin.

   b. East Germany cut off electrical power to West Berlin.

   Effect Countries around the world flew supplies into West Berlin.

2. **Causes** a. The East German economy was poor.

   b. The East German government limited the freedom of its citizens.

   Effect Before the end of the Cold War, many East Germans emigrated to the West.

▶ **Real Life Connections** Name two effects of something that you did or said today. Then name one or more causes for something that happened today, either at home or at school.

Diagrams

Reading a Science Selection

▶ Background Information

This selection is about the nervous system and how it works in the human body. All of our behavior in daily life depends on our nervous system, from serious thinking and emotional responses to physical reactions, such as moving away from a source of pain.

Preview "The Nervous System" before you read it. Read the headings and words in boldfaced type. Four diagrams explain some of the ideas in the selection. These diagrams will help you understand how the information in the selection is organized. The selection begins with the smallest unit of the nervous system, the neuron, and progresses to the larger units of the nervous system.

▶ Skill Focus

Textbooks often contain **diagrams** to show what is being explained in the paragraphs. Diagrams can be best understood when you read the paragraphs first. At the end of a paragraph, you might see a reference to a diagram, such as *See Figure 1*.

At that point, you should study the diagram.

When you study a diagram, be sure to read the **caption** and the **labels.** The caption is the statement under the diagram that tells the reader what the figure shows. The labels are the words or phrases that identify parts of the diagram. They usually contain important information.

Use the following steps for reading a selection with diagrams.

1. Read the paragraph before each diagram. Then study the diagram and read its labels and caption. The paragraph below the diagram may also explain what is pictured. Read that paragraph, too.
2. Read the rest of the paragraphs. Look back at the diagrams whenever you think they will help you.
3. After you have finished reading the paragraphs and studying the diagrams, look away from the selection. Try to picture what you have read and the details in the diagrams. If you are not able to do this, read the material again.
4. Follow this method until you understand all the ideas in the selection.

▶ Word Clues

Read the sentence below. Look for context clues that explain the underlined word.

> It is divided into two hemispheres, or halves, by a deep groove.

If you do not know the meaning of the word *hemispheres,* the phrase, *or halves,* can help you. The phrase *or halves* is an appositive phrase. An appositive phrase explains a word coming before it and is set off from the word by commas or dashes.

Use **appositive phrases** to find the meaning of the three underlined words in the selection.

▶ Strategy Tip

When you read "The Nervous System," be sure to follow the four steps for reading a selection with diagrams. Many training manuals use diagrams. Learning how to read them can be useful to you on a job.

The Nervous System

The nervous system is the body's communication system. It carries messages about the outside world and about the body itself. It carries messages that allow muscles to move. It also keeps the body's organs functioning.

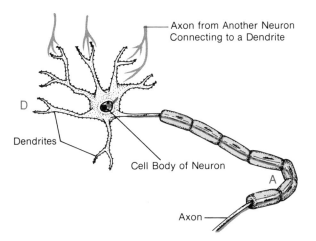

Figure 1. The neuron is the basic unit of the nervous system. Messages are sent by the axon and received by the dendrites.

Neurons

The basic unit of the nervous system is the **neuron** (NOO ron), or nerve cell. A neuron has three parts. It has a cell body and two kinds of threads that extend from it. The long thread is the **axon** (AK son), and the short threads are the **dendrites** (DEN drytz). See Figure 1.

Some neurons have more than one dendrite, but most neurons have only one axon. The dendrites carry messages to the cell body. The axon carries messages away from the cell body. The axon of one neuron connects to the dendrite of another. When a message travels through the nervous system, it is sent by the axon of each neuron. The dendrite receives the message from the axon and passes it on to the next neuron.

Nerves are bundles of neuron fibers, or threads. Different kinds of nerves perform different functions in the nervous system. **Sensory** (SEN sor ee) **nerves** carry messages to the brain and the spinal cord. **Motor nerves** carry messages from the central nervous system to the body's muscles. **Connecting nerves** connect sensory and motor nerves. See Figure 2.

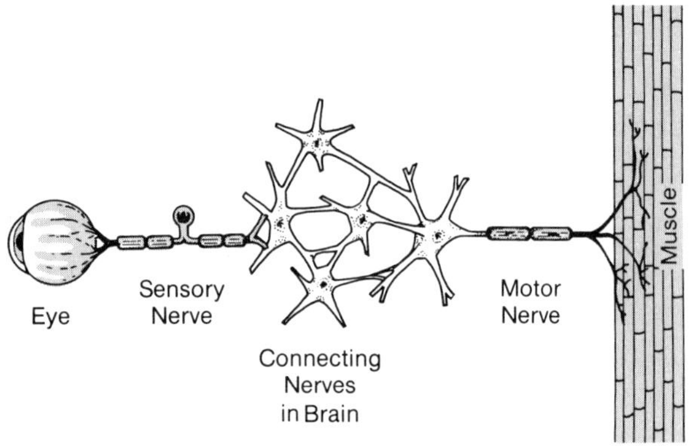

Parts of the Nervous System

The nervous system has two basic parts. The **central nervous system** is made up of the brain and the spinal cord. The **peripheral** (pə RIF ər əl) **nervous system** is made up of the nerves that branch out from the brain and the spinal cord. The **autonomic** (aw toh NOM ik) **nervous system** is a part of the peripheral nervous system. It is made up of the nerves that regulate the internal organs of the body.

Central Nervous System The brain is like the switchboard of a telephone system. Most of the "calls" from the outside world travel through the nerves to the brain. The brain

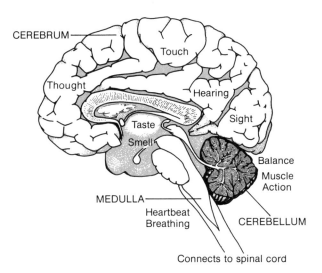

Figure 2. Different kinds of nerves perform different functions.

Figure 3. The brain is the center of the nervous system. It has three parts.

takes in the information from the nerves and sends out orders through the nerves. Although the brain is the principal control center, the spinal cord also plays a major role in receiving and sending messages to the sensory and motor nerves.

The brain itself is divided into three main parts: **cerebrum** (SER ə brəm), **cerebellum** (ser ə BEL əm), and **medulla** (mi DUL ə). See Figure 3. The cerebrum is the largest part of the brain. It is divided into two hemispheres, or halves, by a deep groove. The left hemisphere controls the right side of the body. It is thought to affect the use of language, mathematics, and logical thinking. The right hemisphere controls the left side of the body. Scientists think it affects musical and artistic ability and emotions. Information from the five senses comes to the cerebrum. The cerebrum is the thinking part of the brain. This is where memory is stored. The cerebrum controls all conscious activity, or those activities of which you are aware.

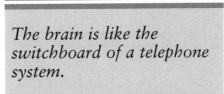

The brain is like the switchboard of a telephone system.

The cerebellum is located underneath the cerebrum. It controls balance and movement of the muscles. The cerebellum also regulates how groups of muscles work together. For example, it <u>coordinates</u> the movements between the hands and the eyes that allow a person to catch a ball—that is, it makes the hands and eyes work well together. The cerebellum affects <u>involuntary</u> activity, the kind of activity of which you are not conscious.

The medulla is the part of the brain that regulates the body's <u>internal</u> organs—the organs inside the body. It controls such vital activities as breathing, the beating of the heart, and the digestion of food. It also controls sneezing, coughing, hiccuping, vomiting, and swallowing.

The medulla connects directly to the spinal cord. The spinal cord is a long bundle of nerves that extends down through the backbone. All messages to or from the brain go through the spinal cord.

Peripheral Nervous System The peripheral nervous system is made up of the nerves that connect the central nervous system to the rest of the body. *Periphery* means "outer edge."

The peripheral nervous system reaches the outer parts of the body, including the hands and feet. See Figure 4.

Nerves of the peripheral nervous system work closely with the central nervous system. The optic nerve, for example, connects the back wall of the eye to the brain. When a person sees something, the eyes receive the image. The image is then sent to the brain by the optic nerve. The brain then "tells" the person what he or she is seeing.

Not all messages are carried to the brain. The nerves can bypass the brain for faster reactions. When a person touches something hot, for example, he or she doesn't first think "hot" before moving. The person moves almost instantly, without thinking. This is called a **reflex action.** In a reflex action, the command to move is sent from the spinal cord instead of the brain.

The autonomic nervous system controls the beating of the heart, the digesting of food, and breathing. *Autonomous* means "independent." The autonomic nervous system works independently of a person's thoughts. The heart beats, food is digested, and breathing continues automatically. The medulla is the

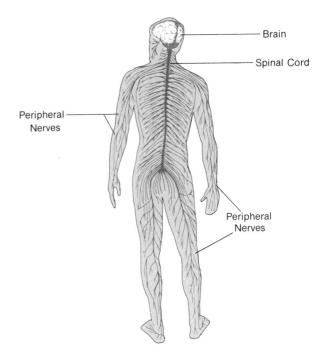

Figure 4. The peripheral nervous system reaches the outer parts of the body.

control center for the autonomic nervous system. Messages that begin in the medulla keep the body's internal organs functioning.

The **sympathetic** (sim pə THET ik) and the **parasympathetic** (par ə sim pə THET ik) systems are the two parts of the autonomic nervous system. The sympathetic system works to speed up the heart and send more blood to the muscles during times of physical activity, anger, or stress. The parasympathetic system works to slow down the heartbeat and send blood back to the digestive system during times of rest. In these ways, the body always gets the power and rest that it needs.

RECALLING FACTS

Recalling details
1. What is a neuron?

A neuron is the basic unit of the nervous system

Recalling details
2. What is the purpose of dendrites?

They carry messages to the cell body.

Recalling details
3. How is the axon different from dendrites?

The axon carries messages away from the cell body.

Recalling details
4. What activities do scientists believe are affected by the left side of the brain?

They believe it affects language, mathematics, and

logical thinking.

Recalling details
5. What activities do scientists believe are affected by the right side of the brain?

They believe it affects musical and artistic activities,

and the emotions.

Recalling details
6. What is the purpose of the autonomic nervous system?

It controls the internal organs of the body.

Using context clues
7. Complete each sentence by filling in the correct word.

   involuntary internal coordinates

   a. The engine and the transmission are

   among the _____internal_____ parts

   of a car.

   b. A social director_____coordinates_____

   activities.

   c. When the pupil of the eye enlarges in

   bright sunlight, it is a(n)

   _____involuntary_____ action.

INTERPRETING FACTS

Making inferences
1. A reflex action is faster than an action that involves thought because the nerve message that causes it

   ▊ a. travels a shorter distance.

   ‖ b. occurs when a person is angry.

   ‖ c. is hotter.

Inferring cause and effect
2. Which of the following would cause a reflex action?

   ▊ a. stepping on a sharp rock

   ‖ b. seeing a good friend

   ‖ c. deciding what to order in a restaurant

Making inferences
3. If a person saw a charging lion, which part of the autonomic nervous system would react?

   ▊ a. sympathetic system

   ‖ b. parasympathetic system

   ‖ c. peripheral system

4. When a person awakens from a nap feeling refreshed, it is because the parasympathetic nervous system has

   ☐ **a.** stopped the body's functions.

   ☐ **b.** speeded up the body's functions.

   ☑ **c.** slowed down the body's functions.

Inferring cause and effect

5. If the heart did not have nerves,

   ☐ **a.** it would expand.

   ☑ **b.** it could not receive the message to beat.

   ☐ **c.** it would not be part of the central nervous system.

Inferring cause and effect

6. If a person is left-handed, which hemisphere of the cerebrum controls the activity of writing?

   ☐ **a.** left

   ☑ **b.** right

   ☐ **c.** both

Inferring cause and effect

7. If a person is ambidextrous and can use both hands equally, then the

   ☑ **a.** two hemispheres of the cerebrum can both control writing.

   ☐ **b.** cerebellum is stronger than the cerebrum.

   ☐ **c.** spinal cord is as strong as the brain.

SKILL FOCUS

1. Look at Figure 1. Put a check mark on the cell body. Put a *D* next to a dendrite and an *A* next to the axon.

2. Look at Figure 2. In your own words, explain how the nervous system might work if a person sees danger and runs from it.

The eyes see the danger. The message is carried by the sensory nerves to the connecting nerves. The connecting nerves carry the message to the motor nerves which send the message to the leg muscles, and the person runs.

3. Look at Figure 3. Name the three parts of the brain and the function of each part.

The cerebrum controls all conscious activity, thinking, and memory and also receives information from the five senses. The cerebellum controls involuntary activity, such as balance, muscle action, and coordination. The medulla regulates the internal organs. It controls breathing, the beating of the heart, and the digestion of food.

4. In your own words, explain what is shown in Figure 4.

The peripheral nervous system connects the central nervous system to the rest of the body. It extends all the way to the hands and feet.

▶ **Real Life Connections** Which part of the human nervous system are you most interested in studying?

Lesson 14

Decimals

___ Reading a Mathematics Selection ___

▶ **Background Information**

You probably do not use the word *decimals* often, but you use decimals almost every day of your life.

Decimals are used to measure the amounts of many things that you buy. Packages of meat, fish, and chicken usually show their weight in decimals, for example, "1.5 lbs." That means the package weighs one and a half pounds. Almost every time that you buy gas for your car, the gas meter shows how much gasoline you have bought in decimals, for example, 10.67 gallons. When you buy boxes of breakfast cereal or cake mix, often the label will tell the amounts of different vitamins in the food in decimal amounts. Bottles and boxes of multiple vitamins tell you how much of each kind of vitamin each pill contains.

Every time that you look at a bill or see the price of your purchases on a cash register, you also read decimals—for example, $12.65, $8.34. The decimals in these amounts of money are cents—65 cents and 34 cents. These decimals show you what part of a

dollar (100 cents) these amounts are: 65 cents is 65 parts of a dollar; 34 cents is 34 parts of a dollar.

The following selection explains decimals. You will learn the names for the four place values to the right of the decimal point.

▶ **Skill Focus**

Some numbers are written with **decimal points.** A decimal point separates the number into two parts. The digits to the left of the decimal point are whole numbers. The digits to the right of the decimal point are parts of a whole.

126.73

In the number above, 126 is the whole number. The decimal point shows that 73 is part of a whole. When you read this number, you use the word *and* in place of the decimal point. It is read like this: one hundred twenty-six *and* seventy-three hundredths.

As a warm-up for this lesson, see if you can give the answer to the following questions.

If your class has twenty students in it, including yourself, what part of the class are you?

If your club dues are one dollar a week and your allowance is fifteen dollars a week, what part of your allowance are your club dues?

▶ **Word Clues**

The suffix *th* can be added to a number word. When *th* is added to ten, hundred, or thousand, the value of the number word is made less. A *hundred* kilometers is very different from a *hundredth* of a kilometer. If you run a *hundred* kilometers, you have run ten thousand times farther than a *hundredth* of a kilometer. The suffix *th is* used with any place value to the right of the decimal point.

▶ **Strategy Tip**

The suffix *th* is an important clue in reading decimals. It is always used when naming any place value to the right of the decimal point. Failure to use this suffix will confuse people about what number amounts you are using.

READING DECIMALS

Each place to the left of the decimal point shows a value. These are whole numbers.

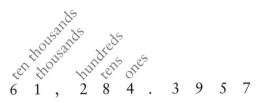

6 1 , 2 8 4 . 3 9 5 7

The whole number in the number above is sixty-one thousand, two hundred and eighty-four. The members in all the places of this number—61,284—have values of one or more. Places to the right of the decimal point are decimal places. They show values of less than one. The suffix *th* is used in naming each decimal place. The places to the right of the decimal point are tenths, hundredths, thousandths, and ten-thousandths.

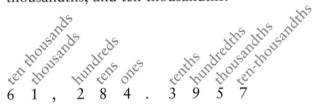

6 1 , 2 8 4 . 3 9 5 7

The tenths place is the first place to the right of the decimal point. A number in the tenths place is $\frac{1}{10}$ as large as the same number in the ones place. Think about a dollar bill. It takes 10 dimes to make a dollar. A dime is one-tenth of a dollar. One-tenth can be written as a decimal, 0.1 or as a fraction, $\frac{1}{10}$. A dime is 0.1 or $\frac{1}{10}$ of a dollar.

The hundredths place is the second place to the right of the decimal point. A number in the hundredths place is one-hundredth of the same number in the ones place. It takes 100 pennies to make a dollar. A penny is one-hundredth of a dollar. One-hundredth can be written as a decimal, 0.01, or as a fraction, $\frac{1}{100}$. A penny is 0.01 or $\frac{1}{100}$ of a dollar.

The thousandths place is the third place to the right of the decimal point. A number in the thousandths place is one thousandth of the same number in the ones place. This is a very small part of a dollar, and no coin is made for that value. One-thousandth of a dollar is called a *mil*. Mils are used in the financial world. It takes 1,000 mils to make a dollar. One-thousandth can be

written as a decimal, 0.001, or as a fraction, $\frac{1}{1,000}$. A mil is 0.001, or $\frac{1}{1,000}$ of a dollar.

The ten-thousandths place is the fourth place to the right of the decimal point. A number in the ten-thousandths place is a ten-thousandth of the same number in the ones place. This is an even smaller part of a dollar than a mil. One ten-thousandth can be written as a decimal, 0.0001, or as a fraction, $\frac{1}{10,000}$.

A number with digits only in the decimal places can be written in two ways.

0.7 or .7

These two numbers have the same value. You read this number as though it were a whole number: seven. Then you add the name of the place value: tenths. The number is read like this: seven tenths.

ones	.	tenths	hundredths	thousandths	ten-thousandths	
0	.	7				seven tenths
0	.	0	4			four hundredths
0	.	6	1			sixty-one hundredths
0	.	0	0	2		two thousandths
0	.	8	3	5		eight hundred thirty-five thousandths
0	.	0	3	4	2	three hundred forty-two ten-thousandths
0	.	9	0	3	1	nine thousand thirty-one ten-thousandths

A number that includes digits on both sides of the decimal point is read in two groups.

9,295.17

First, read the digits to the left of the decimal point as a whole number: nine thousand two hundred ninety-five. The decimal point stands for the word *and*. Then read the decimal value as though it were a whole number: seventeen. Then add the name of the place value of the last digit: hundredths. The number is read like this: nine thousand two hundred ninety-five and seventeen hundredths.

The number can also be written as a whole number and a fraction. The decimal number is written as a fraction. The whole number remains the same. Because 7 is in the hundredths place, the denominator of the fraction is 100. It is read the same as the decimal number.

$$9,295\tfrac{17}{100}$$

Read the following number.

263.783

Read the digits to the left of the decimal point first. Then say the word *and* when you reach the decimal point. Read the digits to the right of the decimal point. Because the last digit is in the thousandths place, add the word *thousandths*. The number is read like this: two hundred sixty-three and seven hundred eighty-three thousandths. The number is written as a whole number and a fraction as follows:

$$263\tfrac{783}{1,000}$$

Look at the following number.

49.5036

It is read like this: forty-nine and five thousand thirty-six ten-thousandths.

Remember, the decimal point separates the whole numbers from the numbers that are less than one whole. The numbers to the right of the decimal point are always less than one.

RECALLING FACTS

Recalling details
1. Write the place values for each digit in this number.

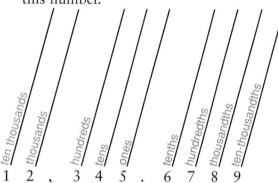

1 2 , 3 4 5 . 6 7 8 9

Recalling details
2. When you hear *and* in a number being read, it means a ___decimal point___.

Recalling details
3. If a dollar bill is one, what part of a dollar is a dime? a penny? a mil? Write each as a fraction and a decimal.

$0.10 = $ ___$\frac{1}{10}$___ = ___0.1___

$0.01 = $ ___$\frac{1}{100}$___ = ___0.01___

mil = ___$\frac{1}{1,000}$___ = ___0.001___

INTERPRETING FACTS

Making inferences
1. Where do you see decimals and fractions used in your daily life?

decimals: money, gas pump, food labels

fractions: recipes, measurements

Inferring cause and effect
2. These numbers all have the same digits. Why do the numbers have different values?
    0.015 .0015 .0105

The digits are in different places.

Making inferences
3. Circle the smallest value in each row.
    a. .7   .04   (.001)
    b. (.04)   .102   .5
    c. .317   (.0146)   .09

Making inferences
4. Circle the largest value in each row.
    a. .08   .095   (.2)
    b. .27   (.41)   .0896
    c. .1   (.275)   .09

A. Write each number in the correct column.

	ten thousands	thousands	hundreds	tens	ones	tenths	hundredths	thousandths	ten-thousandths
54 and 9 tenths				5	4	.9			
6,702 and 8 tenths		6,	7	0	2	.8			
7 hundredths						.0	7		
1 and 38 hundredths					1	.3	8		
7 thousandths						.0	0	7	
91 thousandths						.0	9	1	
643 thousandths						.6	4	3	
56 and 2 thousandths				5	6	.0	0	2	
312 and 54 thousandths			3	1	2	.0	5	4	
6 ten-thousandths						.0	0	0	6
923 ten-thousandths						.0	9	2	3
1,246 ten-thousandths						.1	2	4	6
172 and 73 ten-thousandths			1	7	2	.0	0	7	3
4,317 and 6,431 ten-thousandths		4,	3	1	7	.6	4	3	1
80,008 and 8 ten-thousandths	8	0,	0	0	8	.0	0	0	8

B. Write the fraction for each decimal.

0.2 $\underline{\quad \frac{2}{10} \quad}$ 0.0091 $\underline{\quad \frac{91}{10,000} \quad}$ 884.18 $\underline{\quad 884\frac{18}{100} \quad}$

0.65 $\underline{\quad \frac{65}{100} \quad}$ 6.9 $\underline{\quad 6\frac{9}{10} \quad}$ 329.861 $\underline{\quad 329\frac{861}{1,000} \quad}$

0.634 $\underline{\quad \frac{634}{1,000} \quad}$ 45.05 $\underline{\quad 45\frac{5}{100} \quad}$ 25.0106 $\underline{\quad 25\frac{106}{10,000} \quad}$

0.4372 $\underline{\quad \frac{4,372}{10,000} \quad}$ 2,379.025 $\underline{\quad 2,379\frac{25}{1,000} \quad}$ 7,563.4007 $\underline{\quad 7,563\frac{4,007}{10,000} \quad}$

C. Draw lines to match the decimals and the fractions.

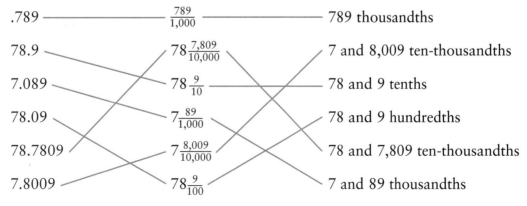

.789 ——— $\frac{789}{1,000}$ ——— 789 thousandths

78.9 $78\frac{7,809}{10,000}$ 7 and 8,009 ten-thousandths

7.089 $78\frac{9}{10}$ 78 and 9 tenths

78.09 $7\frac{89}{1,000}$ 78 and 9 hundredths

78.7809 $7\frac{8,009}{10,000}$ 78 and 7,809 ten-thousandths

7.8009 $78\frac{9}{100}$ 7 and 89 thousandths

▶ **Real Life Connections** Where do you see decimals and fractions used in your daily life?

Vowel–Consonant Combinations

The vowel-consonant combinations *air, ear,* and *are* can stand for the same sound. The words *hair, bear,* and *square* have the same vowel sound, but the letters that stand for the sound are different in each word.

Read the sentences below. Choose a word from the list to complete each sentence. Write the word on the line.

share	**prepare**	**pears**	**stare**
wear	**stairs**	**chair**	**fair**

1. Theo's favorite fruit is ———— pears ————.

2. Clarkstown School is having a book ———— fair ———— next week.

3. Jorge helped his father ———— prepare ———— dinner by making the salad.

4. You should never ———— stare ———— at the sun without protective glasses, or you will damage your eyes.

5. My sister and I ———— share ———— clothes.

6. It is considered proper to push your ———— chair ———— in before you leave the table.

7. Sarah likes to ———— wear ———— heavy sweaters in the winter.

8. You have to walk up two flights of ———— stairs ———— to get to my apartment.

The vowel-consonant combination *ear* can stand for different sounds. The words *bear, earth,* and *beard* have the same vowel letters followed by *r,* but the vowel sound the letters stand for is different in each word.

Read the sentences below. Choose a word from the list to complete each sentence. Write the word on the line.

clear	**search**	**fear**	**early**
heard	**careful**	**learn**	**square**

1. When Warren lost his key, we had to ———— search ———— to find it.

2. Have you ———— heard ———— the news about Governor Harris?

3. We got up ———— early ———— every morning when we camped last summer.

4. Elena will ———— learn ———— how to drive a car next year.

5. Many people ———— fear ———— certain kinds of animals.

6. The sky is always bright blue on a ———— clear ———— day.

7. Please be ———— careful ———— when you cross the street.

8. A ———— square ———— has four equal sides.

Syllables

Guide 3: Words with a Prefix or Suffix

A prefix always has at least one sounded vowel. This means that a prefix always contains at least one syllable. You can divide a word that has a prefix between the prefix and the root word.

misspell   mis spell

Most suffixes have at least one sounded vowel. This means that a suffix usually contains at least one syllable. You can divide a word that has a suffix between the root word and the suffix.

quickly   quick ly

Divide each of the words below into two syllables between the prefix or suffix and the root word. Write each syllable separately on the line to the right of the word.

1. backward	back ward	9. statement	state ment
2. worthless	worth less	10. preheat	pre heat
3. mistrust	mis trust	11. painter	paint er
4. impure	im pure	12. nonsense	non sense
5. fearful	fear ful	13. nearness	near ness
6. biplane	bi plane	14. redo	re do
7. rainy	rain y	15. mistreat	mis treat
8. midday	mid day	16. yearly	year ly

Guide 4: Words with Two Consonants Between Two Sounded Vowels

A word that has two consonants between two sounded vowels is usually divided into syllables between the two consonants.

winter   win ter

Divide each of the words below into two syllables. Write each syllable separately on the line to the right of the word.

1. signal	sig nal	8. window	win dow
2. blanket	blan ket	9. escape	es cape
3. master	mas ter	10. dentist	den tist
4. admit	ad mit	11. walnut	wal nut
5. plastic	plas tic	12. napkin	nap kin
6. sandal	san dal	13. magnet	mag net
7. helmet	hel met	14. perfume	per fume

Lesson 17

Prefixes

A **prefix** is a word part that is added to the beginning of a word to change its meaning. Eight prefixes and their meanings are given below.

Prefix	Meaning
bi	having two, or happening every two
de	away from or undo
mid	middle
non	not
semi	half or partly
sub	under or below
tri	having three, or happening every three
uni	having only one
re	again

Read each word below and the meaning that follows it. Write the correct prefix before each word.

1. __mid__ day — middle of the day

2. __bi__ monthly — once every two months

3. __de__ frost — to become unfrozen

4. __sub__ freezing — below freezing

5. __semi__ sweet — partly sweet

6. __de__ rail — to go off the rails

7. __tri__ angle — a shape with three angles

8. __semi__ circle — half a circle

9. __uni__ cycle — one-wheel vehicle

10. __non__ sense — not making sense

11. __re__ play — play again

Use one of the words above to complete each sentence below.

1. It is so cold outside that it must be __subfreezing__.

2. Another word for twelve o'clock noon is __midday__.

3. We sat in a __semicircle__ around the fire.

4. Mr. Barker had to __defrost__ his refrigerator.

5. A __unicycle__ is difficult to ride because it has only one wheel.

6. I read the letter, but it sounded like __nonsense__.

7. Broken track caused the train to __derail__.

8. Our craft club meets __bimonthly__.

9. The baker used __semisweet__ chocolate to make this cake.

10. In geometry class, we learned how to measure the angles of a __triangle__.

11. Because they tied their last game, the two teams had to __replay__ it.

Stated or Unstated Main Idea

When you read a textbook or reference book for information, the main idea of each paragraph will often be stated in a sentence. The rest of the paragraph will contain the supporting details that give additional information about the main idea.

Sometimes the main idea of a paragraph is not stated in one of the sentences. The information given in the paragraph will help you to **infer**, or figure out, the main idea yourself. To do this, think of a sentence that summarizes the supporting details of the paragraph.

Read the following selection. Decide if the main idea in each paragraph is stated or unstated.

Nō and Kabuki Plays

1. Plays are an important form of entertainment in most countries. Two ki drama unique to Japan are Nō and Kabuki. Music is used in both types of drama. Originally, men performed both men's and women's parts in Nō and Kabuki plays. Bu similarities end there.

2. Kabuki costumes are fancy, bright, and heavy. On the other hand, Nō costumes are quite simple. Kabuki stages are huge and are elaborate. Nō stages are only 18 feet (5.4 meters) square. The only scenery used is a background wall with a tree painted on it. audience must use a lot of imagination.

3. Nō plays started in the 14th century to entertain the upper classes. All parts of a No play must follow a certain set of rules. A Nō actor may look as if he is sleepwalking. The action of the play is slow. Certain actions stand

for certain things. For example, a few steps forward mean the end of a journey. An important part of a Nō play is the choru chants much of the story.

4. Kabuki plays were developed in the 17th century for the common people. Theate was the main amusement of the merchants of that time. Kabuki plays reflect the merchant's happy moods. The players wear thick makeup and exaggerate their movements and facial expressions to communicate feelings

5. Music is important to Kabuki plays. Kabuki actors sing, dance, and speak their lines to music in the background. Musicians play instruments, such as flutes, drums, and gongs They also use the samisen, a three-stringed instrument shaped somewhat like a banjo. Another common instrument has two small blocks of wood that are banged on the floo

For each paragraph in the selection, if the main idea is stated, write the word *stated* on the line. If the main idea is *unstated,* choose a main idea from the sentences given below and write the letter on the line.

   a. Because Kabuki plays are more exciting, they are more popular than Nō plays.
   b. A Nō play is noted for its rules and for the controlled movements of the players.
   c. Kabuki plays reflect the gaiety and showiness of 17th century Japanese merchants.
   d. One difference between Nō and Kabuki plays is that Nō is simpler.
   e. Kabuki actors exaggerate their movements to show emotions.

Paragraph 1 ___stated___   *Paragraph 3* ___b___   *Paragraph 5* ___stated___

Paragraph 2 ___d___   *Paragraph 4* ___c___

Go back to each paragraph that has a stated main idea and underline the sentence with the main idea.

Following Directions

Choking occurs when food or another foreign body completely blocks the air passage, making it impossible to breathe or speak. A person choking on food could die in as little as four minutes. A first-aid technique called **abdominal thrusts** can be used to rescue a choking person. This procedure forces the object blocking the breathing passage out through the mouth.

If a choking victim can either speak or cough, he or she should be encouraged to cough up the object. If the person cannot cough up the object, call an ambulance. If a victim cannot speak or cough, he or she is not getting air, and abdominal thrusts should be used. Choking victims who cannot speak should signal for help by clutching their throat.

Carefully read the information below to learn how to help someone who is choking.

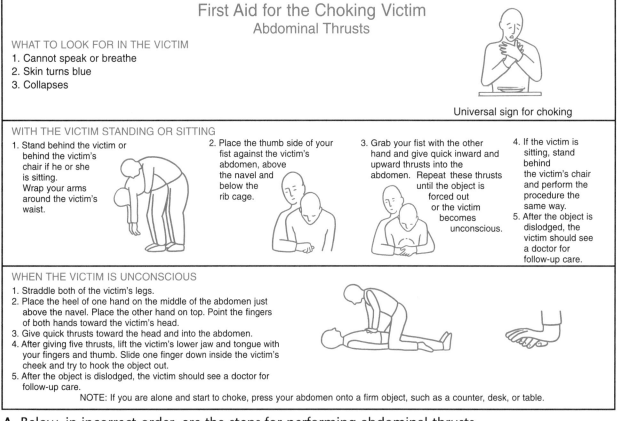

First Aid for the Choking Victim
Abdominal Thrusts

WHAT TO LOOK FOR IN THE VICTIM
1. Cannot speak or breathe
2. Skin turns blue
3. Collapses

Universal sign for choking

WITH THE VICTIM STANDING OR SITTING
1. Stand behind the victim or behind the victim's chair if he or she is sitting. Wrap your arms around the victim's waist.
2. Place the thumb side of your fist against the victim's abdomen, above the navel and below the rib cage.
3. Grab your fist with the other hand and give quick inward and upward thrusts into the abdomen. Repeat these thrusts until the object is forced out or the victim becomes unconscious.
4. If the victim is sitting, stand behind the victim's chair and perform the procedure the same way.
5. After the object is dislodged, the victim should see a doctor for follow-up care.

WHEN THE VICTIM IS UNCONSCIOUS
1. Straddle both of the victim's legs.
2. Place the heel of one hand on the middle of the abdomen just above the navel. Place the other hand on top. Point the fingers of both hands toward the victim's head.
3. Give quick thrusts toward the head and into the abdomen.
4. After giving five thrusts, lift the victim's lower jaw and tongue with your fingers and thumb. Slide one finger down inside the victim's cheek and try to hook the object out.
5. After the object is dislodged, the victim should see a doctor for follow-up care.
NOTE: If you are alone and start to choke, press your abdomen onto a firm object, such as a counter, desk, or table.

A. Below, in incorrect order, are the steps for performing abdominal thrusts when the victim is standing or sitting. Write *1* in front of the step to follow first, *2* in front of the step to follow next, and so on.

___3___ Place the thumb side of your fist against the victim's abdomen, above the navel and below the rib cage.

___1___ Stand behind the victim or behind the victim's chair if he or she is sitting.

___5___ Repeat these thrusts until the object is forced out or the victim becomes unconscious.

___2___ Wrap your arms around the victim's waist.

___4___ Grab your fist with the other hand and give quick inward and upward thrusts into the abdomen.

B. Read the statements about abdominal thrusts and write *true* or *false* on each line.

false   1. A victim is a person who gives first aid.

true   2. When food completely blocks the air passage, it is impossible for a person to breathe or speak.

false   3. Abdominal thrusts require that the choking victim be slapped on the back four times.

false   4. Abdominal thrusts can be done with the victim standing, sitting, or lying on his or her stomach.

true   5. Someone choking can perform abdominal thrusts on himself or herself if no help is around.

true   6. If a choking victim cannot speak or breathe, he or she is not getting any air.

false   7. If a piece of meat blocks a person's air passage, that person will be unaware of it.

false   8. Abdominal thrusts force food down a choking person's throat into the stomach.

true   9. The rescuer faces the victim who is lying down.

true   10. A rescuer may need to repeat abdominal thrusts several times to free the object blocking the air passage.

true   11. You could save a person's life using abdominal thrusts.

true   12. After abdominal thrusts, the victim should see a doctor for follow-up care.

C. Write the answer to each question. Use complete sentences.

1. For what kind of emergency are abdominal thrusts used? They are used on someone who is choking.

2. Why do you think it is important for everybody to know how to perform abdominal thrusts? It is important because abdominal thrusts could save the life of a person who is choking.

3. Why are choking victims unable to speak or breathe? Their air passage is blocked by the food that they are choking on.

4. Rescuers use their hands differently depending on the position of the choking victim. What do they do with their hands for standing or sitting victims? They make a fist.
What do they do for victims lying down? They place one hand on top of the other.

5. How should you let someone know that you are choking? You should clutch your throat with your hand.

6. What is the value of having only one sign to indicate choking? One sign is important so that everyone will recognize it and act immediately.

7. What are the three signs that someone is choking on food? The person can't speak or breathe; and he or she turns blue and collapses.

8. When would some choking victims be lying down rather than standing or sitting? They would be lying down if they had collapsed.

Lesson 20 _____

Mood

Reading a Literature Selection _____

▶ Background Information

Dolphins are intelligent, air-breathing, warm-blooded sea animals. To sailors the sight of a school of dolphins playing in the ocean means good luck. In this story, a whole town mobilizes to help a school of dolphins whose luck has run out.

▶ Skill Focus

Mood is the atmosphere, or feeling, in a story. The mood of a story can be lively, serious, suspenseful, or humorous. An author creates mood by using vivid phrases and details. Sometimes an author repeats a phrase or two to make the mood stronger or more obvious. Setting also influences a story's mood.

Read the paragraph below. Notice the underlined phrases and details that help build a mood of suspense.

The <u>abandoned beach house</u> stood <u>isolated on the dunes</u>. It was <u>too quiet</u> as far as Pat and Chris were concerned. There before them stretched the <u>long, dark, dirty hallway</u>. They

knew that they would have to step through it to get to the other room. Slowly, <u>a door creaked open</u> at the back of the house. Pat felt <u>a sudden chill</u>. <u>A small gust of air ruffled Chris's hair</u>. "Who's there?" they called. "Who's there?" they called again. Still <u>no one answered</u>.

Phrases and details like "a door creaked open," "a sudden chill," "a small gust of air ruffled Chris's hair," and "no one answered" help create a mood of suspense. Repetition of the phrase "Who's there?" heightens the suspense. Even the setting— an "abandoned beach house," "isolated on the dunes," and a "long, dark, dirty hallway"—contributes to the mood. The reader does not know the answer to the question "Who's there?"

An author builds a mood of suspense to keep the outcome of a story uncertain. A mood of suspense also helps catch the reader's interest.

▶ Word Clues

Read the sentence that follows. Look for context

clues that explain the underlined word.

He ran the nylon rope over the <u>winch</u>, which looked like a spool with a crank at the side.

If you don't know the meaning of the word _winch_, the phrase _looked like a spool with a crank at the side_ can help you. The appearance of a winch is compared to that of a spool. A phrase that uses the word _like_ or _as_ to compare two unlike things is called a simile.

Use **comparison** context clues to find the meaning of the three underlined words in the selection.

▶ Strategy Tip

As you read, think about the sounds and sights that an author uses to describe the story's setting. Look for vivid phrases and details. What mood has the author created? How does the setting contribute to the story's mood?

The Dolphin Disaster

Skreek—a single sea gull wheeled across the low, gray sky. The fog was closing in on Port Hegen like a dirty cotton curtain. Most of the lobster boats were still outside the harbor. Ralph Hemming was busy setting his lobster traps when he spotted the first of the dolphins.

"Must be two hundred, maybe three hundred dolphins out there," he said, using the radio that linked his boat to shore. "Odd. Haven't seen them this close to shore in years."

Annie Sloan's voice came over the radio. "Had some up at the Cape last year. Paper said that over a dozen died. Got trapped in shallow water."

The radio crackled as another voice came in. "Hey, Ralph. You got Spooner with you?"

Hemming swung his rumbling boat toward a bright red float that marked one of his sunken traps. He pressed the microphone button. "He's on the wharf mending some of our traps."

"Too bad," said the other voice. "Spooner might have an idea why they're headed so close to the shallows. He knows all about these things."

Other voices on the radio agreed. Meanwhile, Ralph Hemming was busy hooking up his trap line, a rope tied to the trap. He ran the nylon rope over the winch, which looked like a spool with a crank at the side. By turning the crank, the winch would pull the heavy wooden trap up from the bottom, a hundred feet below.

Ralph thought about his son, Spooner. For a sixteen year old, Spooner knew the sea well. He was always reading about the sea and its creatures. In some ways, he knew more about the ocean than some adults who had spent their lives on the water. One thing was sure, though. Spooner wouldn't fish for a living like his grandfather and father. Oh, he'd work with the sea all right, but he'd probably pursue his goal of studying ocean science. Spooner <u>aspired</u> to be an oceanographer just as much as many boys his age dreamed about becoming football players.

Dolphins! Hundreds of them arching out of the water in sleek, dark curves!

Spooner was so struck by the sight that he dropped the lobster trap that he was mending. He ran to the end of the wharf.

The dolphins were in the middle of the channel, moving toward Bald Point. Spooner strained his eyes, but the fog, edging nearer to shore, made it difficult to see the dolphins clearly.

Spooner scrambled down the worn wooden steps to the pebbly beach. His shoes clattered on the smooth stones. The tide had already begun to go out. Pushing his family's rowboat to the water's edge, Spooner floated it and jumped in. He swung the small outboard motor into the water and yanked on the rope several times. This will be the day that the motor won't start, he thought. Finally, the motor buzzed into life.

The fog was getting thicker. In a matter of moments, the dolphins would be swallowed up in the thick folds of the fog. Spooner headed the boat out into the channel. He knew the waters of this rocky coast by heart. He knew that he could track down the dolphins.

Even so, Spooner nearly missed them in the fog. The narrow entrance to Bald Point Cove was only fifty feet wide, with low cliffs rising on both sides. Catching a movement in the water out of the corner of his eye, Spooner swung his boat toward land. Beaching the craft, he sprinted up the low cliff on one side of Bald Point Cove.

The little <u>cove</u> was like a soup bowl three hundred yards across. At high tide, the water in the cove was twenty feet at its deepest. At low tide, the cove was a stretch of mud.

Spooner stood looking down at the cove. Below, he saw hundreds of dolphins swimming around the small pool. They darted this way and that, circling, confused. Something was very wrong.

Then Spooner remembered the story in the paper last year. More than twenty dolphins had died in shallow water off Cape Cod. Some scientists believed that the dolphins' built-in "sonar" had failed for some reason.

Spooner watched as the <u>ebbing</u> tide ran out of the cove like water out of a cracked bowl. The dolphins were swimming faster in crazier circles. He had to get help fast. He'd head for home and get his sister Audrey. She wasn't very interested in the sea, but she was a terrific organizer. She'd help!

Only half an hour later, Spooner and Audrey watched Mr. Shell push back his sleeves and lean against his counter. "Look, kids, I'll be glad to help, but I can't leave the store just now. After six, when I close . . ."

"Then it will be too late!" cried Audrey.

Mr. Shell was the third person in the village Audrey and Spooner had approached. They had gotten lots of sympathy but no help. Spooner had the feeling no one really believed that the danger to the dolphins was so serious! Spooner and Audrey ran out of the store and down toward the town wharf.

"Spooner! Audrey! What's up?" They turned to see Paul Sequeira coming up from the docks. He was seventy two, but he still worked his traps every day as he had for more than fifty years.

"It's dolphins, Mr. Sequeira. Hundreds of them. They're trapped in Bald Point Cove, and the tide will be out soon!" Spooner quickly told Mr. Sequeira what he had seen.

"I heard on the radio that they were close to shore," said Mr. Sequeira. "Fog's so thick, everyone's coming in now. We'll round up some help. Come on."

It seemed only minutes later that Spooner, Audrey, Mr. Sequeira, and nine others hurried to the cove. More help was on the way. Mr. Sequeira had radioed the police, too.

Water was running out of the cove like sand from an hourglass. The water was only three feet deep and getting lower every minute. Spooner couldn't help looking back and forth from his watch to the widening stretch of mud in the cove.

Already a few dolphins were stuck in mud. The others swam frantically in the shallow water. In less than an hour, all the water in the cove would be gone.

How could they get the animals out of danger? Suddenly, Spooner remembered something that he had read. "Form a line! We'll move toward them and herd them into the channel!"

The rescuers moved into the water and did as Spooner said. They forced the dolphins toward the narrow channel leading to the sea. Audrey cheered as some of the dolphins slipped out through the opening.

More people came. They herded more and more animals out to the sea. But the dense fog was making it difficult to see. The dolphins

> *How could they get the animals out of danger? Suddenly, Spooner remembered something that he had read.*

still in the cove darted about desperately. They were frantic and frightened.

"Audrey!" called Mr. Sequeira. "Get out to my boat and radio for some nets. Hurry!"

Audrey splashed through the shallow water, climbed the cliff, and slid down the other side. She rowed quickly but cautiously. The fog had almost totally obscured Mr. Sequeira's lobster boat anchored in the channel. Once on board she made contact with Port Hegen. The nets were on their way. But would they reach the cove in time? Audrey hurried back.

There were about seventy dolphins still in the cove when the water ran out completely. The rescuers couldn't bear to watch the stranded animals die in the mud. They used their heavy nets to drag and tug and slide the heavy animals into the channel.

The workers were able to save about half of the remaining dolphins. The rest had been stuck in the mud too long. Already they were dying.

Later, on the wharf, Ralph Hemming put his arms around his son and daughter. "You did your best, kids. That's all you can ever do."

"Aye," said Mr. Sequeira. "If it hadn't been for you kids, hundreds of dolphins would have died. Think of the hundreds that we saved."

Spooner blinked away tears. "I know we saved most of them. But I can't help thinking that if we knew why they swam into the cove, we could have saved all of them."

In spite of the tragedy, Spooner's dad smiled to himself. He could see that his son planned to spend even more time in the library learning about the ocean. Perhaps there was a positive outcome after all.

RECALLING FACTS

Recalling details

1. Who is the main character?

Spooner Hemming is the main character.

Recalling details

2. Who is Paul Sequeira?

Mr. Sequeira is the 72-year-old lobsterman who helps

organize the dolphins' rescue.

Identifying cause and effect

3. How did the dolphins become trapped?

The dolphins swam into a shallow cove with a narrow

entrance; they couldn't find their way out when the tide

ebbed.

Recalling details

4. Why did Spooner get his sister?

She was good at organizing.

Recalling details

5. List two methods that the rescuers used to save the dolphins.

The rescuers formed a line to herd the dolphins toward

the sea; they later dragged them in nets into the channel.

Identifying cause and effect

6. Why did some dolphins die in spite of the rescue efforts?

The dolphins became stuck in the mud and died before

they could be dragged to the channel.

Identifying plot

7. What was the climax, or the most exciting event, of the story?

Answers may vary. The climax occurred when the

rescuers began herding the dolphins toward the sea.

Using context clues

8. Draw a line to match each word with its meaning.

aspired   small, sheltered body of water

cove   had the ambition to be or do

ebbing   something flowing back, as the tide does toward the sea

INTERPRETING FACTS

Understanding character

1. Circle three character traits that Spooner showed during the rescue.

selfishness   ambition   (concern)

(determination)   (intelligence)   laziness

Understanding character

2. Choose one character trait and tell how Spooner demonstrated that trait during the rescue.

Answers will vary.

Inferring cause and effect

3. What effect did the sighting of dolphins have on the people of Port Hegen?

The townspeople were excited and concerned.

Making inferences

4. Why do you think that some of the people in Port Hegen were willing to work so hard to save the dolphins?

Answers may vary. The people worked so hard to save the dolphins because the dolphins were in trouble and unable

to help themselves. The people were sympathetic to the stranded dolphins.

Drawing conclusions

5. Why was Mr. Hemming proud of Spooner and Audrey?

He was proud because Spooner and Audrey were responsible for alerting the townspeople to the danger that the

dolphins faced. They also worked very hard to save the trapped dolphins.

Inferring theme

6. Circle the letter next to the statement that best states the theme of the story.

     a. Living near the sea is dangerous.

     b. Dolphins often get stranded in coves when the tide goes out.

     c. People working together can overcome almost any problem.

Vivid phrases and details along with setting help create mood in this story. In the following questions, you must decide how the author uses setting and details to catch the reader's interest.

1. Several incidents in "The Dolphin Disaster" have outcomes that are uncertain at first. For example, as you read the story, you may have asked yourself the following questions:

   Will Spooner be able to track down the dolphins?

   Will Spooner get enough help?

   Will the nets arrive in time?

   Will the rescuers save the dolphins before the water runs out of the cove?

   As a result of the uncertainty, what kind of mood, or atmosphere, has the author created?

   The author has created an atmosphere, or mood, of suspense.

2. In the list below, circle the letter next to the phrases and details that do *not* develop the story's mood.
   a. Skreek—a single sea gull wheeled across the low, gray sky.
   b. so struck by the sight that he dropped the lobster trap that he was mending
   c. only minutes later
   d. motor buzzed into life
   e. fast-ebbing tide
   f. Dolphins! Hundreds of them
   g. darted this way and that, circling, confused
   h. water was running out of the cove like sand from an hourglass
   i. Audrey was a terrific organizer
   j. looking back and forth from his watch to the widening stretch of mud in the cove
   k. in the library learning about the ocean

3. Setting often contributes to a story's mood. In this story, a fog "was closing in on Port Hegen like a dirty cotton curtain" and "in a matter of moments, the dolphins would be swallowed up in the thick folds of the fog." What effect does the fog have on the mood of the story?

   The fog makes the mood even more suspenseful by increasing the uncertainty of whether Spooner can track the

   dolphins so that he and the other rescuers can save them.

▶ Real Life Connections Name an instance where you have worked on a team with family, friends, or classmates.

Propaganda

___ Reading a Social Studies Selection _____

▶ **Background Information**

In 1898, the United States went to war with Spain. One of the main causes of the war was the sinking of the battleship *Maine*. There was never any proof that Spain sank the ship, yet most Americans believed that Spain was responsible.

▶ **Skill Focus**

Propaganda is the spreading of information and ideas in a way meant to make others accept them. Often the information and ideas are misleading. Propaganda usually distorts the truth to convince people to believe or to do something that will further a particular cause.

Propaganda may include many facts, but the facts are usually chosen because they support the writer's point of view. Often only one side of a story is told. The facts are usually presented in an emotional way to sway the reader's opinion and to have an effect or impact on a large number of people.

Propaganda can be very dangerous. It can be used for immoral or hurtful purposes. For this reason, knowing how

to recognize propaganda is important.

To recognize propaganda, follow these steps.
1. **Identify the facts.**
   Sort the facts from the opinions. A fact is a statement that is true and can be proven. An opinion is a judgment based on personal beliefs and feelings.
2. **Identify errors of fact.**
   Look for ways that facts have been changed or slanted and information that has been left out to suit the aim of the propaganda.
3. **Analyze the emotional appeal.**
   Decide how the language of the propaganda tries to affect the reader's emotions.
4. **Reach conclusions.**
   Ask what the purpose of the propaganda is and whether this purpose has been achieved.

▶ **Word Clues**

If a reading has no context clues to explain an unknown word or phrase, there may be a clue elsewhere. Read the sentence below.

These newspapers had a great influence on public opinion.[1]

Notice the raised number after the phrase *public opinion.* This number is a signal to you to look for a footnote with the same number at the bottom of the page. A **footnote** gives a brief definition or explanation of the phrase.

[1] public opinion: the expressed views of a group of people about issues of common interest or concern; views not based on what is certain but on what the people as a whole think to be true or likely.

Sometimes the footnote includes a respelling to show you how to pronounce the word.

Use **footnote** context clues to find the meaning of the three other numbered words or phrases in the selection.

▶ **Strategy Tip**

The selection describes the background to the sinking of the *Maine*. It contains two primary sources: a message from Captain Sigsbee and a newspaper report. As you read, notice how propaganda was used to turn the American public against Spain.

Remember the *Maine*

On February 15, 1898, the United States battleship *Maine* sat in the harbor of Havana, Cuba. Suddenly, the *Maine* blew apart in a huge explosion. Two hundred sixty American sailors were killed.

To this day, no one is sure what caused the explosion. The ship's captain gave no cause for the disaster in his report. A navy investigation failed to uncover any clear evidence. Yet, most Americans believed that Spain blew up the ship. Across America people repeated, "Remember the *Maine*." Emotions ran high. Soon the American people demanded war with Spain.

Why did Americans think that Spain had sunk the *Maine*? Why were they so eager to go to war? The story of the *Maine* is an important lesson in American history.

Dangers to Peace

In 1898, the United States was at peace. America had fought in no major war since the Civil War. A generation had grown up without knowing the horrors of war. The nation took peace for granted.

✗ But several events were occuring that were dangerous to peace. Some Americans wanted the United States to become a world power. They were called imperialists, or empire builders. They dreamed of an American empire. Some Americans had an extreme pride in America's growing power. They were called jingoists. Jingoists thought that America should show its strength by a warlike policy toward other nations. Another danger to peace came from several of America's leading newspapers. These newspapers tried to sway their readers' emotions to support a war. They paid little attention to facts in their news stories. These newspapers had a great influence on public opinion.[1] They played an important role in the story of the *Maine*.

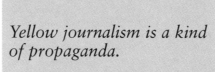

Yellow journalism is a kind of propaganda.

Cuba

The island of Cuba is ninety miles (144 kilometers) off the southeastern coast of the United States. In the 1890s, it became a focus of American interest. Businesses had invested money in Cuba's sugar fields. Politicians recognized Cuba's geographic and military importance to the United States. Americans in general were concerned about the political situation in Cuba.

For years, Cuba had been under Spanish rule. Many Cubans wanted independence. In 1895, some Cubans attempted a revolt against Spain. The revolt failed. Spain sent a new governor, General Weyler, to the island. He treated the rebels cruelly. He set up detention camps[2] in which many Cuban prisoners became sick and died.

Americans were shocked by the news from Cuba. They wanted to know more about what was happening. Two New York newspapers saw a chance to sell more copies. They made Cuba a hot news topic.

Yellow Journalism

The two New York papers were Joseph Pulitzer's *World* and William Randolph Hearst's *Journal*. These newspapers competed with each other for stories about Cuba. They printed shocking stories with screaming headlines. In these stories, Spain was always the villain. A group of Cubans in New York was feeding information to the papers. Its information was slanted in favor of the rebels.

The stories in the *World* and the *Journal* had little to do with the facts. Instead, they tried to catch the readers' attention and sway their emotions. This kind of journalism became known as yellow journalism. Yellow journalism is a kind of propaganda.

✗ ✗ With great emotion, the newspapers

---

[1] public opinion: the expressed views of a group of people about issues of common interest or concern; views not based on what is certain but on what the people as a whole think to be true or likely.

[2] detention camps (di TEN shən KAMPS): places where people are held temporarily as prisoners. In an attempt to cut off supplies to Cuban rebels, General Weyler ordered peasants to gather in detention camps.

reported about conditions in Cuba. One article read: "You would sicken at the sight of thousands of women and children starving to death in Cuba today . . . filthy skeletons dying on bare, foul boards." Another paper stated in an editorial: "If Spain will not put an end to murder in Cuba, the United States must."

✔ The two newspapers urged the United States to go to war with Spain. Hearst told one photographer who was going to Cuba, "You supply the pictures. I'll supply the war." The stories that the New York papers carried had a great effect. They were picked up by newspapers all over the country. Public opinion became set against Spain.

The Sinking of the *Maine*

Riots erupted in Havana, the capital of Cuba, in 1898. President McKinley ordered the battleship *Maine* into Havana harbor. He wanted to protect American citizens in Cuba. Shortly after the *Maine* arrived in Havana, it exploded.

Captain Sigsbee was the officer in charge of the *Maine*. He immediately made the following report about the explosion.

Maine blown up in Havana Harbor at nine-forty tonight and destroyed. Many wounded and doubtless more killed or drowned. Wounded and others

The World

863,956

WORLDS CIRCULATED YESTERDAY

"Circulation Books Open to All."

VOL. XXXVIII. NO. 13,316   NEW YORK, THURSDAY, FEBRUARY 17, 1898.   PRICE

MAINE EXPLOSION CAUSED BY BOMB OR TORPEDO?

Capt. Sigsbee and Consul-General Lee Are in Doubt---The World Has Sent a Special Tug, With Submarine Divers, to Havana to Find Out---Lee Asks for an Immediate Court of Inquiry---Capt. Sigsbee's Suspicions.

CAPT. SIGSBEE, IN A SUPPRESSED DESPATCH TO THE STATE DEPARTMENT, SAYS THE ACCIDENT WAS MADE POSSIBLE BY AN ENEMY.

Dr. E. C. Pendleton, Just Arrived from Havana, Says He Overheard Talk There of a Plot to Blow Up the Ship---Capt. Zalinski, the Dynamite Expert, and Other Experts Report to The World that the Wreck Was Not Accidental---Washington Officials Ready for Vigorous Action if Spanish Responsibility Can Be Shown---Divers to Be Sent Down to Make Careful Examinations.

on board Spanish man-of-war[3] and Ward Line steamer. Send lighthouse tenders[4] from Key West for crew and the few pieces of equipment above water. No one has clothing other than that upon him. Public opinion should be suspended until further report. All officers believed to be saved. . . . Many Spanish officers, including representatives of General Blanco, now with me to express sympathy.

The newspapers reported the explosion to the American people in a very different way. On page 68 is the front page of the *World* on February 17, two days after the explosion.

[3] man-of-war: a fighting ship.

[4] tenders: ships that take care of other ships, supplying food, rescuing crew members, and so on.

War Fever

No one was ever able to prove that Spain sank the *Maine*. The explosion may have been an accident. Or Cuban rebels may have secretly caused it to draw America into war with Spain. Whatever the cause, American public opinion was against Spain.

President McKinley tried to keep war from breaking out. He offered a peace plan to Spain. The plan suggested that Cuba become independent. Spain turned down McKinley's plan.

War fever ran high in the United States. The newspapers kept up their stories against Spain. Finally, President McKinley recognized Cuba as an independent country. As a result, Spain declared war on the United States. The next day, Congress declared war on Spain. The Spanish-American War had begun.

RECALLING FACTS

Identifying cause and effect

1. For the effect described in the sentence below, circle the letter next to the correct cause.

The New York newspapers reported shocking stories about Cuba because

a. they cared about the Cuban people.

(b.) they wanted to sell papers.

c. they owned property in Cuba.

Recalling details

2. Who gave the *Journal* and the *World* information about Cuba?

A group of Cubans in New York gave the newspapers

the information.

Identifying sequence of events

3. Sequence the following events in the order in which they happened.

__2__ General Weyler came to Cuba as governor.

__4__ Congress declared war on Spain.

__1__ Cubans revolted against Spain.

__3__ The *Maine* sank in Havana harbor.

Identifying the main idea

4. Reread the paragraph with an X next to it. Then underline the sentence that best states the paragraph's main idea.

Identifying the main idea and supporting details

5. Reread the paragraph with two X's next to it. Underline the sentence that best states the paragraph's main idea. Then circle two details that support the main idea of the paragraph.

Recognizing cause and effect

6. Why did Spain declare war on the United States?

Spain declared war on the United States because the

United States recognized Cuba as an independent

country.

Using context clues

7. Complete each sentence by writing the answer on the line provided.

detention camps
man-of-war
tenders

a. A ship that fights or is ready to fight is a ___man-of-war___.

b. Many Cubans died from hunger or sickness in ___detention camps___ set up by Spain's General Weyler.

c. Survivors of the *Maine* were rescued by ___tenders___.

Inferring cause and effect

1. Match the words in the left column with the attitudes in the right column.

   _a_   imperialists   **a.** wanted to prove America's strength

   _c_   newspapers   **b.** wanted to use America's power to create an empire

   _b_   jingoists   **c.** wanted to sell papers by printing war stories

   _d_   Americans   **d.** were convinced that Spain had sunk the *Maine*

Inferring comparisons and contrasts

2. In 1898, the Cuban people were fighting for independence from Spain. A comparison can be drawn between this struggle and what event in American history?

A comparison can be drawn between Cuba's struggle for independence and the American Revolutionary War, in

which the colonies fought for their independence from England.

Distinguishing fact from opinion

3. Identify each of the following statements as fact or opinion. Circle the letter next to each statement that expresses an opinion.

   (**a.**) "If Spain will not put an end to the murder in Cuba, the United States must."

   b. The island of Cuba is ninety miles (144 kilometers) off the southeastern coast of the United States.

   (**c.**) America should show its strength by being warlike toward other nations.

Making inferences

4. Cuban rebels might have been responsible for sinking the *Maine*. What could have been their reason for doing it?

They might have wanted to trick Americans into thinking that Spain was responsible for the sinking of the *Maine*

and thus involve the United States in their fight against Spain.

Inferring the unstated main idea

5. Reread the paragraph with a check mark next to it. Write a sentence stating its main idea.

Two New York newspapers helped turn public opinion in favor of war with Spain.

Use Captain Sigsbee's message and the *World*'s front page to answer the questions below.

1. **Identify the facts** (distinguish facts from opinions).

   a. List the facts in Captain Sigsbee's message.   time of explosion (9:40 P.M.); many dead and

wounded survivors aboard Spanish man-of-war and Ward Line steamer; many Spanish officers sympathetic

   b. What opinions can you identify in his message?   He believes that public opinion should be

suspended until further report and that all officers have been saved.

   c. List the facts in the *World* report.   cause of explosion not definite; the *World* has sent tug with

divers to investigate; Lee asks for a court of inquiry

d. What information in the *World* report is based on opinion? explosion caused by bomb or

torpedo; Captain Sigsbee's reported opinion; hearsay evidence from Pendleton; dynamic expert's opinion

2. Identify errors of fact.

a. What does Captain Sigsbee say in his message about the cause of the explosion?

He gives no cause and suggests no cause for the explosion.

b. What does the *World* suggest that Sigsbee thinks is the cause?

The newspaper reports that Sigsbee said the explosion was made possible by an enemy.

c. What does Sigsbee report about the actions of the Spanish after the explosion?

The Spanish were helpful and sympathetic.

d. Does this information appear in the *World*? No

e. How does the newspaper describe Captain Sigsbee's attitude toward the Spanish?

The newspaper says that Sigsbee is suspicious about the Spanish.

3. Analyze emotional appeal.

a. Does Captain Sigsbee seem interested in turning public opinion against Spain? No

b. What effect would the drawing of the explosion in the *World* have on readers? Why?

Because the picture looks as though the *Maine* has been blown up by an enemy in a war, Americans would be

angry and frightened and would want to retaliate or get even.

c. The third headline uses the word *enemy*. What emotional impact does this word have on readers?

It gives the impression that another country has attacked the United States.

4. Reach conclusions.

a. What overall message does the *World* report convey? The United States has been attacked

by an enemy and should be ready to strike back.

b. What emotional effect does the *World* report have on a reader? Because the report

suggests a foreign attack, the reader would probably want the United States to strike back.

c. Why might the *World* have slanted its report as it did? The *World* slanted its report to sell

more copies by using sensational headlines and by feeding U.S. bias against Spain.

d. What effect do you think the *World* report had on readers' attitudes toward Spain?

Most readers would have taken the *World*'s report as fact. The result would be strong anti-Spanish feelings.

e. How might the report have influenced the outbreak of the Spanish-American War?

The report probably led Americans to believe that Spain was responsible for the explosion and was an enemy.

Public opinion against Spain was aroused, which influenced Congress to support immediate intervention in Cuba,

by force, if necessary. The result was a desire for war. The United States declared war on April 16, 1898.

▶ **Real Life Connections** Where could you find an example of yellow journalism?

Cause and Effect

___ Reading a Science Selection ___

▶ **Background Information**

In Chilé, the Alacalufe Indians spend more than three-fourths of their lives in boats on the Pacific Ocean. The ocean is their sole source of food. For this reason, their fishing boats are at sea for weeks at a time. Most of each day is spent fishing.

All over the world, people make their living by fishing. This is true especially of people in coastal towns. However, nearly all of these people have other sources of food. For example, they have farms or gardens where they grow vegetables and fruit to eat. They also buy crops brought from other areas.

Three-quarters of the Earth is ocean. Still, only a small portion of the food that humans eat comes from the sea. This fact may be surprising, but as you will see in this selection, this may change in the future.

▶ **Skill Focus**

The **cause** of an event is the reason it happens. The **effect** is the result of the cause. For example, a blizzard can cause the closing of an airport. The cause is the blizzard. The effect is the closing of the airport.

Sometimes an effect can be the cause of another effect. In this way, a chain of causes and effects is formed. Read the following paragraph.

> There was little rain that year. The lack of rain caused most of the crops to die. As a result, the farmer had few crops to sell. He didn't earn enough money to pay his taxes. Finally, he had to sell his farm.

The following diagram shows this chain of causes and effects.

> little rain → most crops died → few crops to sell → not enough money to pay taxes → sell farm

The first arrow shows how the first cause (little rain) results in an effect (most crops died). This effect is also the cause of an effect (few crops to sell), and so on.

▶ **Word Clues**

Read the sentences below. Look for context clues that explain the underlined word.

> There have been many <u>innovations</u> in farming methods, such as crop rotation and the use of chemical fertilizers. These changes have enabled farmers to grow much more food on an acre of land than they used to.

If you do not know the meaning of the word *innovations*, the word *changes* in the next sentence can help you. The words *innovations* and *changes* are synonyms. Innovations are changes, new ways of doing things. A synonym for an unknown word can appear anywhere in the paragraph.

Look for **synonym** context clues to find the meaning of the three underlined words in the selection.

▶ **Strategy Tip**

When you read "Farming the Ocean," look for chains of causes and effects. Remember, an effect can be the cause of another effect. Understanding cause and effect relationships can help you in all aspects of your life.

Farming the Ocean

The Earth's population has been growing at a tremendous rate. Four hundred years ago, there were only a few million people on the Earth. According to the 1995 U.S. Census, there are over 5.73 billion people, and this number is expected to continue to increase rapidly. One cause of the increase is improved medical care.

The world's supply of food has also been growing very quickly. There have been many developments in farming methods, such as crop rotation and the use of chemical fertilizers. Crop rotation is the practice of planting different crops on a particular piece of land each year. These changes have enabled farmers to grow much more food on an acre of land than in the past. Tractors, reapers, and other farm machinery make it possible to harvest large crops before they die in the field. New methods of transportation and refrigeration make it possible to get food from the farm to the table without spoiling. Special housing and vitamins make it possible to produce more and larger cows, pigs, and chickens.

The growth of the world's food supply must keep up with the growth of the world's population, or people will go hungry. Food shortages in India, Africa, and China have resulted in the starvation of millions of people. In these parts of the world, there is not enough food for the people who live there.

The world's population is growing. Can our world's food supply keep up?

One method that could increase the world's supply of food is called **aquaculture** (AK wə kul chər). Aquaculture is the farming of the oceans. Agriculture is the science and art of farming the land; that is, the <u>cultivation</u> of land to produce crops. The areas of the earth that are covered with water are the <u>marine</u> areas. Aquaculture, then, is the cultivation of the marine areas of the Earth.

People have always used the oceans as a source of food. They have eaten seaweed. They have also gathered and eaten shellfish, such as clams, oysters, and lobsters. They have used spears, hooks, and nets to catch fish. However, none of these traditional methods is aquaculture. These methods take things out of the sea. They do not put anything back into it. Today scientists are thinking about how to care for the oceans and their valuable resources. With special care, the oceans could provide new food supplies.

Agriculturists have learned how to care for the land. They put back in the soil minerals that plants remove. They build shelters for farm animals. They provide all the requirements needed to make their crops and animals healthy. This care has increased the amount of food that the land can produce. The increased production provides food for more people. The same process can work for the oceans.

Aquaculture actually began about three hundred years ago. A Japanese lord was forced to move from one island to another. When he arrived at his new home, he discovered that oysters, his favorite food, were not to be found in the nearby bay. The lord sent his

The ocean continues to be an important source of food.

assistants back to the old island to bring oysters to Japan. Hundreds of oysters were transplanted into the bay. The lord believed that since the oysters lived in one body of water, they could live in another. He was right. The oysters survived in the bay. They produced many young oysters, called **larvae** (LAR vee).

Soon starfish and other predators, like the bat ray, began to eat the oysters. More of the oysters were being eaten by other fish than by people. The Japanese lord had fences built out of bamboo. The long bamboo shoots were stuck into the sand under the water. The other ends of the bamboo reached above the bay's surface. The fences stopped the starfish from crawling into the oyster beds and kept the bat rays from swimming into them.

As the Japanese lord enjoyed his oysters, word of the oyster gardens spread throughout Japan. Other people tried to grow oysters for themselves. Some were successful, but many were not. After many attempts at growing oysters, the Japanese fisher-farmers began to learn from both their successes and their failures. They learned that the oysters needed many things in order to survive. If all of these conditions were not present, the oysters would die. What were some of the requirements for the oysters?

First, it was discovered that water that was too cold would kill the oysters. Then it was found that if the water was too warm, the oysters would also die. The oysters could not survive in lakes or lagoons where the water was not changed by the tides. Moving waters provided the oysters with an unending supply of food called **plankton** (PLANGK tən). Plankton are tiny plants and animals that float in the world's oceans. However, areas with too strong a current would tear the oysters from where they had <u>moored</u> themselves and wash them out to sea. It was also discovered that the

This fish farm in Greece is typical of the aquacultural methods being used in marine areas throughout the world.

oysters would stick to tiles hung in the water. In this position, they got more plankton and thus grew faster and larger.

Before too long, people all over Japan were farming the oceans. Oysters were just one of their underwater crops. They also cultivated, or helped the natural growth of, clams, shrimp, scallops, yellowfish (a kind of free-swimming fish), and many other sea animals.

In more recent times, fish farms have become more numerous in other parts of the world. These farms successfully raise fish, such as salmon, that lay large eggs. The large eggs are easily gathered and moved to protected areas where the newly hatched fish can grow.

Scientists have found that sea animals other than fish can be harvested in tremendous volume. One example is a type of tiny shrimp called **krill**. Krill live in huge swarms in all the world's oceans. They can be processed into a very nutritious food for farm animals. The krill that live in the Antarctic Ocean can be eaten by people.

Today, scientists called marine biologists are observing life in the oceans, seas, and bays all over the world. They are experimenting to improve the methods of aquaculture begun by the Japanese lord three hundred years ago. Many people believe that farming the ocean is the only hope for winning the race between the growth of the world's population and the growth of the world's food supply.

Recalling details

1. Why is it necessary for the world's food supply to keep growing?

The food supply must keep pace with the growth of the

world's population.

Recalling details

2. What is aquaculture?

Aquaculture is the farming of oceans.

Recalling details

3. What are some of the foods people have always taken from the sea?

People have taken seaweed, shellfish, and fish

from the sea.

Recalling details

4. Where did aquaculture begin?

Aquaculture began in Japan.

Recalling details

5. What is plankton?

Plankton is tiny plants and animals that float in the

world's oceans.

Recalling details

6. What are krill?

Krill are a type of tiny shrimp.

Using context clues

7. Answer each question by writing *yes* or *no* on the line provided.

a. Is food produced by the cultivation of land? ___yes___

b. Are seaweeds marine plants? ___yes___

c. Can a tent be moored by safety pins? ___no___

For the following questions, underline the correct answers.

Inferring cause and effect

1. More food gets from the farm to the table without spoiling because of
  a. home refrigerators.
  b. restaurant refrigerators.
  c. refrigerated trucks.

Making inferences

2. Fishing probably provides food mostly in countries that
  a. have large farms.
  b. have coastlines.
  c. have high mountains.

Making inferences

3. One reason aquaculture may have started in Japan is that Japan
  a. is a small country.
  b. is surrounded by the sea.
  c. is a hot country.

Inferring cause and effect

4. Crop rotation produces greater yield because
  a. different crops are used for different purposes.
  b. different crops grow at different rates.
  c. different crops use up different minerals in the soil.

For the following questions, circle the correct answers.

1. What is one cause of the increase in world population?
   a. the spread of diseases
   b. better medical care *(circled)*
   c. lower birthrates

2. What are two causes of the increase in the world's food supply?
   a. crop rotation and chemical fertilizers *(circled)*
   b. more farmland and crop rotation
   c. chemical fertilizers and more farm land

3. What is one effect of new transportation methods and refrigeration?
   a. food gets from the farm to the table without spoiling *(circled)*
   b. improved farm machinery
   c. lower crop production

4. Which one of the following would *not* cause oysters to die?
   a. sea water that was too cold
   b. plankton that was too thick *(circled)*
   c. sea water that was too warm

5. According to the article, aquaculture is
   a. a cause of world population growth
   b. an effect of world population growth
   c. neither a cause nor an effect of population growth *(circled)*

6. Three chains of causes and effects can be made from the events listed below. Connect one event from each column with arrows to show the chains. You will not use all the events. You can use some of the events more than once.

a. Minerals are replaced in soil	Bamboo fences are built	Oysters rot	Fewer people go hungry
b. Japanese lord's oysters eaten by predators	More farm animals survive	More food is produced	More oysters are produced
c. Crops become diseased	More storms occur	Predators are kept out of oyster beds	Weeds grow faster
d. Shelters are built for farm animals	Land produces more crops	Fewer storms occur	Less water is available for crops

▶ **Real Life Connections** Do you think that marine biologists should continue to do research on newer and better methods of aquaculture? Tell why or why not.

Word Problems

__ Reading a Mathematics Selection __

▶ Background Information

A word problem is any practical problem that you need to use math to solve. For example, let's say that one of your parents gives you $10 to go to the movies. You need a ticket, but you also want a small popcorn and a small soda. You ask yourself, "Do I have enough money for all these things?" This question is a word problem.

You can set up the facts of the real-life problem as a math problem in this way: A ticket to the movie costs $6. A small popcorn costs $2.50. A small soda costs $1.50. If Raymond's parents give him $10, will he have enough to buy what he wants?

Add up the numbers. You will see the total cost is exactly $10. The answer is yes.

Knowing how to put the facts of a practical problem into the form of a math problem in this way will help you solve problems that you deal with every day.

▶ Skill Focus

To solve the problems in this selection, you will need to do two mathematical operations.

Use the following five steps in solving word problems.

1. Read the problem. Be sure that you are familiar with all the words, especially the labels. Think about the question that is being asked. Try to picture in your mind the information that is given. Read the problem again to be sure that you understand the question.

2. Decide how to find the answer. It may be helpful to write a sentence about each fact that is given in the problem. Is extra information given that is not necessary to solve the problem? After you determine which information, if any, is not needed, decide what operation to use to solve the problem. In solving some problems, you will need to do two operations. If so, you will need to write two mathematical sentences to find the answer. Be sure to look for key words.

3. Estimate the answer. Use rounded numbers to make an estimate for each mathematical sentence.

4. Carry out the plan. Solve each of the mathematical sentences.

5. Reread the problem. Then write the complete

answer. Is the answer logical? How close is it to your estimate?

▶ Word Clues

As you read word problems, look for key words that will help you find the answer. In problems in which two operations are needed, you must look for key words for both operations. Words, such as *twice as much* and *all together,* often show that you have to combine many groups of the same size, or multiply. Words like *divided, average,* and *per,* often show that you have to break down one big group into smaller groups, or divide.

▶ Strategy Tip

After you read each problem, decide if you have more information than you need to answer the question. If you do, you may find it helpful to cross out the extra information. Then use the five steps with the necessary information to solve the problem.

Solving Word Problems That Have Unnecessary Information

Many facts have been collected about the sea. These facts can be put together to answer new questions about the sea.

Use the following five steps in solving word problems.

1. Read the problem.
2. Decide how to find the answer.
3. Estimate the answer.
4. Carry out the plan.
5. Reread the problem.

READ THE PROBLEM

The *Bathysphere* dove to a depth of 914 meters in 1934. In 1948, the *Benthoscope* dove $1\frac{1}{2}$ times deeper. In 1960, the *Trieste* dove 8 times deeper than the *Benthoscope*. How many meters deep did the *Trieste* dive?

Read the problem again. Be sure that you know the label that is used with each number fact. Are there any words that you do not know? If so, look them up to find their meanings. What question does the problem ask? Often the question is asked in the last sentence. *How many meters deep did the* Trieste *dive?*

DECIDE HOW TO FIND THE ANSWER

The problem gives you many number facts. Written as sentences, the facts are as follows:

1. The *Bathysphere* dove 914 meters.
2. The *Bathysphere* dove in 1934.
3. The *Benthoscope* dove $1\frac{1}{2}$ times deeper.
4. The *Benthoscope* dove in 1948.
5. The *Trieste* dove 8 times deeper than the *Benthoscope*.
6. The *Trieste* dove in 1960.

Enough facts are given in the problem to solve it. However, more information is given than is needed. When extra information is given, decide which facts are not needed and cross them out. In this problem, facts 2, 4, and 6 are not necessary to answer the question.

You will need to do two arithmetic operations to find the answer. You need to find out first how deep the *Benthoscope* dove and then how deep the *Trieste* dove. For the first operation, you must multiply. The key words are $1\frac{1}{2}$ *times deeper*. This is your mathematical sentence:

$$914 \times 1\frac{1}{2} = n$$

For the second operation, you must multiply again. The key words *8 times deeper* tell you to multiply. This is your mathematical sentence:

$$n \times 8 = m$$

In this mathematical sentence, the letter n stands for the answer to the first operation. The letter m stands for the number of meters the *Trieste* dove.

ESTIMATE THE ANSWER

Use rounded numbers to help make an estimate. Round to the nearest one or hundred.

First operation: $900 \times 2 = n$

$1,800 = n$

Second operation: $1,800 \times 8 = m$

$14,400 = m$

Your estimate is 14,400.

CARRY OUT THE PLAN

Do the arithmetic.

First operation: $914 \times 1\frac{1}{2} = n$

$1,371 = n$

Second operation: $1,371 \times 8 = m$

$10,968 = m$

REREAD THE PROBLEM

After rereading the problem, write the complete answer. The *Trieste* dove 10,968 meters. How close is your answer to your estimate? If your answer is not close, you should start over.

Use the five steps to solve this problem.

Read: In 1930, William Dow extracted 90 micrograms of gold from 12,000 liters of sea water. In 1965, Dr. Bayer extracted 1.4 micrograms of gold from 100 liters of sea water. Who extracted more gold per liter of water?

Decide: The problem lists four number facts.

1. Dow extracted gold in 1930.
2. Dow extracted 90 micrograms of gold from 12,000 liters of water.
3. Bayer extracted gold in 1965.
4. Bayer extracted 1.4 micrograms of gold from 100 liters of water.

The question can be answered using facts 2 and 4. Facts 1 and 3 are not necessary.

You will need to do two arithmetic operations to find the answer. You need to find out first how much gold per liter Dow extracted and then how much gold per liter Bayer extracted. For both operations, you must divide. The key word is *per*. These are your mathematical sentences.

$$90 \div 12{,}000 = d$$
$$1.4 \div 100 = b$$

Estimate: Round each number.

$$100 \div 12{,}000 = d$$
$$.008 = d$$
$$1 \div 100 = b$$
$$.01 = b$$

Carry Out: $90 \div 12{,}000 = d$
$$.0075 = d$$
$$1.4 \div 100 = b$$
$$.014 = b$$

Reread: Bayer extracted more gold per liter of water than Dow.

RECALLING FACTS

Recognizing sequence of events
1. In which step do you figure out which information isn't needed?

Step 2, Decide

Recalling details
2. How do you make an estimate?

Round the numbers and solve the mathematical sentences.

Recalling details
3. What should you do if you have extra information in a problem?

Do not use it. Cross it out.

Recalling details
4. Match each operation to its key word.

multiply ——— **a.** times

divide ——— **b.** per

INTERPRETING FACTS

Making inferences
1. Why might a word problem have extra information?

Extra information might be related to the necessary information and be interesting to know. It might also help in

solving other problems.

Making inferences
2. Why are labels important in word problems?

They let you know what the numbers mean.

Making inferences
3. In the second problem in the selection, why are the letters b and d used?

b stands for Bayer and d stands for Dow

4. Why was the letter *n* used in the first problem and not the second?

In the first problem, the answer to the first operation is needed to solve the second operation. This isn't true of the

second problem.

SKILL FOCUS

To solve these word problems, you will use one or both of only two mathematical operations: multiplication and division. You may find it helpful to write a sentence on another sheet of paper for each number fact that is given. Some problems have extra information. Cross out the facts that are not needed.

1. Read: In 1950, the United States used 757 billion liters of water. Fifteen years later, in 1965, 1.7 times as much water was used as in 1950. Forty-four years later, in 1994, 2.4 times as much water was used as in 1965. How much water was used in 1994?

Decide: Multiply to find how much water was used in 1965. Multiply again to find how much was used in 1994.

$757 \times 1.7 = n$; $n \times 2.4 = w$

Estimate: $800 \times 2 = n$; $1,600 = n$; $1,600 \times 2 = w$; $3,200 = w$

Carry Out: $757 \times 1.7 = n$; $1,286.9 = n$; $n \times 2.4 = w$; $1,286.9 \times 2.4 = w$; $3,088.56 = w$

Reread: 3,088.56 billion liters of water were used in 1994.

2. Read: A seaweed farm that covers 10 square kilometers produces 72,576 metric tons of seaweed. A dredging site that covers 21 square kilometers produces 272 metric tons of gold for a profit of $150 million. Is there more seaweed or more gold in a square kilometer of sea water?

Decide: Divide to find tons of seaweed per square kilometer of sea water. Divide to find tons of gold per square

kilometer of sea water. $72,576 \div 10 = s$; $272 \div 21 = g$

Estimate: $70,000 \div 10 = s$; $7,000 = s$; $300 \div 20 = g$; $15 = g$

Carry Out: $72,576 \div 10 = s$; $7,257.6 = s$; $272 \div 21 = g$; $12.95 = g$

Reread: There is more seaweed than gold in a square kilometer of sea water.

3. Read: At sea level the air pressure is 1.033 kilograms per square centimeter. This is called *1 atmosphere*. The pressure increases by 1 atmosphere every 10 meters of water depth. At what depth would you find 4 atmospheres of pressure, and how great is the pressure?

Decide: Multiply to find depth at 4 atmospheres. Multiply to find pressure. $10 \times 4 = d$; $1.033 \times 4 = p$

Estimate: $10 \times 4 = d$; $40 = d$; $1 \times 4 = p$; $4 = p$

Carry Out: $10 \times 4 = d$; $40 = d$; $1.033 \times 4 = p$; $4.132 = p$

Reread: 4 atmospheres of pressure are present at a depth of 40 meters; the pressure is 4.132 kilograms per

square centimeter.

▶ **Real Life Connections** Describe an everyday problem or situation that you would solve using two mathematical operations.

80 Lesson 23 *Solving word problems that have unnecessary information*

Syllables

Guide 5: Words with One Consonant
Between Two Sounded Vowels

Many words have only one consonant between two sounded vowels. This guide will help you in dividing such words. Such words are divided differently depending on whether the first vowel is long or short.

> **Guide 5a:** A word that has one consonant between two sounded vowels, with the first vowel long, is usually divided into syllables before the consonant.

spider   spi der

Use Guide 5a to divide each word below into two syllables by writing each syllable separately on the line to the right of the word.

1. pilot	pi lot		9. bacon	ba con
2. robot	ro bot		10. odor	o dor
3. music	mu sic		11. flavor	fla vor
4. private	pri vate		12. major	ma jor
5. even	e ven		13. locate	lo cate
6. human	hu man		14. total	to tal
7. spiral	spi ral		15. moment	mo ment
8. minus	mi nus		16. student	stu dent

> **Guide 5b:** A word that has one consonant between two sounded vowels, with the first vowel short, is usually divided into syllables after the consonant.

rapid   rap id

Use Guide 5b to divide each word below into two syllables by writing each syllable separately on the line to the right of the word.

1. shiver	shiv er		9. pedal	ped al
2. robin	rob in		10. magic	mag ic
3. closet	clos et		11. seven	sev en
4. dragon	drag on		12. planet	plan et
5. clever	clev er		13. second	sec ond
6. medal	med al		14. melon	mel on
7. travel	trav el		15. robin	rob in
8. river	riv er		16. shovel	sho vel

Say each of the words below to yourself. If the first vowel is long, use Guide 5a to divide the word into two syllables. If the first vowel is short, use Guide 5b.

1. cabin	cab in		8. model	mod el	
2. paper	pa per		9. wagon	wag on	
3. lilac	li lac		10. clover	clo ver	
4. lemon	lem on		11. petal	pet al	
5. silent	si lent		12. spinal	spi nal	
6. lizard	liz ard		13. satin	sat in	
7. meter	me ter		14. tiger	ti ger	

Guide 6: Words with Blends

The word *zebra* has two consonants between two sounded vowels. Because the consonant blend *br* makes one sound, it is treated in the same way that a single consonant is treated. The word is divided in this way: *ze bra*.

In a word that has three consonants between two vowels, it is possible that two of the consonants are a blend or a digraph. You treat the blend or digraph as one consonant. For example, *congress* has a *gr* blend. You divide the word between the consonant and the consonant blend: *con gress*.

Circle the blend or digraph in each of the words below. Then divide the word into two syllables by writing each syllable separately on the line to the right of the word.

1. explore	ex plore		8. bushel	bush el	
2. leather	leath er		9. surprise	sur prise	
3. athlete	ath lete		10. gather	gath er	
4. other	oth er		11. central	cen tral	
5. pumpkin	pump kin		12. compress	com press	
6. detract	de tract		13. imply	im ply	
7. camphor	cam phor		14. children	child ren	

When a word ends in *-le*, the *-le* and the consonant before it make up a syllable, as in *bun dle*.

Divide the words below into two syllables by writing each syllable separately on the line to the right of the word.

1. cradle	cra dle		8. fable	fa ble	
2. gentle	gen tle		9. dimple	dim ple	
3. bugle	bu gle		10. noble	no ble	
4. handle	han dle		11. rifle	ri fle	
5. sample	sam ple		12. title	ti tle	
6. stable	sta ble		13. maple	ma ple	
7. thimble	thim ble		14. uncle	un cle	

Accented Syllables

When words contain two syllables, one of the syllables is stressed, or accented, more than the other. In dictionaries, the **accent mark** (') is placed at the end of the syllable that is said with more stress. For example, the first syllable in the word *picnic* is said with more stress than the second syllable.

pic'nic

Words that have three syllables usually are accented on one of the first two syllables. When you are trying to pronounce a word with three syllables, say the word with more stress on the first syllable. If the word does not sound right, say it again, giving the most stress to the second syllable.

Say each of the following words to yourself. Write an accent mark after the syllable that should be stressed.

1. peo´ple	8. di rec´tion	15. car na´tion
2. riv´er	9. hu´man	16. mo tel´
3. con tain´	10. im por´tant	17. buf´fa lo
4. chem´i cal	11. gar´den	18. ca noe´
5. pos´si ble	12. de vel´op	19. wag´on
6. fig´ure	13. or´gan ize	20. tor pe´do
7. con´so nant	14. por´cu pine	21. for get´ting

Words of four or more syllables usually have two accented syllables. In the word *caterpillar*, the first syllable, *cat*, has the most stress. This syllable receives the primary accent mark ('). The third syllable, *pil*, has more stress than the remaining two syllables, but less stress than the first syllable. The secondary accent mark (') is placed after that syllable.

cat'er pil'lar

Say each of the following words to yourself. Write the primary accent mark ' after the syllable that has the most stress. Write the secondary accent mark ' after the syllable that has the second most stress.

1. sec' re tar´y	6. e lec´tro mag´net
2. bron´to sau fus	7. al´li ga´tor
3. ar´ma dil´ lo	8. mar´i o nette´
4. hip´po pot´a mus	9. in´vi ta´tion
5. cem´e ter´y	10. en cy´clo pe´di a

Schwa Sound

The vowels *a, e, i, o,* and *u* can all have the same sound. This is a soft sound like a short *u* pronounced lightly.

Pronounce *around.* Did the *a* sound like a soft, short *u*? ___yes___

Pronounce *harden.* Did the *e* sound like a soft, short *u*? ___yes___

Pronounce *animal.* Did the *i* sound like a soft, short *u*? ___yes___

Pronounce *collect.* Did the *o* sound like a soft, short *u*? ___yes___

Pronounce *circus.* Did the *u* sound like a soft, short *u*? ___yes___

This short, soft *u* sound is called the **schwa** sound. In dictionary respellings, the symbol ə stands for the schwa sound. If you look up the word *lament* in the dictionary, you will find it respelled this way.

lə ment'

Say each of the words below to yourself. Write an accent mark after the syllable that is stressed. Then circle the letter that stands for the schwa sound.

1. wag(o)n	6. gar´ m(e)nt	11. (a)p pear´	16. stan´ z(a)
2. (a) ware´	7. pos´ si(ble)	12. mov (a) ble	17. choc´(o) late
3. gal´ l(o)p	8. s(u)p ply´	13. ash´ (e)n	18. sug´ (a)r
4. eas´(i) ly	9. ze´ br(a)	14. (a)t tack´	19. mir´ r(o)r
5. (a)p ply´	10. op´ p(o) site	15. se´ r(u)m	20. med´ (i) cine

Look at the words in the list above. Does the *schwa* sound come in the accented or unaccented syllable? Write the correct word in the sentence below.

The *schwa* sound always falls in an ___unaccented___ syllable of a word.

Read the selection that follows. Circle the letter or letters in each underlined word that stand for the schwa sound.

Animals in Africa

Afric(a) has many large an(i)mals. One of the largest of all beasts is the elephant. It lives in a fam(i)ly herd of blood rel(a)tives and trav(e)ls (a)bout eating grass and leaves. The g(o)rilla is (a)nother fairly big an(i)mal. It is the largest of the apes. It looks fierce, but it is really a peacef(u)l an(i)mal.

The li(o)n and the leop(a)rd are (a)mong the fiercest of the land beasts. The croc(o)dile, which lives in lakes, riv(e)rs, and marsh(e)s, is much feared. The hyen(a) is disliked because of its horr(i)ble shrieks.

Main Idea and Supporting Details

When you are reading a paragraph that is packed with information, the first step is to find the **main idea**. The second step is to find the **supporting details** that give more information about the main idea. These details are important because they help develop, or support, the main idea.

The following paragraph is about the American colonists. The main idea and supporting details are listed after the paragraph.

> The American colonists were unhappy under the rule of England. In 1774, colonial leaders formed the First Continental Congress to decide on possible actions to take. They asked the King of England to cancel certain laws that the colonists thought unfair. They also asked that British troops leave the colonies.

Main Idea The American colonists were unhappy under the rule of England.

Supporting Details
a. They formed the First Continental Congress to decide on possible actions to take.
b. They asked the King of England to do away with laws that the colonists thought unfair.
c. They asked that the British troops leave.

On the next page, write the sentence that states the main idea for each paragraph. Then write the supporting details in your own words.

1. Both the British and the colonial armies wanted control of two hills near Boston—Bunker Hill and Breed's Hill. In June, 1775, the Americans took control of them first and posted armed troops on Breed's Hill. After two unsuccessful attempts to take the hills, the British defeated the Americans in a battle known as the Battle of Bunker Hill. However, most of the battle was fought on Breed's Hill, not Bunker Hill.

2. In 1775, a new congress, the Second Continental Congress, decided to end British rule and govern the colonies itself. It formed an army to fight the British and made George Washington commander-in-chief. It issued and borrowed money. It set up a postal system and created a navy.

3. The idea of independence spread throughout the colonies. *Common Sense,* written by Thomas Paine, convinced the colonists that they must fight. The colonists in Massachusetts, New Jersey, and South Carolina rebelled against their British governors. A committee set to work on a statement telling the King of England why the colonies believed that they must break away from England. Thomas Jefferson, with suggestions from the committee, wrote this statement, the Declaration of Independence.

4. A young Frenchman named Lafayette offered to help the colonial army. Later, France declared war on Great Britain. In 1780, France sent 6,000 soldiers to the colonies. The British kept them in Newport Harbor for eleven months. The following spring, the French sent a large squadron of ships and a lot of money. The French had come to the aid of the colonists.

5. In 1781, the colonists won the battle at Yorktown. The British General Cornwallis had marched his soldiers to Yorktown, Virginia. Knowing of Cornwallis's movements, the colonists put into action a plan that ended the Revolutionary War in their favor. Washington and his French allies pretended to move to New York, but marched to Yorktown instead. Meanwhile, the French fleet took control of the waters off Yorktown so that Cornwallis could not get help from the British fleet. Surrounded by these forces, Cornwallis had no choice but to surrender.

Paragraph 1

Main Idea After two unsuccessful attempts to take the hills, the British defeated the colonists in a battle known as the Battle of Bunker Hill.

Supporting Details

a. Bunker Hill and Breed's Hill are near Boston.

b. The colonists and British wanted these hills.

c. The colonists set up troops on Breed's Hill.

d. The battle was fought mostly on Breed's Hill, not Bunker Hill.

Paragraph 2

Main Idea In 1776, a new congress, the Second Continental Congress, decided to end British rule and govern the colonies itself.

Supporting Details

a. It formed an army with Washington as commander.

b. It controlled money.

c. It set up a postal system and a navy.

Paragraph 3

Main Idea The idea of independence spread throughout the colonies.

Supporting Details

a. *Common Sense* convinced colonists to fight.

b. Three states rebelled against their British governors.

c. Thomas Jefferson wrote the Declaration of Independence.

Paragraph 4

Main Idea The French had come to the aid of the Americans.

Supporting Details

a. A Frenchman named Lafayette offered to help.

b. France declared war on Great Britain.

c. France sent 6,000 soldiers.

d. France sent a squadron of ships and a lot of money.

Paragraph 5

Main Idea Knowing of Cornwallis's movements, the colonists put into action a plan that ended the Revolutionary War in their favor.

Supporting Details

a. Cornwallis marched his soldiers to Yorktown.

b. Washington and the French marched to Yorktown.

c. The French controlled the waters off Yorktown.

d. Cornwallis had to surrender to Washington.

Inferences

In order to understand what an author has not stated, you must gather clues from the details that are stated. In this way, you can **infer**, or figure out, information that is not stated directly in a selection.

If you go through the following steps, you will find it easier to infer information.

1. Read carefully.

2. Think about what you've read. Be sure that you understand the information that is stated.

3. Read again and look for clues to information that is not stated.

4. Put together the information stated with the information that you already know. Use clues to help you make inferences.

As you read the following selection on Phillis Wheatley, pay close attention to the facts. Use the facts to infer information that is not directly stated in the selection.

Phillis Wheatley

1. The year was 1761. Mrs. Wheatley walked out of her large house on an upper-class Boston street. The wife of a successful tailor, she was headed for a slave ship that had docked in the Boston harbor. Although the Wheatleys had a few elderly slaves in their household, Mrs. Wheatley needed a slave who would serve as her personal maid for years to come.

2. Mrs. Wheatley boarded the slave ship. She found hundreds of people cramped in small, dark, stuffy rooms. As she looked around, she was drawn to a thin, frightened-looking girl in a corner. The girl had been kidnapped from her home in West Africa to be sold in America. The long journey had been difficult for her. Mrs. Wheatley paid a small amount for this sickly girl. The ship's captain was pleased because he was afraid that the girl looked too sick to sell at all.

3. The sad life of the young girl was about to undergo a complete change. She couldn't have been bought by a finer master and mistress. The girl reminded Mrs. Wheatley of a tiny tree in need of warmth, food, and care. Mrs. Wheatley named her Phillis, which means "a green branch of a tree." Although the girl spoke only the language of her West African tribe, Mrs. Wheatley explained to her the meaning of her new name. Phillis was pleased with it.

4. Phillis learned quickly. Although she was a servant in the Wheatley home, she was treated more like a member of the family. Instead of doing hard chores, Phillis learned to read English and Latin. She hungrily studied the Bible, mythology, ancient history, and eighteenth-century English poetry. Gradually, Phillis became a well-read woman.

5. Phillis started to write poetry as a teenager. Her first poem, written in 1767, was about the death of George Whitefield, a famous English evangelist. When it was published three years later, Phillis became the first black woman and only the second woman to publish in the colonies. Soon all of Boston knew of her. Her fame spread to England and the rest of Europe as well.

6. Phillis became ill in the early 1770s, and the Wheatleys' family doctor recommended a change in climate. So Phillis accompanied Mr. Wheatley on a business trip to England. She met the best of British society and was well received. With the help of her English friends, her book *Poems on Various Subjects, Religious and Moral* was published.

7. George Washington became commander in chief of the Revolutionary army in 1775. Phillis was delighted that the colonists finally had a strong leader in the fight against England. To express how she felt, Phillis wrote a poem about Washington. She sent it to him with a letter. Much to Phillis's surprise, George

Washington sent her a thank-you note praising her for her beautiful verses and inviting her to visit him. Phillis accepted his invitation.

8. After Mr. and Mrs. Wheatley died, Phillis was left alone. She married John Peters, a freed slave like herself. But he was never able to support the family. Phillis tried to raise money by publishing a second book. She put an advertisement in the newspaper seeking buyers for her book. Much to her disappointment, almost no one showed interest in her work. Shortly thereafter, at the age of 31, she died. Despite all of her hardships, Phillis Wheatley earned great fame as a poet in her time.

For each of the following statements, decide which items can be inferred from the paragraph listed. Put a check mark next to the statement or statements. On the lines that follow, write the phrase or sentence that has the clue that you found. Then explain how you inferred the information.

Paragraph 1 (check two)

a. __✔__ The Wheatleys were wealthy.

b. _____ The Wheatleys had several children.

c. __✔__ Mrs. Wheatley was looking for a young maid.

Clue: _her large house on an upper-class Boston street_

Explanation: _People must be wealthy to own a large house on a fine street._

Clue: _The Wheatleys had a few elderly slaves. She needed someone for years to come._

Explanation: _A young slave would be able to serve for years._

Paragraph 2 (check two)

a. _____ Many of the slaves died on the trip to America.

b. __✔__ The slave ship carried its passengers as if they were cargo.

c. __✔__ The healthy-looking slaves brought higher prices.

Clue: _hundreds of people cramped in small, dark, stuffy rooms_

Explanation: _These conditions were unsuitable for people._

Clue: _Mrs. Wheatley paid a small amount for this sickly girl._

Explanation: _Someone healthy would be worth more money._

Paragraph 4 (check two)

a. _____ Phillis was not very good at doing household chores.

b. __✔__ Phillis had an excellent mind and was eager to learn.

c. __✔__ The Wheatleys allowed Phillis to read many books in their home.

Clue: _She learned to read English and Latin._

Explanation: _Someone who learns two languages probably is smart._

Clue: _She hungrily studied the Bible, mythology, ancient history, and eighteenth-century English poetry._

Explanation: _Someone studying these works would have to read many books._

Suffixes

A suffix is a word part that is added to the end of a word to change its meaning. Eight suffixes and their meanings are given below.

Suffix	Meaning	Suffix	Meaning
ity	condition or quality	ous	having, full of
let	small, little	ship	condition of or state of
ly	like or every	ure	act or result
or	person or thing that	ward	toward

Read each word below and the meaning that follows it. Write the correct suffix after each word.

1. mother ___ly___ like a mother
2. back ___ward___ toward the back
3. acid ___ity___ condition of being acidic
4. courage ___ous___ having courage
5. direct ___or___ person who directs
6. book ___let___ little book

7. fail ___ure___ act of failing
8. week ___ly___ every week
9. friend ___ship___ state of being friends
10. invent ___or___ person who invents
11. west ___ward___ toward the west
12. partner ___ship___ state of being partners

Use one of the words above to complete each sentence below.

1. Karen looked _____backward_____ to see if she had dropped anything.
2. Tabitha Babbit, the _____inventor_____ of the circular saw, got the idea for it while watching her spinning wheel.
3. Because a _____booklet_____ is little, it often has a paper cover.
4. The _____friendship_____ between Joe and Ben started in second grade.
5. Jumping into the water to save a frightened child is a _____courageous_____ act.
6. The author was discouraged by his _____failure_____ to write a successful novel.
7. The drink's _____acidity_____ made it taste bitter.
8. Every Friday, Pete bought a _____weekly_____ supply of groceries.
9. The _____director_____ watched the play from backstage.
10. On Monday, the employees had their _____monthly_____ meeting.
11. Bill and Pat formed a _____partnership_____ in order to buy a toy business.
12. The wind was blowing in a _____westward_____ direction.

Library Catalog

To locate a book in the library quickly and easily, use the **library catalog**. In most cases, the catalog will be a computer database. Although formats may vary, most library databases are set up to give the same basic information. You find information by choosing items from a menu, or list. The main menu often lists other resources as well as the library catalog. When you choose the catalog, a second menu will appear. You can then search for a book by its title, by the author's name, or by its subject. If you don't have exact information about the book, you may be able to choose an item called **keywords**. The computer will search its database using one or two important words that you give it.

A library catalog gives more information than just the author, title, and subject of a book. Usually an entry for a book gives a summary, a description (size, number of pages, kind of illustrations), the publisher and date it was published, and a list of related subjects. It may tell how many copies exist, which branches have the book, and whether it is available.

Subject Search

Suppose you want to read a true story about survival in the wilderness. First, you select "Subject" from the catalog menu to do a **subject search**. Then enter a phrase such as *wilderness survival*. A list of subjects will appear. Choose one that is the same as, or close to, the phrase that you entered. A list of books about that topic will appear. Then choose a particular book to find out more about it.

Author Search

If you want to find out which books by a particular author are in the library, you can do an **author search**. Choose "Author" from the catalog menu and enter the author's name, last name first (for example: Ansell, Rod). A list of authors will appear. Choose your author to see a list of his or her books. You can then choose a particular book to find out more about it.

Title Search

If you already know what book you want, you can do a **title search**. Choose "Title" from the catalog menu and enter the exact title. An alphabetical list of titles will appear, including the one that you entered. If the title begins with *A*, *An*, or *The*, the book will be listed by the second word in the title. You can then select the title of the book that you want.

In each kind of search, the last step is to select a particular book. When you do, a screen similar to this one appears:

```
Call Number  Young Adult Nonfiction  Status:
             613.69 An82T            checked
                                     out

AUTHOR: ANSELL, ROD
TITLE: To fight the wild
PUBLISHER: New York: Harcourt Brace
           Jovanovich, c. 1986

DESCRIPTION: 151 p.; ill.; 22cm.
SUMMARY: A man struggles to survive on his
         own in one of the most isolated
         corners of Australia for two months
         before he is rescued.

SUBJECTS: 1) Wilderness areas - Australia
          2) Wilderness Survival
          3) Survival
          4) Australia
```

Notice the call number at the top of the screen on page 90. This number appears on the spine, or narrow back edge, of the book. Every nonfiction book has its own call number that tells where it is shelved in the library. Nonfiction books are kept in numerical order. This book would come before a book with the number 613.7 and after one numbered 612.06. The letters immediately following the number are the first two letters of the author's last name. Across from the call number is the word *status*, which means condition or position. This tells you whether the book is on the shelf or is checked out.

A. Now use the screen on page 90 to do the following:

1. Circle the year that the book was published.

2. Is this book illustrated? Put two lines under the information that tells you.

3. If you wanted to learn more about the setting of this story, what other subjects might you search under? Draw a box around each.

B. Circle the kind of search that you would do in order to answer each question.

1. Who wrote the book *Cowboy: An Album*?

   author search   (title search)   subject search

2. Which of Virginia Hamilton's books does the library have?

   (author search)   title search   subject search

3. Does the library have any new books about World War II?

   author search   title search   (subject search)

4. What is the call number for *The Forgotten Heroes: The Story of the Buffalo Soldier*s?

   author search   (title search)   subject search

5. Does the library have books on martial arts?

   author search   title search   (subject search)

6. Does the library have Laurence Yep's newest book?

   (author search)   title search   subject search

C. Use the information on the computer screen below to answer each question.

1. When was this book published?

   _____ 1985 _____

2. The summary mentions a polar expedition. Under what subjects could you look for more information about it?

   Arctic regions–Discovery and exploration
   _____

3. Suppose you want to find other books by this author. What name would you look

   under? _____ Dolan, Edward F. _____

4. Would this book be shelved before or after one with call number

   J919.804 FAR? _____ before _____

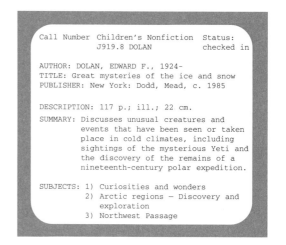

```
Call Number  Children's Nonfiction   Status:
      J919.8 DOLAN                checked in

AUTHOR: DOLAN, EDWARD F., 1924-
TITLE: Great mysteries of the ice and snow
PUBLISHER: New York: Dodd, Mead, c. 1985

DESCRIPTION: 117 p.; ill.; 22 cm.
SUMMARY: Discusses unusual creatures and
      events that have been seen or taken
      place in cold climates, including
      sightings of the mysterious Yeti and
      the discovery of the remains of a
      nineteenth-century polar expedition.

SUBJECTS: 1) Curiosities and wonders
          2) Arctic regions — Discovery and
             exploration
          3) Northwest Passage
```

Outlining

Sometimes you write a summary of a selection or a chapter in a textbook to help you understand or study it. Another good way to understand and remember something that you read is to make an **outline** of it. An outline can be written quickly and read easily. A good outline shows how the main ideas and supporting details in a selection are organized.

In a paragraph, the most important idea is the main idea. In an outline of a selection or chapter, the main idea of each paragraph is restated in a few words and written next to a Roman numeral: I, II, III, and so on.

The details that give important supporting information about the main idea are the major details. The major details are written next to capital letters: A, B, C, and so on. These letters are indented, or moved a little to the right, underneath the Roman numerals.

The details that give information about the major details are the minor details. The minor details are written next to numbers: 1, 2, 3, 4, and so on. These numbers are indented underneath the capital letters.

Read the following paragraph. Then look at the outline next to it.

Cargo ships can be classified into different groups according to the kinds of cargo they carry. *General cargo ships* carry packaged items—goods that are put in packages. These include such items as chemicals, food, and furniture. *Tankers* carry liquid cargo. This might include petroleum—the thick natural oil that fuel oil and gasoline are made from—or molasses. *Dry bulk carriers* haul products, such as iron ore and coal, that can be loaded loose on the vessels.

Cargo Ships

I. Classification of cargo ships
  A. General cargo ships
    1. Carry packaged items
    2. Examples—chemicals, food, furniture
  B. Tankers
    1. Carry liquid cargo
    2. Examples—petroleum, molasses
  C. Dry bulk carriers
    1. Carry loose items
    2. Examples—coal, iron ore

Notice that *Classification of cargo ships*, the main idea of the paragraph, is written next to Roman numeral I. *General cargo ships* is written next to capital letter A. This phrase is the first major detail about cargo ships. *Carry packaged items* is written next to number 1. This phrase is a minor detail about general cargo ships.

Every outline should have a title. When you outline a selection, always include at least two main ideas. An outline of a selection can never have a I without a II. There should also be at least two major details under each main idea. An A should always be followed by a B. Finally, there should always be at least two minor details under each major detail.

Each of the following paragraphs compares a type of cargo ship of the past with a type that is in use today. By completing the outline, you will organize information in a way that will help you understand and remember the main ideas and details.

During the early 1900s, the standard general cargo ship was a three-island ship. The first island, called the forecastle, held the crew's quarters. The bridge, from which the ship was navigated, formed the second island in the middle of the ship. The poop, which held the officers' cabins, formed the third island. Today, freighters have one island for the bridge and living quarters. Having one island leaves room for more and bigger hatches and makes it easier to load and unload cargo.

In 1866, the first oceangoing tanker, the *Gluckauf*, was launched. This ship was built in Great Britain for a German oil company. It was 300 feet (91 meters) long and 37 feet (11 meters) wide. It carried 2,300 tons (2,090 metric tons) of oil and could travel at a speed of 9 knots. Large tankers are often called supertankers today. The largest tankers carry about 555,000 deadweight tons. They can travel at a speed of about 15 knots (15 sea-miles per hour).

The first dry bulk carriers were specially designed boats that began hauling iron ore on the Great Lakes during the 1800s. Like tankers, these vessels were designed to carry only one kind of cargo. But unlike tankers, the ore carriers hauled solid cargo. As a result, they required more complicated loading and unloading arrangements than tankers, which needed little more than hose connections and pumps. Today oceangoing bulk carriers have grown larger and larger. Most can carry more than 100,000 short tons (91,000 metric tons) of cargo. Motor-driven equipment on board quickly removes the enormous hatch covers so that the cargo can be reached easily.

II. General cargo ships

   A. Early 1900s—three islands

      1. First island—forecastle: crew's quarters

      2. Second island—bridge: navigation

      3. Third island—poop: officers' cabins

   B. Today—one island

      1. Bridge and living quarters

      2. More and bigger hatches—easier to load and unload

III   Tankers

   A. *Gluckauf* first oceangoing tanker—launched 1866

      1. Built in Great Britain for German oil company

      2. 300 feet long and 37 feet wide

      3. Carried 2,300 tons

      4. Traveled at 9 knots

   B. Modern supertankers

      1. Carry 555,000 tons

      2. Travel at 15 knots

IV.   Dry bulk carriers

   A. First carriers hauled iron ore on Great Lakes in 1800s

      1. Carried only one kind of cargo

      2. Hauled solid cargo

      3. Complicated loading and unloading arrangements

   B. Modern oceangoing carriers are larger

      1. Carry 100,000 short tons

      2. Motor-driven equipment removes hatch covers

Reading Drug Labels

Medicine can be helpful in curing an illness but dangerous if taken incorrectly. It is very important to read the label on the bottle or box *before* taking any medication. The label states the medical problems that the medication may help. It gives the dosage—how much medicine should be taken and how often. A label may also provide certain warnings to help prevent the wrong use of the medicine. Anyone using medication should read the label carefully to be familiar with the proper dosage and use.

Read the labels below from two different medications.

FORMULA D—
For coughs due to colds and flu
—quiets coughs
—relieves stuffy nose
—soothes sore throat

DIRECTIONS FOR USE
ADULT DOSE
12 years and over—2 teaspoonfuls
CHILD DOSE
6 to 12 years—1 teaspoonful
2 to 6 years—$\frac{1}{2}$ teaspoonful

Repeat every 4 hours as needed
No more than 6 doses daily
Drink a full glass of water with each dose

WARNINGS
Do not administer to children under 2 years old unless directed by physician. Persons with a high fever or persistent cough or with high blood pressure, diabetes, or heart disease should not use this medication unless directed by physician.

KEEP OUT OF REACH OF CHILDREN

DRAMADON *is the most widely prescribed product for the prevention and treatment of seasickness—including nausea, dizziness, or vomiting.*

DIRECTIONS FOR USE: To prevent motion sickness, take first dose $\frac{1}{2}$ to 1 hour before boarding a ship, boat, plane, car, or bus.

Dosage: Adults: 1 to 2 tablets every 4 to 6 hours, not to exceed 8 tablets in 24 hours. Children 6 to 12 years: 1 tablet every 6 to 8 hours, not to exceed 3 tablets in 24 hours. Children 2 to 6 years: $\frac{1}{2}$ tablet every 6 to 8 hours, not to exceed $1\frac{1}{2}$ tablets in 24 hours.

Warnings: **DRAMADON** may cause drowsiness. Do not operate automobiles or dangerous machinery while taking this medication. Avoid alcoholic beverages while taking this medication. Not for use in the presence of asthma or glaucoma. Keep this and all medication out of reach of children.

A. Use the information on the labels to complete each sentence.

1. The medication used to prevent seasickness is ___Dramadon___.

2. The medication used to quiet coughs is ___Formula D___.

3. You can tell that Formula D is not a tablet because the directions tell how many ___teaspoons___ to take.

4. Each container of Dramadon contains ___90___ tablets.

5. The symptoms—or signs—of seasickness are ___nausea, dizziness, or vomiting___.

6. To prevent seasickness from occurring, you should take Dramadon ___one-half to one hour before boarding.___

7. Adults can take ___1 or 2___ Dramadon tablets every 4 to 6 hours. If an adult takes 2 tablets every 4 hours, then ___12___ tablets will be taken within one day. However, not more than ___8___ tablets should be taken in a day. This means you can take up to two tablets at one time, but no more than ___4___ two-tablet doses in a 24-hour period.

8. The Dramadon label warns against driving an automobile while using the medication because the medication may cause ___drowsiness___.

9. If an adult uses the maximum number of Dramadon tablets recommended for one day, then a container of Dramadon will last for ___11 1/4___ days.

10. The medication that should be taken with a glass of water is ___Formula D___.

11. If an eleven-year-old takes the maximum number of recommended doses of Formula D in one day, then he or she will take ___6___ teaspoonfuls of the medication. If a four-year-old takes the maximum number of doses in a day, he or she will take ___3___ teaspoonfuls.

12. If a one-year-old is given Formula D, then a ___physician___ has recommended it.

13. "No more than 6 doses daily" means no more than 6 doses in ___one day___.

B. Circle the letter in front of the one, two, or three answer(s) to each question.

1. Which warning(s) is (are) given on both medications?
   (a.) Keep out of reach of children.
   b. Do not drive an automobile while using medication.
   c. Do not use if you have glaucoma.

2. Both medications have different dosages for which age group(s)?
   (a.) children two to six years old   (b.) children six to twelve years old   (c.) adults

3. How many teaspoonfuls of Formula D can an adult take every four hours?
   a. 1   b. 8   (c.) 2

4. What is the most Formula D an adult should take in one day?
   a. 2 teaspoonfuls   (b.) 12 teaspoonfuls   c. 8 teaspoonfuls

5. What are the benefits of Formula D Cough Syrup?
   (a.) It helps to relieve a cough.   (b.) It clears a stuffy nose.   (c.) It makes a sore throat feel better.

Lesson 33 _____

Setting

Reading a Literature Selection _____

▶ **Background Information**

Today many people know about the sport of mountain climbing.Climbers today make use of the most modern tools and equipment. However, the early mountain climbers were not so lucky. They were pioneers, preparing the way for others in this dangerous sport.

The following selection is a true story about Edward Whymper, the first person to climb the Matterhorn. One of the steepest mountains in the European Alps, the Matterhorn is a challenge to even the most experienced mountain climbers. As you will find out, this great triumph for Whymper ended in tragedy.

▶ **Skill Focus**

Setting is the place and time of the events in a story. Events can happen in any place and at any time. A story can take place on the streets of a city, on a country farm, along a seacoast, or in a foreign country. The time can be the present, several years ago, or far in the future.

In many stories, the setting creates difficulties for the characters. In a story set in a deserted cabin, a person might have to cope with loneliness. In a story set on a ship in a stormy sea, the crew might have to deal with physical danger.

The following questions will help you identify setting and understand how setting can cause difficulties for characters. Ask yourself the following questions as you read a story.

1. Where and when do the events of the story take place?
2. What details does the author use to reveal the setting?
3. What difficulties does the setting create for the characters?
4. How do the characters overcome the difficulties that arise because of the setting?
5. What effect does the setting have on the characters in the story?

▶ **Word Clues**

Read the sentence below. Look for context clues that explain the underlined word.

> Young Edward Whymper grew up in England among rolling hills, fertile farmlands, and craggy <u>moors</u>.

If you do not know the meaning of the word *moors*, the words *hills and farmlands* can help you. The word *moors* is grouped with other things in the same category, so that you can figure out that moors are a landform.

Use **groupings** as context clues to find the meaning of the three underlined words in the selection.

▶ **Strategy Tip**

As you read, look for details that describe the setting. Notice how the place and time of the events in this true story cause difficulties for Whymper, the members of his party, and other climbers.

Triumph and Tragedy

Young Edward Whymper grew up in England among rolling hills, fertile farmlands, and craggy moors. He had never seen a mountain or even climbed a hill. That is, not until he came to the Alps at the age of twenty. These fabled mountains stretch through several European countries, including France, Italy, Switzerland, and Austria. Whymper was an engraver who was assigned by a publishing company to make pictures of tall mountains. Since there are no large mountains in England, he came across the English Channel and journeyed over land to see the mountains for himself. And see them he did! These towering snowcapped peaks were like nothing in England. Out of green valleys and clear lakes, the majestic mountains seemed to reach for the sky.

It was 1860, and mountaineering was just becoming known as a sport. A hundred years earlier, Horace Bénédict de Saussure, a scientist from Geneva, offered a reward to whomever could climb the highest peak of the Alps. This peak was Mont Blanc, at 15,771 feet. Six years later, physician Michel Gabriel Paccard and his guide, Jacques Balmat, succeeded. Before Mont Blanc was conquered, mountain climbing was almost unheard of. By the middle of the nineteenth century, however, at least a hundred large peaks in the Alps, such as Ortles, the

Jungfrau, and the Zugspitze, had been climbed for the first time.

The possibilities for conquering <u>sheer</u> peaks for the first time seemed limitless to the earliest mountaineers. However, the surge of interest in climbing prompted one concerned climber to ask sadly in 1854, "Will our grandsons succeed in the future in conquering the last of all the alpine peaks?" The "Golden Age" of alpinism, the climbing of the Alps, had begun. So many English climbers came to explore the peaks of Europe that the Alps became known as the "Playground of Europe." In the two decades that followed, nearly all the important peaks had been conquered.

As difficult as it may be to believe today, the earliest alpine hikers didn't realize that climbing was dangerous, because they had no experience that alerted them to the particular dangers of the sport. It was the ascent and alarming descent of the dramatic Matterhorn that brought about an understanding of the dangers of mountaineering. That is where Edward Whymper returns to the story.

Located on the Swiss-Italian border, the Matterhorn looks like a sharp, pointed pyramid when viewed from the nearby town of Zermatt, Switzerland. Its steep face challenges even the most experienced climbers today.

After journeying in the Alps for almost a year, Whymper first saw the Matterhorn in the summer of 1861. Though he had never climbed a hill before coming to the Alps, he had become interested in climbing during his year in the mountains, and he immediately attempted to climb it. His first attempt failed. Whymper was inexperienced, and the equipment he had was not good enough for climbing such a steep mountain. Even the best mountaineers said that the Matterhorn was impossible to climb. That did not stop Whymper. He resolved to succeed in his climb someday. He spoke of the mountain in the battle terms that many mountaineers use. His plan was "to return with a companion and besiege [or attack] the mountain for so long that either it or we will be beaten."

Whymper thought he had found his companion in Jean Carrel. Carrel grew up in Italy at the foot of the Matterhorn. It had been his dream since he was a young boy to be the

first person to climb it. Back in 1857, he had tried to climb it with his brother and another mountaineer, Abbé Aimé Gorret, but the mountain proved overwhelming to the trio. Still, Carrel had every intention of returning to the mountain again, and he knew in his heart that he would succeed.

The two determined men could surely make it together. Whymper went back to England, where he devoted his time to planning for the trip. He created a mountaineer's tent that could be carried. By using it, the climbers could bivouac—make a camp—with some protection from the wind, snow, ice, and cold. A bivouac allows climbers to spend nights on steep rock faces when getting to a flat space would take more than one day. Whymper built new kinds of equipment, such as a <u>grappling</u> iron that could help the climbers grab onto the impossibly steep rock faces. He also built two ladders that could be folded up, which the climbers could carry with them.

In 1863, Whymper was ready. He and Carrel had decided their best route up would be the Italian ridge, but they had to wait for conditions that were suitable for climbing. Certainly there is snow on these high peaks all year round, but the height of summer in a good year is the best chance for success. Finally, in the summer of 1865, all signs indicated that it was time! When Whymper arrived in Italy, he got in touch with Carrel. He found out that his would-be companion had decided to go up with some Italian climbers. What had been a partnership had turned into a rivalry.

Whymper was disappointed but not beaten. He had come this far. There was no way he would turn back now. He found other companions and used his special equipment and newfound expertise to scale the mountain. As it turned out, he and Carrel reached the top on the same day, July 14. Carrel's party was 300 feet below Whymper and his party on the Italian side, so Whymper is considered to be the first person to climb the mountain. Finally, he had realized his dream! The young engraver who had never until five years earlier rested his eyes on a mountain peak had climbed a mountain most people said was impossible to climb.

> *After an avalanche buried three climbers in 1896 near Vienna, Austria, the first mountain rescue service was founded.*

According to one account by Whymper, his triumphant cries and those of his fellow climbers were heard by Carrel and his party on the Italian side of the peak. Whymper said that he and another climber sent rocks sliding down the mountain to be sure that the Italians knew of their victory. An exultant Whymper said, "The Italians turned and fled."

It didn't take long for Whymper's great joy to turn to grave <u>catastrophe</u>. On the way down the mountain, one of the men in his party slipped. Three of his companions who were attached to the same rope were pulled off the mountain with him. When the rope snapped and the four men fell from the mountain, Whymper could only watch in horror. Afterward, he described the accident: "For a few seconds we watched our unfortunate companions tumble down the slope, fighting with outstretched hands for some kind of finger-hold. They were still unhurt as one by one they disappeared from view and crashed from cliff to cliff down a drop of almost 4,000 feet."

No one knows whether the rope broke in midair or whether it was cut as it slid against a rock. Some people have even suggested that some member of the party cut the rope or gave the climbers who fell a weaker rope. Historians do not believe these theories and point out that until this time, climbers weren't really aware of just how dangerous the sport could be.

Although there had been other deaths and accidents, this disaster quickly changed the way that people thought about mountain climbing. People all over the world heard about the accident. Climbers and nonclimbers began to realize how truly dangerous the pursuit of mountain peaks can be. The more people climbed mountains, the more accidents happened. People can die from slipping off footholds, from pieces of mountain breaking off the main rock face, from exposure to the wind and cold, and from equipment failures. Accidents in which people are injured but not killed make the trip much more dangerous for those in the party who have to carry the injured person. Climbing down a sheer rock wall is already a life-risking course of action.

Trying to do it while carrying a badly hurt climber might be called suicidal.

In 1896, near Vienna, Austria, three climbers were buried by an avalanche. After this, the first mountain rescue service was founded. The service responds to climbers all over the world, and its members have been called "The Angels of the Mountains." Today's climbers wear up-to-date safety equipment and generally train and practice before attempting to climb great peaks. Lightweight but warm clothes, shoes with spikes, and belts that help hold hikers to the mountain are just some of the modern inventions that now help climbers. In addition, climbing clubs and schools around the world teach people proper safety techniques. In the United States, there are even indoor climbing clubs, where people can practice climbing with the safety of soft mattresses to cushion their falls.

Of course, climbing remains dangerous. Avalanches, snowstorms, equipment failures, and carelessness have led to injuries and deaths, but the sport has come a long way since Whymper's climb of triumph and tragedy.

RECALLING FACTS

Recalling details

1. Who was Edward Whymper?

A young engraver from England, Whymper was the

first person to climb the Matterhorn.

Recalling details

2. Who was his rival from Italy?

Jean Carrel was his rival.

Identifying cause and effect

3. Why was Whymper's first attempt at the Matterhorn unsuccessful?

He was inexperienced, and the equipment that he had

was not good enough to climb such a steep mountain.

Identifying cause and effect

4. Why did Whymper need years of preparation before he was ready to return to the Matterhorn?

He needed time to build new equipment.

Recalling details

5. What kind of equipment did Whymper build that he hoped would help him in his climb?

He built a tent that could be carried, ladders that would

fold up, and a grappling-iron tool.

Recognizing sequence of events

6. What did Whymper and his party do when they reached the top of the Matterhorn?

They gave triumphant cheers, and they sent some

rocks sliding down the mountain.

Identifying mood

7. Circle the word that best describes the mood or atmosphere in this story.

　　adventurous　terrifying　peaceful

8. Answer each question by writing *yes* or *no* on the line provided.

    a. Would a beginning skier learn to ski on a mountain's sheer slopes?

           no

    b. Would a sailor use a grappling tool to anchor his boat to another boat?

           yes

    c. Would a wonderful birthday party be a catastrophe?   no

---

INTERPRETING FACTS

Making inferences

1. Why do you think Whymper thought that Carrel was his rival?

Whymper had planned his whole trip hoping that Carrel would come along, and then he found out that Carrel

planned to go with several Italian climbers.

Making inferences

2. Why might mountain climbers tie ropes around themselves that attach them to one another?

If one falls, the others who are hooked more securely to the mountain can keep him or her from falling.

Making inferences

3. How do you think Whymper felt when he returned from the mountain?

Answers may vary. He might have been proud at his achievement, but sad that four of his fellow climbers had fallen

to their death.

Drawing conclusions

4. Whymper had resolved "to return with a companion and besiege the mountain for so long that either it or we will be beaten." Which happened?

Answers may vary. Whymper beat the mountain because he reached the top. The mountain beat Whymper and his

party because four men died.

Understanding character

5. Circle three traits of character demonstrated by Edward Whymper in his climb of the Matterhorn.

    (determination)   laziness   shyness

    (inventiveness)   (resolve)   fearfulness

Making inferences

6. a. Using the illustration on page 97, describe in one sentence the clothing climbers wore in the mid-nineteenth century.

They wore heavy boots, hats, and coats, and they carried ropes and walking sticks.

b. Using details from the story, how do you think modern climbers would be dressed?

They would be wearing lightweight and warm clothing, shoes with spikes, and belts that would help them latch onto

the mountain.

Predicting outcomes

7. Do you think that Edward Whymper would have likely climbed the Matterhorn again?

Answers may vary. No. Once he had succeeded, the mountain had lost its challenge for him and returning would

have brought back a tragic memory. Yes. He wanted to help others go up the mountain safely.

SKILL FOCUS

Use information in the story and the photographs on pages 97 and 98 to answer the following questions.

1. Where and when does Edward Whymper's climb take place?

It took place on the Matterhorn in July 1865.

2. **a.** Using details from the story, describe the setting in one sentence.

The Matterhorn is steep and dangerous, with snow, ice, and wind.

b. Using details from the photographs, describe the setting in one sentence.

The Matterhorn is sharp, pointed, and snow-covered.

3. What difficulties did the setting create for Whymper and his party?

The steep, snow-covered slopes made climbing difficult. When the four men fell, rock might have broken their rope.

4. How did Whymper prepare for the setting?

He constructed new equipment that would make climbing easier.

5. What effect did the setting have on Whymper and his party?

They struggled to get up the mountain, and in the end, four men died.

▶ Real Life Connections Have you ever engaged in a sport or activity and later realized its dangers? What was your reaction to your earlier behavior?

Reading a Map

Reading a Social Studies Selection

▶ Background Information

The highest landforms on earth are mountains. By definition, a mountain rises at least 1,000 feet (300 meters) above the land that surrounds it.

At the top of a mountain, the air is thinner than it is at sea level. The thinner air makes it more difficult for people to breathe. Very high mountaintops are covered by snow year round and have very little plant life. This is because mountains are above the **treeline**—the point at which trees can no longer grow.

In many parts of the world, great mountains rise together in groups called ranges. Do you know which mountain range is closest to where you live? It may be one of the eight mountain ranges that are discussed in "The Great Mountain Ranges of the World."

▶ Skill Focus

A **relief map** shows the differences in height of various parts of the earth's surface, called *landforms*. Some landforms, such as mountains, rise high into the air. Between mountains are landforms called valleys. Other landforms, such as plains, are low and level.

The height of a landform is its **elevation**. Elevation is measured in feet or meters above sea level. Sea level is the point from which the height of all landforms is measured, beginning at zero feet or meters.

Relief maps use colors to show the different elevations and depths of the earth's landforms. Each relief map has a key that is color-coded. This key indicates, in feet or meters, the elevations that the colors on the map stand for.

Another way to compare the height of landforms is to use an illustration drawn with a scale of elevation. This sort of illustration makes it possible to compare landforms that are not close together geographically. The elevation illustration has a **vertical elevation scale.** At the bottom of the scale is sea level. Landforms, such as mountains, are drawn to their proper height according to the elevation scale.

Use both relief maps and elevation illustrations to help you better understand the earth's landforms.

▶ Word Clues

Read the sentences below. Look for context clues that explain the underlined word.

> The Rockies were formed millions of years ago when there was a great underlined upheaval in the earth's crust. Hot, liquid rock inside the earth pushed the crust upward thousands of feet above sea level, forming the Rockies.

The word *upheaval* in the first sentence is explained in the sentence that follows it. This sentence gives details that help you to understand the meaning of the word *upheaval.*

Use **detail** context clues to find the meaning of the three underlined words in the selection.

▶ Strategy Tip

Before you read "The Great Mountain Ranges of the World," preview it. First read the boldfaced headings. Then study the relief map on page 105. Also look at the illustration on page 103. Do you know the elevation of your hometown?

The Great Mountain Ranges of the World

During the long history of the Earth, the mighty forces of nature have been tirelessly at work. These natural forces have shaped the landscape of our world. Among nature's greatest works of art are mountains. Eight major mountain ranges crown the continents of the earth. To the people who live among them, these mountains are things of both beauty and danger.

The Rocky Mountains

The largest mountain range in North America is the Rocky Mountains. This range stretches for more than 3,000 miles (4,800 kilometers) from Canada's Yukon Territory to New Mexico. In places, the Rockies are 350 miles (560 kilometers) wide. The highest peak is Mount Elbert in Colorado. It rises 14,433 feet (4,399 meters) above sea level.

The Rockies were formed millions of years ago when there was a great upheaval in the earth's crust. Hot, liquid rock inside the earth pushed the crust upward thousands of feet above sea level, forming the Rockies. Glaciers, wind, and rain have, over time, carved them into a variety of shapes and sizes. The Rockies form a huge, high wall. For this reason, they are called the Continental Divide. On one side of the Divide, rivers flow east toward the Gulf of Mexico and the Atlantic Ocean. On the other side, rivers flow west toward the Pacific.

The Rockies were an obstacle for settlers in the East who wanted to move to the West. When the South Pass was discovered, wagons rolled through this and other passes, opening the West to settlement.

The Appalachian Mountains

The Appalachian (ap ə LAY chən) Mountains stretch through eastern North America from Quebec in the north to

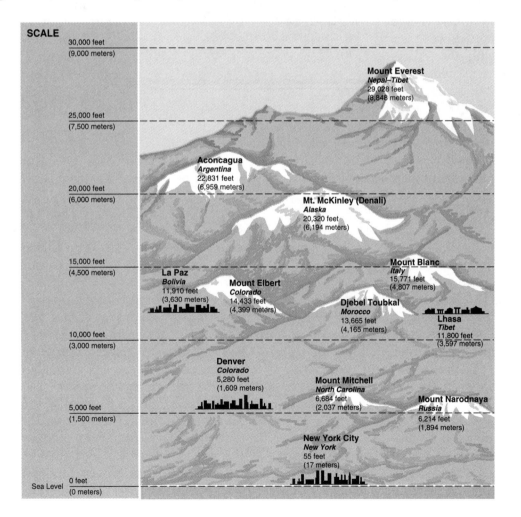

Alabama in the south. This mountain range is more than 1,500 miles (2,400 kilometers) long. The Appalachians are a relatively low range. Their highest point is Mount Mitchell in North Carolina, 6,684 feet (2,037 meters) above sea level.

The Appalachians also stood as a barrier to early pioneers as they tried to settle the continent. In the late 1700s, Daniel Boone led a group of settlers through the Cumberland Gap in Kentucky to open up for settlement the land west of the Appalachians.

Today hikers can walk 2,000 miles (3,200 kilometers) through the range on the Appalachian Trail. This trail is a marked footpath that stretches from Maine to Georgia, running mostly along the crest of the mountains.

The Alaskan Mountains

The Alaskan range includes the highest peak in North America, Mount McKinley, also called Denali. McKinley reaches a height of 20,320 feet (6,194 meters) above sea level. The Alaskan Mountains are truly Arctic mountains. Huge glaciers move down their slopes and fill the valleys with great ice fields. The climate of the range is so threatening that some areas remain unmapped. The Alaskan mountains contain some of the most beautiful scenery in the world. Mount McKinley National Park is in the northern part of the range.

The Andes Mountains

The Andes form the longest mountain chain in the world. It stretches 4,500 miles (7,200 kilometers) from the northern tip to the southern tip of South America along its west coast. The highest peak is Aconcagua (ah kawn KAH gwah), which stands 22,831 feet (6,959 meters) above sea level.

The Andes were formed millions of years ago by a great uplift of the earth's crust. Many active volcanoes in the Andes can still spread disaster when they explode with fire and liquid rock.

The Indians of South America live in many of the high regions of the Andes. Because of the altitude, the air is very thin. The Indians have adapted to their environment over the centuries. They have larger-than-average lungs to take in more air. They also have 20 percent more blood than a lowlander, which allows them to carry more oxygen to their body cells.

The Atlas Mountains

✘ The Atlas range in northwest Africa is rich in legend and history. Ancient Greeks believed that the mountains were the home of the Titan Atlas. Atlas was thought to hold up the heavens on his mighty shoulders. For many centuries, the Atlas Mountains were a mystery because they were impossible to cross.

The people living in the Atlas range have always been proud and independent. The Berber people from the Atlas region swept across North Africa and Spain in the twelfth century. They created an empire that lasted a century. The French gained control of much of northern Africa in the late 1800s. The mountain people, however, resisted their control until the 1930s.

From the north, the Atlas range is especially beautiful. The mountains begin as foothills and then climb higher and higher on the horizon. The highest peak, Djebel Toubkal, reaches 13,665 feet (4,165 meters).

The Alps

The Alps are the largest mountain range in Europe, extending from northern Italy across Austria, the Balkan regions, Switzerland, and France. The highest peak is Mont Blanc, 15,771 feet (4,807 meters) above sea level. The beautiful peaks of the Alps are separated by deep valleys dotted with clear lakes.

✔ Today alpine villages nestle under the towering mountains in scenes out of picture postcards. The beauty of the mountains can suddenly turn to terror, however. In winter and spring, an avalanche is a common occurrence. During an avalanche, tons of snow and ice suddenly break off the mountains and slide into the valleys below. The force of the snow can destroy everything in its path. To protect themselves, villagers plant trees and erect snow fences around their homes. Mountain roads are sheltered by snow sheds. Still, avalanches claim many lives every year in the Alps.

> *The Andes form the longest mountain chain in the world.*

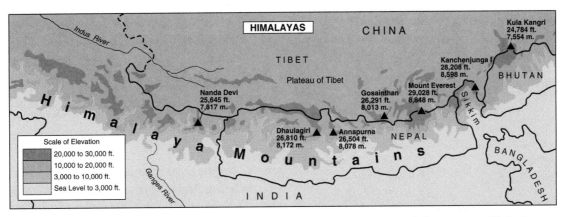

The Ural Mountains

The Ural Mountains stretch for about 1,500 miles (2,400 kilometers) through Russia and Kazakhstan. The Urals form a north-to-south line that is often considered the dividing point between Europe and Asia. Because the Urals are very old mountains that have been worn down by time, they are of only moderate height. Their rounded hills are generally low and rolling, with steeper slopes on the eastern side. In the north, they average 1,000 to 1,500 feet (305 to 460 meters) high. The highest point is Mount Narodnaya at 6,214 feet (1,894 meters) above sea level.

Much of the Ural range is covered by thick forests. Within the mountains are rich mineral deposits. As early as the 1500s, miners found salt, silver, and gold in the Urals. In the 1800s, the mountains became a famous source of gemstones. Takovaya emeralds are especially prized. During World War II, the Urals supplied the Soviet Union with such valuable resources as iron, copper, asbestos, and potash. Today the Ural range is a leading industrial region.

The Himalaya Mountains

The Himalayas are truly the giants of the earth. They are the highest mountain range in the world. Located in Asia, the Himalayas stretch across parts of Pakistan, India, Kashmir, Tibet, Nepal, Sikkim, and Bhutan. The Himalayas are also the world's youngest mountain range. They are still being pushed higher by earthquakes and other mountain building forces.

The Himalayas are a complex and beautiful group of mountains. There are many famous peaks in the range, but the most famous of all is Everest. Mount Everest is the highest mountain in the world. It reaches an altitude of 29,028 feet (8,848 meters).

The name *Himalaya* comes from the Sanskrit language and means "house of snow." For several different groups of people, the Himalayas are home. In some areas of the mountains, holy men of the Hindu and Buddhist religions live in mountain monasteries. In the Tibetan Himalayas, nomadic tribes live as herders of yaks. Yaks provide them with wool, leather, milk, cheese, meat, and transportation. On the lower slopes of the Himalayas in Nepal, native Sherpas eke out a living as herders and farmers. They have a difficult time raising crops. The farmers cut terraces, like huge steps in the mountainside, to make room for the crops. Rice, wheat, corn, and lentils are the chief terrace crops. They also grow barley, jute, pepper, and tobacco. Sherpas are often among the climbers who attempt to climb Mount Everest.

All the great mountains of the world have now been conquered by mountaineers. Even Everest, the roof of the world, has been scaled.

RECALLING FACTS

Recognizing sequence of events

1. What happened after a pass was discovered in the Rocky Mountains?

Pioneers were able to settle the land west of the

Rockies.

Inferring unstated main idea

2. One paragraph in the selection is marked with an *X*. Reread that paragraph and underline the sentence that states its main idea.

Comparing and contrasting

3. List one similarity between the Rocky Mountains and the Appalachian Mountains.

Answers may vary. They are both in North America;

they both slowed migration west.

Recalling details

4. Match each peak in the left column with its mountain range in the right column. Write the letter of the range on the line next to the mountain.

c	Aconcagua	a.	Alps
d	Everest	b.	Alaskan Mountains
a	Blanc	c.	Andes
e	Elbert	d.	Himalayas
b	McKinley	e.	Rockies

Comparing and contrasting

5. List one similarity and one difference between the Berber tribes and the Sherpa herders.

Answers may vary. The Berbers and Sherpas are both

mountain people; the Berbers live in the Atlas Mountains,

the Sherpas live in the Himalayas.

Using context clues

6. Complete each sentence with the correct word below.

moderate   avalanche   eke

a. Actors without acting jobs often ___eke___ out livings as waiters.

b. A ___moderate___ amount of rainfall is neither very great nor very small.

c. The mountain was closed to skiers because of an ___avalanche___.

INTERPRETING FACTS

Inferring details

1. a. Which of the eight great mountain ranges is farthest north? the Alaska range

b. How does its location affect its climate? It is an Arctic mountain range with glaciers and ice fields.

Making inferences

2. Why do mountains no longer prevent travel as they used to?

Airplanes can cross mountains easily. Also, mountain roads and railroads have been built.

Inferring cause and effect

3. Many mountain tribes have lived the same way for hundreds of years. Why might their lives not have changed as much as those of other people?

Answers may vary. Mountain tribes are isolated geographically from the rest of civilization.

Making inferences

4. The Himalayas are the world's highest mountain range. They are also the world's youngest mountain range. What effect does time have on mountains?

Over time, mountains are worn down by wind, rain, glaciers, and so forth.

Inferring unstated main idea

5. Reread the paragraph with a check mark. Write a sentence stating its main idea.

Avalanches are a great danger to people living in the villages of the Alps.

A. Study the relief map of the Himalayas on page 105. Read the map key. Then answer the questions that follow.

1. How many elevation ranges are shown on this map? _____4_____

2. What is the highest elevation shown? What is the lowest elevation shown?
   29,028 feet (8,848 meters)   24,784 feet (7,554 meters)

3. In what elevation range is Mount Everest? ___the highest (20,000 ft. to 30,000 ft.)___

4. Which area has the higher elevation, the Tibetan plain to the north of the Himalayas or the Indian plain to the south of the Himalayas? ___the Tibetan plain___

5. In what two countries do the Himalayas reach their greatest height?
   Nepal, India

6. Is there any mountain on the map that is not in the same elevation range as Mount Everest? _____no_____

B. The elevation illustration on page 103 compares the heights of the highest peak in each of the major mountain ranges. Several cities are also included in the map. Study the elevation scale and the mountain peaks. Then answer the questions that follow.

1. Which mountain shown has the lowest elevation? What is its elevation?
   Mt. Narodnaya   6,214 feet (1,894 meters)

2. Which mountain has an approximate elevation of 20,000 feet (6,000 meters)?
   Mt. McKinley

3. Which two mountains are close in elevation to Mount Elbert?
   Djebel Toubkal, Mont Blanc

4. What is the approximate difference of elevation between Mount Everest and Aconcagua?
   6,000 feet (1,800 meters)

5. Which city shown in the illustration is closest to sea level?
   New York City

6. Which city shown in the illustration has the highest elevation?
   La Paz

7. Which city is closest to the elevation of Mount Mitchell?
   Denver

▶ **Real Life Connections** Research facts about mountain ranges in or near your own state. Which are accessible for climbing? How high is the highest point?

Cause and Effect

__ Reading a Science Selection __

▶ Background Information

Humans have been on Earth for a fraction of its existence. Science only recently has developed the instruments and the methods needed to explore this planet. These modern methods have greatly increased our knowledge of Earth.

Scientists work constantly to explain how the different parts of the earth interact. Scientific theory explains not only what is going on now in the earth. It also describes how the continents and oceans came to be arranged the way that they are, over many millions of years. One theory states that all the continents were once one huge land mass. Such a study sheds light on the land that we live on and the land under the oceans, which cover most of the earth's surface.

However, in the 1950s, scientists studied ocean floors for the first time. They found that they were made of very young rock, which made them question whether all the earth's continents had indeed once been connected.

▶ Skill Focus

The **cause** of an event is the reason it happens. The **effect** is the result of the cause. For example, an earthquake can make a building collapse. The cause is the earthquake. The effect is the collapse of the building.

Sometimes a single cause has many effects. Read the following sentences.

Last night, a fire broke out in our building. Smoke poured out of the upper stories. People ran out into the street. The fire department was alerted.

The cause is the fire. It is given in the first sentence. The effects are given in the next three sentences. Sometimes a single effect has many causes. Read the following sentences.

Janice earned an *A* in science. She often answered the teacher's questions in class. She studied for every test. She did a project for extra credit.

The effect is that Janet earned an *A* in science. It is given in the first sentence. The causes are given in the next three sentences.

Sometimes words signal cause and effect. Look for words, such as *because, cause,* and *as a result.*

▶ Word Clues

Read the sentence below. Look for context clues that explain the underlined word.

Although scientists are certain of the boundaries of the plates, they are <u>dubious</u> about how the plates move.

If you do not know the meaning of the word *dubious,* the word *certain* can help you. *Dubious* and *certain* are antonyms, words that are opposite in meaning. *Dubious* means "not certain."

Use **antonym** context clues to find the meaning of the three underlined words in the selection.

▶ Strategy Tip

As you read the selection, study the diagrams. The labels and captions will help you understand the theories about the movement of the earth's crust.

The Theory of Plate Tectonics

A **theory** (THEE ə ree) is an explanation of observed facts. Scientists base their theories on facts that have been observed or examined. The most recent theory about the movement of the earth's crust is the theory of **plate tectonics** (tek TAHN iks). It begins with the idea that the crust of the earth is made up of seven major plates, or sections, and several smaller plates. These crustal plates make up the topmost, solid part of the earth. The topmost part of the earth is called the **lithosphere** (LITH ə sfir). It covers the floor of the oceans and all the continents.

The seven major lithospheric plates are the Pacific, the North American, the South American, the Eurasian, the African, the Antarctic, and the Australian. The boundaries of the continents are not necessarily the same as the boundaries of the plates. For example, the eastern edge of North America and the western edge of Europe are not the boundaries of plates. The plates that these continents rest on extend into the Atlantic Ocean. These plates include part of the ocean floor.

Two of the smaller plates are the Caribbean and the Arabian. The Arabian plate includes the Arabian Peninsula, the Red Sea, and the Persian Gulf. The Caribbean plate lies between North America and South America.

Although scientists are certain of the boundaries of the plates, they are dubious about how the plates move. The lithospheric plates float like rafts on the **asthenosphere** (as THEN ə sfir). The asthenosphere is made up of hot, liquid rock. The hot liquid and gases flow outward from the inner part of the asthenosphere. This flow of hot, liquid rock below the lithosphere causes the plates to move.

Ocean-Floor Spreading

Midocean ridges are large systems of underwater volcanic mountains. They are found in all the oceans. Deep <u>rifts</u> run through the center of these otherwise solid ridges. When hot, liquid rock flows up from the asthenosphere, it erupts, or explodes upward out of the rifts. This action pushes the plates apart. When the liquid rock, or lava, cools and hardens, new crust is formed. The eruption of lava from between plates can cause the opposite edges of the plates to be pushed down into the asthenosphere. This process is called

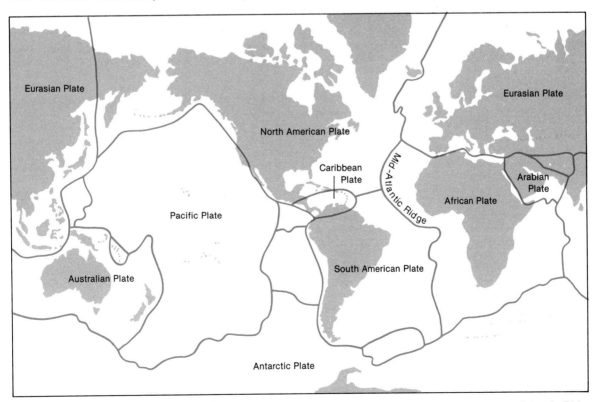

Figure 1. This map shows the seven major lithospheric plates and two smaller plates. The Mid-Atlantic Ridge is one of the midocean ridges.

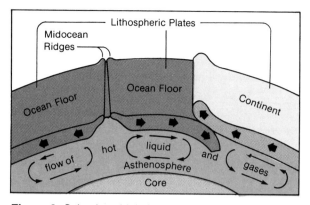

Figure 2. Scientists think that the flow of currents in the asthenosphere causes the movement of lithospheric plates. The boundaries between plates are zones of volcano and earthquake activity.

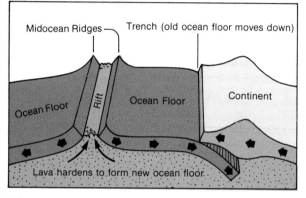

Figure 3. Under the ocean, lava erupts from the rift in the midocean ridge.

ocean-floor spreading. The theory of plate tectonics resulted in part from scientists' discovery of ocean-floor spreading.

In the 1950s, scientists discovered that rocks directly next to the midocean ridges on either side are younger than rocks farther away. The youngest rocks are in the center of the ridges. Based in part on the difference in ages of ocean-floor rocks, scientists believe that new ocean floor is being formed along the ridges. The creation of new ocean floor causes ocean-floor spreading.

Continental Drift

Ocean-floor spreading supports an earlier theory about the movement of the earth's crust. The theory of **continental drift** was first suggested in the early 1900s by a German scientist named Alfred Wegener. Wegener <u>advocated</u> this theory, although most other scientists opposed it. Wegener believed that all the continents were once part of a single landmass. He named the landmass **Pangaea** (pan JEE ə). The landmass broke into separate continents that <u>gradually</u> drifted apart. This did not happen suddenly, but over a long period of time. As a result, there are now seven continents. Many scientists believe that the continents are still drifting.

The theory of plate tectonics is of great interest to scientists today because it helps explain many natural occurrences. For example, earthquakes can be caused by crustal plates sliding past each other, moving apart, or colliding. Volcanic activity and mountain building are also related to such movements. When the plates move apart, hot liquid rock can erupt from the asthenosphere. As the rock cools and hardens, mountains or volcanoes can be formed.

The theory of plate tectonics also combines the ideas of continental drift and ocean-floor spreading.

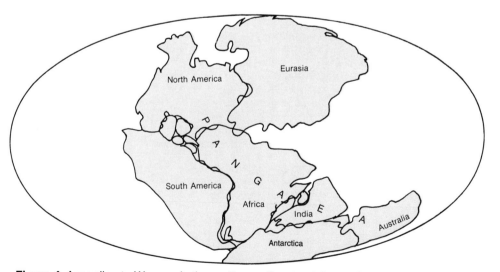

Figure 4. According to Wegener's theory, the continents of the earth were once part of one large landmass. This map shows how the continents may have once been connected.

110 Lesson 35 *Identifying cause and effect*

RECALLING FACTS

Recalling details

1. What is a theory?

A theory is an explanation of observed facts.

Recalling details

2. What is the lithosphere?

It is the topmost, solid part of the earth.

Recalling details

3. How many major plates are there?

There are seven major plates.

Recalling details

4. What is the asthenosphere made up of?

It is made of hot, liquid rock.

Recalling details

5. What are midocean ridges?

They are large systems of underwater volcanic

mountains.

Recalling sequence of events

6. Alfred Wegener developed the theory of

continental drift

_____ fifty

years before scientists found proof of ocean-floor spreading.

Identifying cause and effect

7. What natural occurrences can be explained by the movement of crustal plates?

earthquakes, volcanic activity, and mountain building

Using context clues

8. Decide if each statement is true or false. Write *true* or *false* on the lines.

a. A baby's growth from infancy into adulthood is gradual.

true

b. If you advocate building a new library, you are against it.

false

c. Lightning hitting a tree could result in a rift.

true

INTERPRETING FACTS

Making inferences

1. The fact that some of the continents look as if they could fit together like a jigsaw puzzle supports the idea that

  a. the continents were once of equal size.

  b. the continents can float on water.

  (**c.**) the continents were once joined together.

Making inferences

2. The hot liquid rock and gas in the asthenosphere flows

  (**a.**) from a hot area to a cooler area.

  b. from a cold area to a warmer area.

  c. from a high area to a lower area.

Making inferences

3. The volcanic mountains that make up the midocean ridges

  a. are made up of shells and coral.

  b. are made up of the skeletons of deep-sea fish.

  (**c.**) are made up of lava from the asthenosphere.

Making inferences

4. The rift in the midocean ridge is a

  (**a.**) boundary between crustal plates.

  b. very deep lake.

  c. continental shelf.

Making inferences

5. Ocean-floor spreading does not cause the crustal plates to become larger because
   a. parts of them evaporate.
   b. parts of them are pushed down into the asthenosphere.
   c. parts of them burn up.

SKILL FOCUS

1. What in the asthenosphere causes the movement of lithospheric plates?

The flow of hot liquid rock and gases outward from the inner part of the asthenosphere causes the movement of the

lithospheric plates.

2. What causes the lithospheric plates to be pushed apart?

The eruption of lava between plates causes the lithospheric plates to be pushed apart.

3. What was an effect of scientists' discovery of ocean-floor spreading?

Discovery of ocean-floor spreading led to the development of the theory of plate tectonics.

4. What was the effect of the breakup of Pangaea?

The breakup of Pangaea caused the formation of seven continents.

5. What are three movements of crustal plates that can cause earthquakes?

The three movements of crustal plates that can cause earthquakes are sliding past each other, moving apart,

or colliding.

6. What are two effects that can occur when crustal plates move apart?

When the crustal plates move apart, they can cause the formation of mountains; formation of volcanoes.

7. Underline two effects of ocean-floor spreading.
   a. heats up the asthenosphere
   b. pushes apart crustal plates
   c. pushes opposite edge of plates down into asthenosphere
   d. causes movement of icebergs
   e. makes oceans deeper

8. What makes scientists believe a new ocean floor is being formed?

Rocks near the midocean ridges or at the center of them are younger than those further away from the ridges.

▶ Real Life Connections Research what might have caused a particular geographic feature in your state.

Percents

Reading a Mathematics Selection

▶ Background Information

Percents are an extremely useful mathematical tool to learn. Percents are used in many parts of daily life. A sale at a store claims that you can buy certain items for "15 percent off" the original price. Interest rates on loans and mortgages are stated in percents. When you make up a budget, you often will figure out what percentage of your income you have to spend on each expense.

Much of the information that we get every day from reading and watching television also contains percents. Open up a newspaper, magazine, or book, and you will probably find something about percents. Watch the nightly news on television, and you will see percents are often used to show such information as the rise or fall in the cost of living, the rate of inflation, or the rate of employment. The weatherperson will report that, for example, there is a 20 percent chance of rain tomorrow. If you did not know about percents, you would not understand these different kinds of information.

After reading "Percents" you will have a better understanding of this important and very useful part of mathematics. Because percents are often about money and amounts of goods that are measured in fractions, you will learn in this lesson how to change percents into fractions and decimals, and vice versa.

▶ Skill Focus

The symbol % stands for **percent**. The word *percent* refers to a certain number compared to 100. For example, 83% means 83 parts compared to 100.

Percents are very useful when comparing amounts. For example, you might know that 3 out of every 7 mountains in the world are taller than 8,000 meters and that 5 out of every 9 mountains are snow-covered during the summer. It is difficult, however, to compare these two groups of mountains.

Another way to write 3 out of 7 is 43%. Another way to write 5 out of 9 is 56%. When you compare 43% tall mountains with 56% snow-covered mountains, you can easily see that there are more snow-covered mountains in summer than mountains that are more than 8,000 meters tall.

Percents can be written as fractions and as decimals. Decimals and fractions can be changed to percents.

▶ Word Clues

The word *percent* comes from two Latin words, *per centum*, meaning "per one hundred or for each hundred." Knowing the meaning of this word will help you understand how to use percents.

When reading the following selection, also look for these important words: *fraction, decimal,* and *change*.

▶ Strategy Tip

Study each section of the selection carefully before going on to the next section. Use the headings to help you understand how the selection is organized.

Reading Percents

The word *percent* refers to a certain number compared to a hundred. Many facts about the mountain systems of the earth can be stated using percentages.

Mountains cover about 20 percent of the earth's surface.

If the earth's surface were divided into 100 equal sections, mountains would cover about 20 of them.

The symbol % stands for percent: 20 percent can be written as 20%. You can think of the percent symbol as two zeros separated by a one. These are the same digits that make up 100.

$$\% = 100$$

Because 20% means 20 out of 100, you can write the same value as the fraction $\frac{20}{100}$. Therefore, 20% and $\frac{20}{100}$ are the same. You can write the fraction $\frac{20}{100}$ as a decimal. Because $\frac{20}{100}$ means 20 one-hundredths, you can write the same value as 0.20. Therefore, 20%, $\frac{20}{100}$, and 0.20 all express the same value.

North America covers about 16 percent of the earth's surface.

16 percent can be written as 16%.

$$16 \text{ out of } 100 = \frac{16}{100}$$

$\frac{16}{100}$ written as a decimal is 0.16.

$$16\% = \frac{16}{100} = 0.16$$

The number in the next example can also be stated as a percent, a fraction, or a decimal.

Approximately 75 percent of the active volcanoes lie in one area of the world.

$$75\% = \frac{75}{100} = 0.75$$

Changing a Percent to a Decimal

To change a percent to a decimal, move the decimal point *two places to the left*. Then remove the % sign.

$$92.6\% = \underset{\smile}{92.6}\% = .926$$

Sometimes you have to put in one or more zeros.
$$3.7\% = \underset{\smile}{03.7}\% = .037$$

Often a decimal point is not shown in the percent. You then have to put a decimal point

at the end of the number and move it two places to the left to make it a decimal.

$$27\% = \underset{\smile}{27.}\% = 0.27$$
$$9\% = \underset{\smile}{09.}\% = .09$$

Changing a Decimal to a Percent

To change a decimal to a percent, move the decimal point *two places to the right*. Then add the % sign.

$$.132 = \underset{\smile}{.132} = 13.2\%$$

Sometimes you have to put in one or more zeros.

$$.7 = \underset{\smile}{.70} = 70\%$$

Sometimes a decimal point is not shown.

$$3 = 3. = \underset{\smile}{3.00} = 300\%$$
$$17 = 17. = \underset{\smile}{17.00} = 1700\%$$

Changing a Percent to a Fraction

To change a percent to a fraction, remove the percent sign to form the numerator, and add the denominator 100.

$$93\% = \frac{93}{100}$$

The numerator of this fraction is 93. The denominator of all percent fractions is 100.

$$8\% = \frac{8}{100}$$
$$137\% = \frac{137}{100}$$
$$16\% = \frac{16}{100}$$

Changing a Fraction to a Percent

Two different types of fractions may be changed to a percent. If the denominator of the fraction is 100, just remove the denominator and add a percent sign.

$$\frac{29}{100} = 29\%$$
$$\frac{7}{100} = 7\%$$

If the denominator is not 100, it must first be changed to 100. You need to multiply the numerator and denominator by a number that will change the denominator to 100. For example, to change $\frac{3}{4}$ to a percent, multiply by 25 to change the fraction to $\frac{75}{100}$.

$$\frac{3}{4} = \frac{75}{100} = 75\%$$

To change $\frac{1}{5}$ to a percent, do the following:
$$\frac{1}{5} = \frac{20}{100} = 20\%$$

Study these four rules.

1. To change a percent to a decimal, move the decimal point two places to the *left*. Add a decimal point and zero when they are needed.
2. To change a decimal to a percent, move the decimal point two places to the *right*. Add a decimal point and zeros when they are needed.
3. To change a percent to a fraction, first remove the percent sign. Then put the number over 100.
4. To change a fraction to a percent, remove the denominator if it is 100, and add a percent sign. If the denominator is not 100, multiply the numerator and denominator by a number that will change the denominator to 100. Then add a percent sign to the numerator.

RECALLING FACTS

Recalling details
1. What does the word *percent* mean?

The word *percent* refers to a certain number compared

to 100.

Recalling details
2. What is the symbol for percent?

The symbol % stands for percent.

Recalling details
3. How do you change a percent to a decimal?

To change a percent to a decimal, move the decimal

point two places to the left. Add a decimal point and

zeros when needed.

Recalling details
4. How do you change a percent to a fraction?

To change a percent to a fraction, remove the percent

sign. Put the number over 100.

Recalling details
5. How do you change a fraction to a percent?

If the denominator is 100, remove it and add a percent

sign. If the denominator is not 100, change the fraction

so that the denominator is 100. The numerator

becomes the percent.

INTERPRETING FACTS

Making inferences
1. Why does moving the decimal point two places change a percent to a decimal and a decimal to a percent?

Moving it two places multiplies or divides by 100.

Making inferences
2. How might percents be used in ads?

They are often used to show discounts, price reductions, or interest rates on loans and credit cards.

Making inferences
3. Why are percents used to score tests?

They compare scores on a scale of 100.

4. What part of something is 100% of it?

One hundred percent (100%) refers to all of it.

Making inferences

5. If you had $10 and you earned 100% more, how much would you have all together?

You would have $20.

SKILL FOCUS

A. Fill in the blanks. The first one is done for you.

1. 15% = $\frac{15}{100}$ = .15

2. 13% = $\frac{13}{100}$ = .13

3. 137% = $\frac{137}{100}$ = 1.37

4. 36% = $\frac{36}{100}$ = .36

5. 8% = $\frac{8}{100}$ = .08

6. 34.7% = $\frac{34.7}{100}$ = .347

7. 1.1% = $\frac{1.1}{100}$ = .011

8. 3% = $\frac{3}{100}$ = .03

9. 75% = $\frac{75}{100}$ = .75

10. 50% = $\frac{50}{100}$ = .50 or .5

B. Change the percents to decimals and the decimals to percents.

1. 14% = .14

2. 73% = .73

3. 5% = .05

4. 100% = 1.00

5. 83.9% = .839

6. .16 = 16%

7. .84 = 84%

8. .03 = 3%

9. 1.04 = 104%

10. .752 = 75.2%

C. Change the fractions to percents and the percents to fractions.

1. $\frac{79}{100}$ = 79%

2. $\frac{7}{100}$ = 7%

3. $\frac{3.7}{100}$ = 3.7%

4. $\frac{1}{4}$ = 25%

5. $\frac{3}{5}$ = 60%

6. 67% = $\frac{67}{100}$

7. 29% = $\frac{29}{100}$

8. 2% = $\frac{2}{100}$

9. 125% = $\frac{125}{100}$

10. 43% = $\frac{43}{100}$

D. Write the percent, fraction, and decimal for the following amounts.

1. Twenty-five and nine tenths percent. $25.9\% = \frac{25.9}{100} = .259$

2. Eight twenty-fifths $\frac{8}{25} = \frac{32}{100} = 32\% = .32$

3. Twelve tenths $\frac{120}{100} = 120\% = 1.2$

4. Forty-two hundredths $\frac{42}{100} = 42\% = .42$

▶ **Real Life Connections** Where do you read percents in your daily life?

Evaluating Opinions

What is the difference between a fact and an opinion? A fact is a statement that can be checked and proven. An opinion is a statement that tells how someone feels or what someone thinks about something. Some opinions may be more sound than others because they have one or more facts to back them up. When you find an opinion in your reading, decide whether it is sound.

Read the following selection.

The Sierra Nevada is a huge mountain range in eastern California. Sierra Nevada means "snowy, saw-toothed mountain" in Spanish. The Sierra Nevada is the site of three national parks—Yosemite, Sequoia, and Kings Canyon—and beautiful Lake Tahoe. Donner Memorial State Park, a historic landmark, is also in this mountain range.

The Sierra Nevada is like a granite wall extending north and south for 430 miles (692 kilometers) through California. It is about 70 miles (110 kilometers) wide. At one time, the earth's crust lifted and tilted to the west to make a long gentle slope on the mountain's western side and a steep slope on its eastern side. The highest point of the Sierra Nevada is Mt. Whitney. Its altitude, or height, is 14,494 feet (4,418 meters). In fact, Mt. Whitney is the second highest point in the United States. Several other peaks of the Sierra Nevada are close to the height of Mt. Whitney.

Rivers, such as the Feather, American, and San Joaquin, flow in the Sierra Nevada. Rushing mountain waters have cut deep canyons in the long western slope of the mountain range. Yosemite Valley is the most outstanding of these canyons. Yosemite was originally cut by streams. Later, glaciers moved down the valley, eroding it further. The glaciers created the Sierra Nevada's granite cliffs and impressive landscapes. On the shorter, steeper eastern slope, many creeks descend and join the Owens, Walker, Carson, and Truckee rivers. The cliffs, meadows, evergreen forests, lakes, and waterfalls make the Sierra Nevada a beautiful mountain range.

The higher up the mountain range, the greater the rainfall. This is true up to 4,500 feet (1,350 meters). From there to the top, the rain decreases. In a typical winter, 30 to 40 feet (9 to 12 meters) of snow accumulates at Lake Tahoe and Donner Pass, but as much as 60 feet (18 meters) of snow can fall. It is no wonder that skiers are attracted to this region.

A variety of vegetation grows on the Sierra Nevada at different elevations. Shrubs and grasses grow near the Sacramento and San Joaquin valleys at the western base of the Sierra Nevada. From 3,000 to 4,000 feet (900 to 1,200 meters) are forests of yellow pine, sugar pine, cedar, and fir. These trees are a valuable source of timber. Within the forest is the *Sequoia gigantea*, or "big tree." This is the largest plant on the earth. At 6,000 to 7,000 feet (1,800 to 2,150 meters), lodgepole pine, Jeffrey pine, and red fir grow. Above the timberline is rocky land that is barren except for scattered evergreens. The rivers of the western slope of the mountain range supply water for irrigation. The farms in the Sacramento and San Joaquin valleys and the Tulare Basin receive this water. The largest cities in California receive their water supply from these rivers, too. Hydroelectric plants on the rivers generate the power for farmlands and cities.

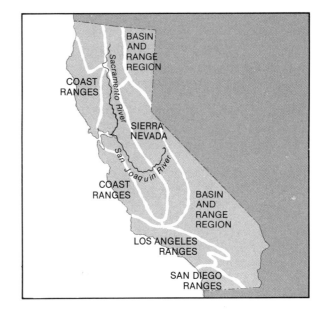

The Sierra Nevada forms a barrier to east-west travel. Cars, trucks, and buses can cross the mountains through several passes. Major highways use six passes, each at a different elevation. A road at 9,625 feet (2,935 meters) over Tioga Pass connects Yosemite Valley and Mono Lake. But this road is usually closed nine months of the year because of snow. Railroads travel over the Sierra Nevada. Hikers and pack trains, or groups of mules, use the various trails to cross the mountain range.

The gold rush of 1849 began when gold was discovered in the Sierra Nevada. This attracted many people to the foothill region in the 1800s. Mining of gold and other metals is no longer important. Now tourism is the area's chief industry. All kinds of camping and recreational facilities are located throughout the Sierra Nevada for people who enjoy summer or winter sports. Other industry in the region includes fruit-growing, lumbering, and grazing.

Read the opinions about the Sierra Nevada in the left column. Select none, one, or two of the facts in the right column that support each opinion. Write the letter of each supporting fact on the line before the opinion. Leave the line blank if the opinion has no supporting facts.

1. __d, g__ The Sierra Nevada is a huge mountain range.

2. __e__ The Sierra Nevada is the nation's best recreation area.

3. _____ Lake Tahoe is one of the most beautiful lakes in the world.

4. __i__ Yosemite Valley is the most outstanding canyon in the United States.

5. __b, n__ The Sierra Nevada is a beautiful mountain range.

6. __a, h__ The best skiing in the West is in the Sierra Nevada.

7. __c, m__ No forests can offer as large a selection of timber as those of the Sierra Nevada.

8. __l__ A better road is needed over Tioga Pass.

9. _____ Visitors to California should spend their time seeing the Sierra Nevada rather than Disneyland.

10. _____ Some of the best fruit in the United States is grown in the Sierra Nevada.

11. __f, k__ If not for the rivers of the Sierra Nevada, California would be without water.

12. __j__ Mt. Whitney seems very high.

13. _____ There is no need for trails for pack trains.

a. Each year, the Sierra Nevada receives 30 to 40 feet (9 to 12 meters) of snow.

b. The range has meadows, cliffs, and forests.

c. At 4,000 feet (1,200 meters) is yellow pine, sugar pine, cedar, and fir.

d. The Sierra Nevada is over 400 miles (640 kilometers) long.

e. It is the site of three national parks.

f. Rivers on the western slope supply California's largest cities with water.

g. The Sierra Nevada is about 70 miles (110 kilometers) wide.

h. Some winters, 60 feet (18 meters) of snow fall.

i. Glaciers moved down the Yosemite Valley and created cliffs and impressive landscapes.

j. The peak of Mt. Whitney is 14,494 feet (4,418 meters) high.

k. Rivers on the western slope irrigate farmlands.

l. Heavy snow at Tioga Pass keeps it closed nine months out of the year.

m. At 7,000 feet (2,150 meters) is lodgepole pine, Jeffrey pine, and red fir.

n. The range has waterfalls, such as those in Yosemite Valley.

Improving Reading Rate

People have so much to read today that the ability to read quickly has become important. The typical reader of a century ago had fewer books, newspapers, and magazines to read. For this reason, you may read more in a week than your great-grandparents did. Being able to read rapidly helps you to read more in a short period of time. However, it is always important to keep in mind that to read material without understanding it is a waste of time no matter what the speed.

A rapid rate of reading has no particular value in itself. A good reader is able to read at several speeds depending on the material being read. When reading materials are difficult or unfamiliar, a good reader reads slower. For example, social studies, science, and mathematics may be more difficult to read than literature. So these materials are read more slowly. Even literature can be difficult. Sometimes a reader needs to reread a paragraph to understand a complex idea. A good reader needs to slow down when words or sentences are difficult or unfamiliar. A good reader also stops to read diagrams and maps. This requires increased attention, making a slower reading rate necessary.

The first thing to do to increase your reading rate is to get rid of bad reading habits. Any of the habits listed below will prevent you from increasing your reading rate.

To answer each question, write *yes* or *no* on the line provided.

_____ 1. Do you move your lips when reading silently?

_____ 2. Do you point to words with your finger as you read?

_____ 3. Do you move your head from side to side as you read?

_____ 4. Do you read one word at a time?

Perhaps you have been doing some of these things for years. If so, it may take you some time to overcome them. But it can be done if you try. If you have any of these habits, practice the suggestions below for overcoming them.

Lip moving	Hold your finger over your lips, or hold a piece of paper between your lips.
Finger pointing	Hold your book with both hands, one on each side of the book.
Head moving	Rest your chin in the palm of one hand and hold it still.
Reading one word at a time	Work hard at trying to take in several words at each glance.

The following paragraph is marked off into word groups. See if you can read it by taking in each group of words in one glance.

Bertela lives / on an island / that belongs / to Denmark. / There are / beech trees / in the woods / near her home. / Every fall / she gathers beech nuts / in these woods. / The squirrels gather / the nuts, too. / The nuts are so plentiful / that there are / enough of them / for both Bertela / and the squirrels.

Below is a selection that can be used in checking your reading rate. Use a watch or a clock with a second hand to time yourself. Start right on a minute, such as four minutes past ten o'clock. Write your starting time at the beginning of the selection. Then read the selection. Write your ending time at the end of the selection.

Starting time _____

The Mistake

At the top of the hill, the three riders reined their horses to a stop. They wore blue coats, tan trousers, high boots, and three-cornered hats. The tallest of the riders lifted a pair of field glasses to his eyes and looked out over the fields and woods.

"Tell us, General Washington, what do you see? British soldiers? campfires?" asked one of the riders.

Washington smiled. "Remember, Lafayette, it will take the British a few days to reach this area from the Delaware River."

Lafayette looked disappointed. Then General Greene, the third rider, spoke. "General Washington, we have ridden all over this land today, and we still have not found a good place for battle against the British."

"True enough," Washington sighed.

Greene looked up at the darkening sky. "Look, sir, it's going to storm."

The three riders started toward a field below them. Black clouds raced across the sky. It began to thunder.

"There's a house ahead!" shouted Lafayette. "Let's stop there."

"Yes, hurry!" Washington led the dash to the farmhouse.

Just as the riders reached the barn near the house, the rain came pouring down. They got off their horses and looked around. A farmer was staring at them. "Why, it's General George Washington. Here on my farm! General, sir, welcome. Come into my house and have some food. My son Tom will look after your horses. Our name is Small."

Washington smiled and went into the house with the farmer. Lafayette followed the general. But Greene stayed with the horses. He was worried. Suppose these were friends of the British. The boy might hide their horses, and they would be trapped. Finally, however, he decided to follow the others.

Inside the warm house, Washington sat at the table talking with the farmer. Lafayette was pacing from window to window. Washington looked out the window and said, "Mr. Small, I see this storm will last for hours. I wonder if you would let us stay the night?"

Both Lafayette and Greene looked worried. Greene whispered to the general, "Sir, we can't stay. We don't know if these people are friends or enemies. We might be in British hands by morning!"

Washington said coldly, "We will stay."

Dinner was good, and even Greene enjoyed it. For a while, he felt at ease and almost forgot his fears. Lafayette also seemed to relax and was talking a mile a minute. But when they went upstairs, all of Greene's fears returned. Without undressing, he lay on top of the bed with his gun at his side and his eyes open. He jumped up with each new sound.

Just before sunrise, Greene heard a horse whinny and a dog bark. Silently he went downstairs and out to the barn. The horses seemed safe. He put his hand on his gray horse.

"Don't do it, sir." A low voice cut the darkness.

"Who's there?" His hand on his gun, Greene whirled around.

"Me! Tom Small! And I say don't run away. The general needs you."

"Run away? What do you mean?" asked Greene.

Tom looked at his feet. "I've been standing watch because I was afraid you were going to slip away with your horse."

"Fool!" shouted Greene. "You think me a traitor?"

Tom looked uneasy. "Well, you acted so strange, sir. I just thought . . . There have been lots of deserters—traitors, too."

Suddenly Greene laughed. "Tom, we're a pair! We both were worried about the same thing. I came down here because I heard some noise and thought the British had trapped us."

Two hours later at breakfast, Washington looked at Greene and said, "You look like you didn't sleep all night. What's wrong?"

Greene winked at Tom. "Nothing, sir. Tom and I just stood watch all night."

Washington looked from one to the other but said nothing. Later, after they had left the Smalls', they stopped to rest. Washington broke the silence. "You know, you were right. I did take a risk last night. I was quite wrong."

Greene could only nod. But Lafayette held out his hand to Washington. "Ah, my general, only a great man will say, 'I was wrong.'"

To find the total time that it took to read the selection, do the following: (1) Subtract your beginning time from your ending time. (2) Divide the number of words in the selection by the remainder expressed in seconds. If it took you 3 minutes and 5 seconds ($3 \times 60 + 5 = 185$ seconds) to read the selection, you would have read 3.7 words per second ($695 \div 185 = 3.7$). (3) To find the number of words per minute (WPM), multiply your rate per second by 60. Your answer would be 222 WPM.

Words in selection: 695

	Hr.	Min.	Sec.
Ending time:	_____	_____	_____
Starting time:	_____	_____	00
Total time:	_____	_____	_____

No. words: 695 = ___ × 60 = ___ WPM

No. seconds: _____

To check your understanding of the selection, fill in the circle in front of the correct answer to each question.

1. Where did the three riders stop the first time?
   - a. at a farmhouse
   - b. under a tree
   - ● c. at the top of a hill

2. Who looked through the field glasses?
   - a. General Greene
   - ● b. General Washington
   - c. Lafayette

3. Where does the farmer greet the general?
   - a. in his house
   - ● b. at his barn
   - c. in the field

4. Who looks after the riders' horses?
   - a. General Greene
   - b. General Washington
   - ● c. Tom Small

5. Why is Lafayette pacing from window to window?
   - a. He is hungry.
   - b. He is afraid of thunder.
   - ● c. He is worried about the British.

6. Which of the three riders seems to enjoy his stay with the Smalls?
   - a. General Greene
   - b. General Washington
   - ● c. Lafayette

7. How do you know that Greene did not sleep very much at the Smalls'?
   - a. He doesn't undress.
   - b. He has his gun at his side.
   - ● c. He keeps his eyes open.

8. Why does Greene go down to the barn?
   - ● a. He hears some noises.
   - b. He wants to talk to Tom.
   - c. He can't sleep.

9. Why does Tom stay up all night?
   - a. He is afraid the British will come.
   - b. He can't sleep.
   - ● c. He thinks Greene might run away.

10. What does Tom mean when he says, "There have been lots of deserters ...'?
    - a. Many U.S. soldiers stole horses.
    - b. Many farmers hid U.S. soldiers.
    - ● c. Many U.S. soldiers ran away.

Taking Notes

When reading new information that you need to remember, it is a good idea to take notes. **Taking notes** will help you remember the information as you read it. Taking notes is especially helpful in recording the information from several references before writing a report.

Not everything you read is necessary to remember. When taking notes, write down only the important information, especially main ideas and supporting details. Following are some suggestions to help you take notes.

1. Find the main idea of each paragraph and include it in your notes.
2. Look for major details that answer such questions as *who, what, when, why,* and *how.* Write these details under the main ideas. Leave out minor details, or information that is not needed.
3. Arrange your notes in the same order in which the information appears in the selection. Group each main idea and its supporting details together.
4. Label your notes by writing the subject at the top of the page. Write your notes in your own words. Do not copy entire sentences, but write down key words and phrases. Be brief so that you can read your notes quickly.

The following selection is written in chronological order, the order in which the events take place. Using the space provided on page 123, take notes as you read the selection. Make sure your notes show the sequence of the visits of the Spanish explorers to the New World.

Explorations to the New World

Columbus's voyages to the New World led the way to further exploration of North and South America. By the Treaty of Tordesillas, Spain claimed the right to most of the New World. Early Spanish explorers heard stories of wealthy kingdoms in the Americas. Such reports encouraged new expeditions. Until 1519, Spanish control of the New World was limited to small settlements in the West Indies. With the many Spanish expeditions that followed Columbus, Spain gradually gained control of most of South and Central America and parts of North America.

Hernando Cortés

In 1519, Hernando Cortés, a clever fighter and skillful leader, landed on the coast of Mexico in search of gold. He soon heard about the powerful Aztec Empire that demanded huge payments from the people it conquered. Cortés sought out the support of the many Indian tribes who hated their Aztec rulers. He marched his small army of 400 soldiers and 16 horses into the crowded Aztec capital of Tenochtitlan where he confronted the Aztec ruler Montezuma.

After months of negotiations, Montezuma agreed to become a subject of the Spanish king. In 1520, the Aztecs revolted against the Spanish. Cortés and his army barely escaped with their lives. However, with the help of his allies, Cortés surrounded Tenochtitlan. In 1521, he attacked and destroyed the Aztec capital. Within a few years, the Aztec Empire crumbled.

Francisco Pizarro

Nine years later, in 1530, Francisco Pizarro, another explorer, received permission to explore the Inca Empire of present-day Peru. With 180 metal-clad soldiers—less than half of Cortés's force—Pizarro marched into the Andean kingdom. Luck was with him. When he arrived, the Incas were caught up in a civil war.

Pizarro launched a surprise attack, imprisoned the Inca leader Atahualpa, and killed most of his attendants. The attack stunned the Incas, weakening their resistance to the Spanish. By 1535, Pizarro had captured Cuzco, the Inca capital, and crushed nearly all opposition.

Francisco Coronado

In 1540, Francisco Coronado led an expedition in search of the "seven cities of gold" reportedly nestled in the hills of present-day New Mexico. For about two years, Coronado, along with many Spanish soldiers, searched in vain for these cities of gold that did not really exist. In the process, he explored much of the future southwestern United States. One of his lieutenants was the first European to see the Grand Canyon.

Hernando de Soto

While Coronado was looking for gold in the west, Hernando de Soto led another gold-hunting expedition into what would become the southeastern United States. From 1539 to 1542, his army wandered as far north as the Carolinas and as far west as present-day Oklahoma. When de Soto died, the expedition returned without finding any large supplies of gold. Even before de Soto's death, the Spanish had begun to concentrate on settling the area to the south, in present-day Mexico, the Caribbean, and South America.

Answers will vary.

Early Exploration

_____

_____

_____

_____

_____

_____

_____

_____

Taking notes can help you remember and review what you have read. Use the information from your notes to complete the chart. The first explorer has been started for you.

Explorer	Areas Explored	Dates	Importance
Cortés	Mexico	1519–1521	He defeated the Aztecs.
Pizarro	Peru	1530–1535	He defeated the Incas.
Coronado	southwestern United States	1540–1542	He explored much of present-day southwestern United States.
de Soto	southeastern United States	1539–1542	He explored present-day southeastern United States from Carolinas to Oklahoma.

Reading a Road Map

Whether you are driving to a park across town or to a scenic spot across the country, it is a good idea to have a road map with you. A road map shows how to get from one place to another and how far it is between places. It also shows the location of points of interest.

The road map below shows the Great Smoky Mountains National Park and some of the surrounding areas.

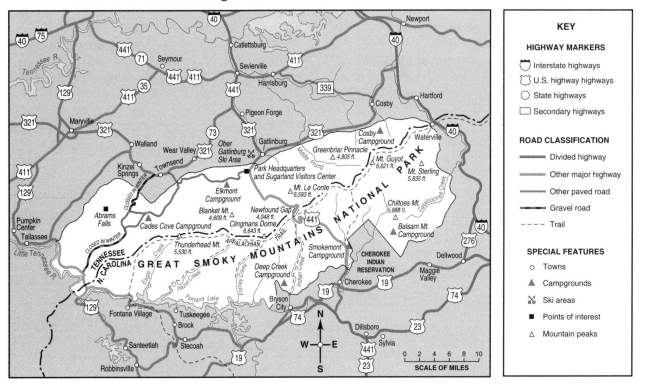

Notice the key to the right of the map. A key explains the symbols used on a map. The scale of miles helps you figure out the distance from one place to another. The road classification symbols identify different kinds of roads. Special symbols also mark such features as towns, campgrounds, ski areas, and other points of interest. Maps usually include a direction symbol known as a compass. The compass indicates north, south, east, and west with the abbreviations N, S, E, and W.

A. Read the definitions in the left column. Then read the words in the right column. On the line next to each definition, write the correct word.

1. _____key_____   explains map symbols   scale of miles

2. _____compass_____   indicates directions   road classification

3. ____scale of miles____   shows distance from one place to another   key

4. ___road classification___   identifies different kinds of roads   special features

5. ___special features___   campgrounds, ski areas, mountains   compass

B. Decide if each of the following questions can be answered using the map on the opposite page. Write *yes* or *no* on the line.

___yes___ 1. Are there hiking trails in Great Smoky Mountains National Park?

___yes___ 2. What towns are south of the park?

___no___ 3. How long does it take to drive through the park?

___yes___ 4. Are there campgrounds inside the park itself?

___no___ 5. Are there hotels and motels near the park?

___yes___ 6. Which roads are closed in the winter?

___yes___ 7. Which rivers run through the park?

___yes___ 8. How high is Newfound Gap?

___no___ 9. How many miles is it from the park to New York City?

___yes___ 10. How do you get from Gatlinburg to the Cherokee Indian Reservation?

___no___ 11. Is fishing permitted in the park?

___yes___ 12. Are there any gravel roads in the park?

___no___ 13. If you leave Gatlinburg at 9:00 A.M., when will you get to Mt. Le Conte?

C. Fill in the circle next to the phrase that correctly completes each sentence.

1. The Great Smoky Mountains National Park is in the states of
   ○ North Carolina and South Carolina.
   ● Tennessee and North Carolina.
   ○ Tennessee and Kentucky.

2. If you travel south through the park from Gatlinburg, you will first reach
   ● Park Headquarters and Sugarland Visitors Center.
   ○ Newfound Gap.
   ○ Smokemont Campground.

3. To get from Gatlinburg to Cosby, you can travel on
   ○ US 441.   ○ Route 339.   ● US 321.

4. The Interstate Highway that is closest to the park is
   ○ Interstate 82.   ○ Interstate 75.   ● Interstate 40.

5. The highest point in Tennessee is
   ○ Newfound Gap.   ● Clingman's Dome.   ○ Mt. Le Conte.

6. The trail that goes from the western part of the park to the eastern part is
   ● the Appalachian Trail.   ○ the Gatlinburg Trail.   ○ the Forney Ridge Trail.

7. A large body of water on the southern border of the park is called
   ○ Rainbow Falls.   ● Fontana Lake.   ○ Forney Creek.

8. When going from Newfound Gap to Smokemont Campground, you would travel
   ○ southwest.   ○ northwest.   ● southeast.

Lesson 41

Conflict and Resolution

Reading a Literature Selection

▶ **Background Information**

Training for an Olympic sport demands a lot from competitors. These athletes must either commit themselves totally to their sports or risk failure. This play is about a young woman who must make a decision that will affect her life for several years. Can she commit herself to years of working hard and practicing constantly?

▶ **Skill Focus**

Often the characters in a story have a goal to achieve or a problem to solve. The struggle to achieve the goal or solve the problem is called **conflict**.

A character can face three main types of conflict.

Conflict with Self

A character may struggle with emotions or feelings within himself or herself. This struggle is an internal conflict. An example is a person trying to overcome a fear of high places.

Conflict with Another Character

A character may struggle against another person. This struggle is an external, or outside, conflict. An example is two marathon, or long-distance, runners competing for a place on the U.S. Olympic Team.

Conflict with an Outside Force

A character may struggle against nature, society, or some danger over which he or she has no control. This struggle is also an external conflict. An example is a firefighter battling flames to save people inside a burning building.

By the end of a story, the character facing a conflict succeeds or fails in achieving the goal or solving the problem. The way a conflict is settled is called the **resolution**. Conflict and resolution are part of a story's plot, or main action.

Stories sometimes have more than one conflict. As you read, look for conflicts and their resolutions.

▶ **Word Clues**

Often when you read, you may find words that you don't know because they are not part of your experience. Read the following sentence.

> Besides, my eyes are always red from the <u>chlorine</u> in the pool.

You can tell from the context clues that *chlorine* is something in the pool. However, there are no context clues to tell you what chlorine is. You will need a **dictionary** to help you. You may find it more convenient to finish what you are reading first and then look up the word.

Use a dictionary to find the meaning of the four underlined words in the play.

▶ **Strategy Tip**

As you read the play, be alert to the playwright's use of dialogue, scene changes, and stage directions. Also notice how the main conflict develops. Remember to look for other conflicts in addition to the main conflict of the story.

The Campaign for Kate

Cast
Kate Fenton, member of a swim team
Maria Cortez, member of a swim team
Mr. Meacham, coach of the swim team

Scene 1

Late in the afternoon at the Hillside High School pool. Mr. Meacham stands at the edge of the pool, stopwatch in hand. When Mr. Meacham speaks, the team stops doing laps. Everyone leaves the pool but Kate and Maria, who hang on to the edge and talk.

Mr. Meacham *(loudly):* All right, team, that's enough for today. I'll see you all tomorrow, bright and early. Remember, be here no later than 6:30 A.M.

Kate *(to Maria):* He'll see me, but I won't see him. I'll be swimming, but I'll probably nap through my first four laps! I don't know if I can keep this up.

Maria: Mr. Meacham says it's important to work out every day for several hours, especially with the all-county meet coming up Saturday.

Kate: Well, I'm beginning to get tired of this stuff. Besides, my eyes are always red from the chlorine in the pool. And it doesn't do my hair

any good, either. And furthermore, practicing five hours a day doesn't leave me time or energy for anything else. And for what—so I can someday say I'm a great swimmer in the <u>butterfly</u> event?

Maria: I know; I'm tired, too. But now I take Mr. Meacham's advice and go to bed an hour earlier. Maybe you should try that.

Kate: Agh! I go to bed early as it is. I need some time to myself, to do other things. If I go to bed any earlier I'll sleep away my whole life. You know, I used to love swimming. I had dreams *(pause)* . . . dreams of becoming an Olympic champion like Summer Sanders or Qian Hong. Now it's more like a nightmare than a dream.

Maria: I heard Mr. Meacham say you have the talent to make the Olympic team some day.

Kate: He did—but I keep wondering if I can throw myself into swimming and train the way he wants me to. I don't know if I'm ready to give up everything just to try for it.

Maria: Here comes Mr. Meacham. We'd better talk about this later.

Mr. Meacham *(very enthusiastic):* Good workout, Maria. Your time is improving. *(turns toward Kate, showing concern)* Kate, you've just got to think about your kick as you finish each lap. It's cutting down your speed. You could lose a race that way. Tomorrow morning we'll work on it. I think you're either daydreaming or not getting enough sleep.

Kate: I'll be all right, Mr. Meacham.

Mr. Meacham: Well, you'd better hit the showers and then go home to hit the books. I want my team to get decent grades, too!

Kate and Maria <u>clamber</u> out of the pool and head for the showers.

Kate *(takes off her swimming cap):* By the way, some of the kids want me to run for the student senate. What do you think?

Maria *(throws a towel over her shoulders):* It sounds great, but do you have the time? Mr. Meacham says swimming has top <u>priority</u>.

Kate: I'll just have to make the time. Anyway, Maria, you take Mr. Meacham too seriously. Just because you want to be a swim coach someday.

Maria: I have to work harder than you, Kate! *(getting angry) You* have a natural talent that I could never match. I'll be glad if I can be a coach someday . . . You can set your sights even higher. I get angry when you won't!

Kate: OK! OK! Sorry. Friends?

Maria *(pause):* Friends.

Scene 2

Saturday. Kate and Maria sit on a bench in the locker room before the swim meet begins.

Maria *(concerned):* You look tired, Kate.

Kate *(<u>fatigue</u> shows in her voice):* I'm beat. I was at a campaign meeting last night until all hours. We were painting posters and writing slogans. How does this one sound? "Get in the swim—Vote for Kate!"

Maria: Sounds great. I love slogans. They can say a lot in a few words. They can appeal to emotions and make something popular. Now let's get in the swim ourselves. Let's go out there so you can beat me and everyone else without even trying, as usual!

Kate and Maria rise and walk toward the locker room doors.

Scene 3

Maria and Kate cling to the edge of the pool after the race.

Kate *(in spite of her disappointment):* Congratulations, Maria! First place, and your best time ever! You even beat my best time!

Maria *(happy and relieved):* I can hardly believe it myself, beating you and everyone else in the pool! I've never done that before!

Kate: You deserve it; you work hard, Maria.

Mr. Meacham *(walks toward Maria and Kate):* Maria! That was great! Congratulations! *(turns to Kate)* Now Kate. *(becomes very serious)* I want to talk to you. You've got to work on your kick as you make the turn.

Kate *(raises her voice, becomes angry):* Mr. Meacham, can't you leave me alone? I hate my kick! I hate this pool! I'm not meant for this. Some Olympic athlete! I can't even win a high school race! *(gets out of the pool and walks over to the starter's table)*

Mr. Meacham *(follows Kate):* You certainly won't make the Olympic team with that attitude.

Kate: Well, you saw today that I haven't got what it takes.

Mr. Meacham *(very calmly):* All I saw today was a swimmer who wasn't concentrating. Kate, you have a natural talent. It's far greater than that of any other member of the team. Maria knows it. Today was a lucky break for her. It may not come again. Maria knows her best shot is to study to be a coach. But you could be a star if you work to develop your talent.

Kate: I don't know if I can work that hard at swimming. You said it was important to be well rounded. Some kids want me to run for a place as representative in the student government. On a day like today, that sounds like a good idea. Why shouldn't I do it?

Mr. Meacham *(very patiently)*: For most kids, it would be a great idea. But your talent is special, Kate. You shouldn't give up your chance at an Olympic medal someday because you spread yourself too thin. *(pause)* I have an idea. You continue to come to practice, but don't compete for the next three weeks. Run for the student senate. But you must make up your mind by the end of the three weeks. If you decide to swim in the meet on the fourteenth, you've committed yourself to swimming. If you don't race on the fourteenth, you're off the team.

Kate: OK. *(walks slowly toward the locker room)* I can accept that.

Scene 4

The following week. Kate and Maria chat in the pool.

Maria: Did you hear, Kate? I won again yesterday! Our whole team won.

Kate: I heard, I heard! Mr. Meacham must be pleased.

Maria: Oh, sure. But he misses you. I even miss swimming four strokes behind you!

Kate: Maria, you put yourself down too much. You work hard. You deserve to win.

Maria: Speaking of winning, how is your campaign coming?

Kate: I have until the fourteenth to officially begin my campaign.

Maria: That's the day of the next race!

Kate: I know, I know.

Kate and Maria swim to the end of the pool to start their laps.

Scene 5

The fourteenth. Hillside High School pool, less than 20 minutes before the swim meet. Kate is nowhere in sight.

Mr. Meacham: Maria, have you seen Kate? Is she coming?

Maria *(sits on the bench near the locker room door)*: I don't know. Last night on the phone she said something about showing us her new campaign posters.

Mr. Meacham *(his disappointment is obvious)*: Then she's decided.

Kate *(bursts into the pool area)*: I thought you'd like to take a look at these. Here's one for you, coach. *(Mr. Meacham slowly takes the poster from Kate)* And one for you, Maria.

Maria *(eagerly reads)*: "Get in the swim with Kate—and vote for someone else!"

Mr. Meacham: Great Kate! Let's get ready for the Olympics!

Curtain

RECALLING FACTS

Recalling details

1. Who is the main character in this play?

Kate is the main character.

Comparing and contrasting

2. How is Kate's goal different from Maria's?

Kate wants more in her life than swimming. Maria wants

to concentrate on swimming and on becoming a

swimming coach.

Comparing and contrasting

3. Why does Maria feel she is not as good a swimmer as Kate?

She feels that Kate has a natural swimming talent that

she, Maria, does not have.

Identifying cause and effect

4. Why is Kate so tired the day of the first swim meet?

Kate was tired because she was at a campaign

meeting late the night before.

Identifying cause and effect

5. What does Mr. Meacham say was the cause of Kate's loss at the swim meet?

He says that her loss was due to a bad attitude and a

lack of concentration.

6. Why does Kate tell Maria that she deserves to win first place?

Maria worked hard; all her practicing helped her beat

her best time.

_____

7. Fill in the circle in front of the word that correctly completes each sentence.

a. Something thought of as being more important than something else is a

_____.

○ lap   ○ campaign   ● priority

b. Someone swimming on his or her stomach combining a kick and double overarm pull is doing the _____.

● butterfly   ○ side stroke   ○ crawl

c. Very young children _____ on a jungle gym.

○ swim   ● clamber   ○ somersault

d. Someone who is extremely tired is suffering from a feeling of

_____

● fatigue   ○ disgust   ○ failure

INTERPRETING FACTS

1. How are Maria and Kate different?

Answers may vary. Maria is not a naturally gifted athlete but is committed to swimming. She does all that her coach

tells her to do. On the other hand, Kate has interests other than swimming. Although she is a natural, she is not as

dedicated to the sport as Maria.

2. If Kate and Maria are friends, why do they argue?

Answers may vary. Kate and Maria are concerned about what is good for each other; they are also competitors on

the swim team.

3. Why is training as a swimmer so demanding?

Answers may vary. Training takes a lot of time every day; it's fatiguing and hard on the body.

_____

4. How do you think Kate felt when she heard about Maria's second victory?

Answers may vary. Kate was probably pleased for Maria but probably also regretted not having competed herself.

_____

5. From the stage directions in Mr. Meacham's dialogue, what kind of person do you think Mr. Meacham is?

Answers may vary. Mr. Meacham is concerned about the swimmers on his team. He is patient with his swimmers'

conflicts, but wants each to perform as well as Maria can.

_____

6. What is the message of this play?

Answers may vary. Worthwhile goals usually demand hard work and hard choices.

_____

Think about the conflict Kate faced and how she solved it. Then answer these questions.

1. Of the three conflicts described at the beginning of the lesson, which conflict did Kate face?

Kate faced conflict with herself.

2. What was Kate's conflict? The demands and pressures of swim training clashed with Kate's other

interests.

3. How did Mr. Meacham, the coach, help Kate with her problem?

Mr. Meacham gave Kate a deadline by which she had to decide if she really wanted to dedicate herself to swimming.

4. How was the conflict finally resolved? Kate finally realized that she wanted to compete in swimming

even if it meant sacrificing other activities.

5. Was Kate's conflict internal or external? Explain.

Kate's conflict was an internal conflict. Kate had to struggle with her feelings of anger, confusion, indecision, and

so on.

6. There is also a minor conflict in the story. It is an external conflict. Circle the letter of the statement that identifies this minor conflict. Then tell how it was resolved.
   a. Maria had to deal with being second best.
   b. Maria got angry with Kate over her unwillingness to work hard.
   c. Maria did not get along with her coach.

Maria's anger disappeared when Kate realized how necessary hard work and practice were to becoming a winner.

7. Maria also has a conflict with herself about her love of swimming and her knowledge that she is not a first-class swimmer. How does she resolve this conflict?

She works hard at her swimming and plans to be a swimming coach.

8. How does the title of this play, "The Campaign for Kate," have two meanings?

One campaign is Kate's campaign for a position in the student government. The other is her struggle to make a total

commitment to swimming.

▶ Real Life Connections Describe a recent conflict in your life. How did you resolve it?

Reading a Timeline

Reading a Social Studies Selection

▶ Background Information

The Olympic Games are the biggest sporting event in the world. Competitors from around the world come together to compete in various sports. These athletes are the best at what they do.

Almost everyone has an Olympic memory. You may remember Michael Jordan and the "Dream Team" winning the gold medal in basketball, or Nancy Kerrigan skating her way to the silver medal in figure skating in 1994.

While you probably have watched the Olympics on television, you may not know about the history of the Olympics.

The history of the Olympic Games can be divided into two parts. The games began in ancient Greece, even before recorded history. These games went on, uninterrupted, for 1,200 years, until they were ended by the Roman emperor Theodosius (thee ə DOH shee əs). The games were not played again until 1896, when the modern Olympic Games began. They have continued to this time.

This selection describes the early Olympics in ancient Greece. It also describes the revival of the games in 1896. The timeline on pages 133 and 134 presents information not included in the text.

▶ Skill Focus

Historical events are usually studied in chronological order. Chronological order is the order in which events take place. In addition to describing historical events in paragraphs, textbooks sometimes use **timelines** to show the sequence of events.

A timeline is a kind of graph of events in chronological order. Each section on a timeline stands for a certain period of time— one year, ten years, a century, or some other length of time. The timeline shows the important events that occurred in each time period.

A timeline shows information in a brief, clear form. It helps you understand when an event happened in relation to other events. A timeline also gives you a quick overview of the history of a particular region, topic, or period.

▶ Word Clues

Read the sentence that follows. Look for context clues that explain the underlined word.

> The Olympics started in ancient Greece so long ago that their <u>origin</u>, or beginning, is not recorded in history.

If you don't know the meaning of the word *origin*, the word following the word *or* can help you. An origin is a beginning. The word *origin* is explained in this appositive phrase set off by a comma. An appositive phrase gives the meaning of the word that comes right before it.

Use **appositive** phrases to find the meaning of the three underlined words in the selection.

▶ Strategy Tip

Before you read "Swifter, Higher, Stronger," preview it. The headings and the timeline give you an overview of the games from ancient Greece to today. Do you know in which years the U.S. athletes won the most gold medals?

Swifter, Higher, Stronger

Superior athletes from around the world gather together to compete against each other as individuals. They also come as representatives of their countries. These men and women are Olympic athletes.

The Olympic Games have a history reaching back to ancient Greece. Many people think that the modern Olympics are the most exciting of sports spectacles. Athletes the world over devote their lives to training for the games. Like the early Greeks, these athletes have as their goal the motto *Citius, altius, fortius,* meaning "swifter, higher, stronger."

The oldest event in the Olympic Games is track and field. It was, and still is, the heart of the games. Even the Olympic motto is directed to the track-and-field athlete, for the Latin words encourage the athlete to run faster, jump higher, and throw harder.

The Beginning of the Olympics

The Olympics started in ancient Greece so long ago that their origin, or beginning, is not recorded by history. The ancient Greeks believed in excellence in every area of life. A Greek citizen was expected to have both a sound mind and a sound body. The Olympics were a celebration of the human body and what it could achieve.

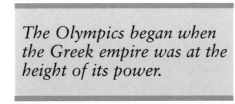

The Olympics began when the Greek empire was at the height of its power.

The first Olympics recorded in history took place in 776 B.C.E. The Greeks have left us a picture of what the event was like. The games took place in the beautiful valley of Olympia. This was a sacred place where the Greeks came to worship their gods.

The grassy slopes of the valley served as a stadium for the games. In 776 B.C.E., over 45,000 Greeks watched and cheered the athletes competing in the games. The first person ever to have his name put in an Olympic record was Coroebus (kə REE bəs). Coroebus was a cook from the city of Elis (EE lis). He was the winner of a footrace of about 200 yards (180 meters). An Olympic winner became a great hero in ancient Greece. He was crowned with an olive wreath. The people of his city welcomed him

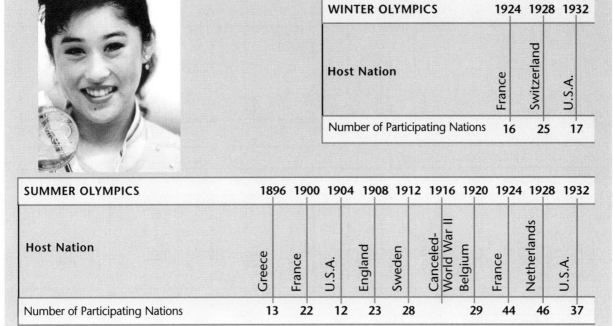

The Modern Olympic Games

WINTER OLYMPICS	1924	1928	1932
Host Nation	France	Switzerland	U.S.A.
Number of Participating Nations	16	25	17

SUMMER OLYMPICS	1896	1900	1904	1908	1912	1916	1920	1924	1928	1932
Host Nation	Greece	France	U.S.A.	England	Sweden	Canceled—World War II	Belgium	France	Netherlands	U.S.A.
Number of Participating Nations	13	22	12	23	28		29	44	46	37

home with parades. Poems were written about him, and statues were erected in his honor.

The physical strength and skill of the Greek athlete was so admired because the Greek nation was often at war. Warfare at the time meant hand-to-hand battle. Young Greek men had to be in good physical shape to be good soldiers. They might be called upon at any time to defend their country.

The Early Games

✔ In the first Olympic Games, there were only footraces. The pentathlon (pen TATH lon)—a contest consisting of five events—was later added to the games. The pentathlon tested an athlete in the long jump, javelin throw, footrace, discus throw, and wrestling. Wrestling soon became a favorite event in the games. Other events, including chariot racing—races between horse-drawn, two-wheel cars—came later.

One of the stories of outstanding Greek athletes is about the famed Milo (MY loh) of Croton (KROHT ən). He won the wrestling crown in six Games. He developed his great strength, it is said, by lifting a baby calf on his shoulder every day until it was a huge bull.

Another famous wrestler was Arrachion (ə RAK ee on) of Phigalia (fi GAYL ya). In one match, Arrachion was being strangled by an opponent. As he gasped for breath, Arrachion twisted his opponent's foot out of its socket. The opponent raised his hand to show he was defeated. Meanwhile, Arrachion died of strangulation. The Greeks crowned Arrachion's dead body with the winner's olive wreath.

The Olympics began when the Greek empire was at the height of its power. When Greece declined as a world power, the games lost their noble spirit. In 67 C.E., the Roman emperor Nero came to compete in the Olympic chariot races. Unjustly, he declared himself the winner.

The last of the early games was held about 390 C.E. Then, in 394 C.E., they were outlawed by the Christian emperor Theodosius I. After 1,200 years, the Olympics ended. During that long time, they had not been interrupted once, not even by war. And though the games were no longer played, their memory and spirit lived on.

The Modern Olympic Games

In 1896, the Olympics were reborn. For the first time in 1,506 years, an Olympic winner was crowned with an olive wreath. Once again, athletes met in competition.

The credit for the rebirth of the Olympics belongs to one person, the Baron de Courbertin of France. Courbertin believed that the Olympic games could serve the modern world as they had ancient Greece. The games would encourage physical fitness in young people. They would also promote world understanding and peace.

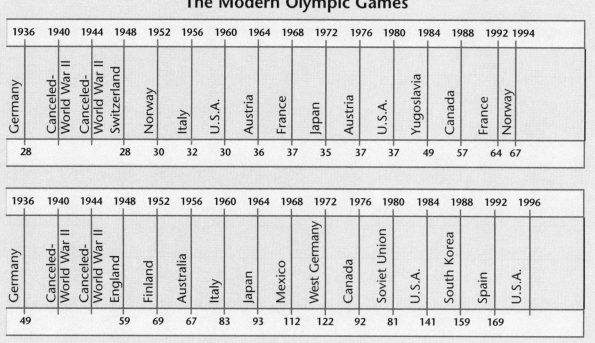

The Modern Olympic Games

1936	1940	1944	1948	1952	1956	1960	1964	1968	1972	1976	1980	1984	1988	1992	1994
Germany	Canceled-World War II	Canceled-World War II	Switzerland	Norway	Italy	U.S.A.	Austria	France	Japan	Austria	U.S.A.	Yugoslavia	Canada	France	Norway
28			28	30	32	30	36	37	35	37	37	49	57	64	67

1936	1940	1944	1948	1952	1956	1960	1964	1968	1972	1976	1980	1984	1988	1992	1996
Germany	Canceled-World War II	Canceled-World War II	England	Finland	Australia	Italy	Japan	Mexico	West Germany	Canada	Soviet Union	U.S.A.	South Korea	Spain	U.S.A.
49			59	69	67	83	93	112	122	92	81	141	159	169	

Alone, Courbertin began a campaign to revive, or bring back, the Olympics. Finally, in 1894, he gained support for his idea, and two years later, the first modern Olympic Games were held. Appropriately, the first modern Olympics took place in Athens, Greece. The games created excitement and enthusiasm throughout the world. At first, the United States as a nation did not support the Olympics. But after the 1896 games, the country caught Olympic fever. A major reason for the sudden interest in the Olympics was that the American athletes who competed in the track-and-field events in 1896 won nine out of the twelve events.

Many new games were included in the Olympics in 1896. The original track-and-field events were still the center of the games. But gymnastics, shooting, swimming, fencing, weight lifting, and other events were also added.

In 1912, the challenging decathlon—a track-and-field contest of ten events—was added to the Olympics. Athletes compete in this contest for two days. There are five events the first day. These include the 100-meter dash, long jump, shot put, high jump, and 400-meter run. Five more events follow on the second day. They are the 110-meter hurdles, discus throw, pole vault, javelin throw, and 1,500-meter run.

Over the years, the number of participants and the number of events in the games have grown. Women as well as men compete in today's Olympics. At their best, the Olympics reach the goal that the Baron de Courbertin had in mind when he revived them. In 1896, Courbertin wrote these words about the games: "The important thing in the Olympic Games is not to win, but to take part, just as the important thing in life is not the triumph but the struggle; the essential thing is not to have conquered but to have fought well."

RECALLING FACTS

Recognizing sequence of events

1. Number the following events in the order in which they happened.

   _3_ The emperor Nero won an Olympic chariot race.

   _1_ Coroebus set an Olympic footracing record.

   _5_ The first modern Olympic Games were held in Athens, Greece.

   _4_ The emperor Theodosius outlawed the Olympics.

   _2_ Wrestling was added to the games.

Identifying cause and effect

2. What effect did the decline of the Greek empire have on the early Olympic Games?

   The Olympic Games declined in their seriousness and sense of fair play; they lost their noble spirit.

Recalling details

3. Where were the early Olympics and the first modern Olympics both held?

   They were both held in Greece.

Recalling details

4. What new events were added to the Olympics in 1896?

   Wrestling, gymnastics, swimming, fencing, and weightlifting, were added.

Recalling details

5. Why did the Baron de Courbertin revive the Olympics?

   The Baron de Courbertin believed that the Olympic Games would encourage physical fitness in young people and would promote world understanding and peace.

Recalling details

6. Match the events in the right column with the dates in the left column.

   _b_ 776 B.C.E.   a. beginning of the modern Olympics

   _c_ 390 C.E.   b. first Olympic Games ever recorded

   _a_ 1896 C.E.   c. last recorded early Olympic Games

7. Reread the paragraph in the selection marked with an X. Underline its main idea. Then circle two or more details that support the main idea.

Using context clues

8. Draw a line to match each word with its meaning.

revive   a contest of five events

decathlon   to bring back or make popular

pentathlon   a contest of ten events

INTERPRETING FACTS

Inferring cause and effect

1. Write the cause for the effect described below.

   Cause Young Greek men had to be fit to fight in wars.

   Effect Many of the early Olympic events tested physical skills needed by Greek soldiers.

Inferring comparison and contrast

2. The ancient Greeks believed in both a sound body and a sound mind. Compare their belief about this with the feelings of Americans today.

   Answers may vary. Because so many people today are conscious of physical fitness, they would agree with the need for a sound body and a sound mind.

Inferring details

3. During what span of time were the Olympic Games not held?

   The Olympics were not held before 776 B.C.E. and from 390 C.E. to 1896.

Inferring cause and effect

4. Why did the events in the Olympics change over the years?

   New sports developed over the years.

Inferring the unstated main idea

5. Reread the paragraph in the selection that has a check mark next to it. Write a sentence that expresses the main idea.

   The number of events in the early Olympic Games increased over the years.

Drawing conclusions

6. Do you think the Baron de Courbertin's statement about the Olympics on page 135 is still true about the Olympics today? Explain.

   Answers will vary.

Distinguishing fact from opinion

7. a. Is the Baron de Courbertin's statement a fact or an opinion?

   opinion

   b. In two sentences, tell why you agree or disagree with the statement.

   Answers will vary.

Drawing conclusions

8. Do you think the Olympic motto "Swifter, higher, stronger" is still appropriate? Explain.

   Yes. The motto is still appropriate because athletes must still run fast, jump high, and throw with strength. No. The motto is not appropriate because the modern games also test such skills as skiing, skating, and so on.

9. Explain how the Olympic Games have always been democratic in spirit.

Both ancient and modern games allow the best

athletes to compete and win regardless of race,

religion, or economic status.

10. Why might the decathlon be considered the supreme Olympic event?

Answers may vary. As a two-day, ten-event competition

in a range of running, jumping, and throwing, as well as

in pole vaulting and hurdles, it is the fullest test of an

athlete's strength, speed, and skill.

SKILL FOCUS

Use the timeline on pages 133 and 134 to answer the following questions.

1. How frequently are the Olympic Games held? _____ every four years _____

2. In what year did the greatest number of nations participate in the games? _____ 1992 _____

3. a. In what years were the Olympic Games canceled?

   _____ 1916 _____   _____ 1940 _____   _____ 1944 _____

   b. Why were the games canceled? The garmes aim to promote world peace and understanding;

   athletes from around the world meet in peaceful competition. This is not possible when nations are fighting against

   each other in a world war.

4. Where were the summer and winter Olympics held in the first games after World War II?

   summer–England; winter–Switzerland

5. Where and when were the first winter Olympic Games held? _____ France, 1924 _____

6. In what year were both the summer and the winter games held in Germany? _____ 1936 _____

7. As of 1994, how many games, summer and winter, had been held in the United States?

   _____ 7 _____

8. In which two countries have the most Olympic Games been held? _____ France, United States

9. Look at the number of nations participating in the summer Olympics. What trend do you

   see from 1896 to 1994? The number of participating nations has been on the rise since 1896.

10. Have the winter Olympics ever been held in Greece? _____ no _____ In one sentence,

    explain why this might be so. _____ Greece is not cold enough for outdoor winter sports. _____

▶ Real Life Connections What sport would you like to see as a new Olympic event? Give your reasons.

Lesson 43

Following Directions

___ Reading a Science Selection ___

▶ **Background Information**

Following directions is an important skill. You will need to follow directions countless times in your life.

In the following selection, you will be asked to follow directions to carry out a scientific experiment. The selection has five sections. The first two describe the scientific meaning of work and the different forces that are involved. Read these sections carefully and study the diagrams. Be sure that you understand each of the boldfaced terms and equations.

The third and fourth sections describe how two simple machines—levers and pulleys—make work easier. While you read these sections, review the equations in the first part of the selection.

▶ **Skill Focus**

Following directions is an important skill. For example, to carry out an experiment in a science textbook, you must follow directions.

Directions for an experiment are set up in a certain way. Most sets of directions have five parts: Problem, Aim, Materials,

Procedure, and Observations or Conclusions. Like recipes, science experiments are always set up the same way so that they can be repeated any number of times exactly as they were done the first time. The following describes each part.

Problem: The question that you should be able to answer at the end of the experiment

Aim: What will be done in the experiment

Materials: Equipment or objects needed for the experiment

Procedure: The steps that must be carried out in order to complete the experiment

Observations or Conclusions: Questions to answer or conclusions to draw about the outcome of the experiment

Use the following steps to read a science selection with directions for an experiment.

1. Read the paragraphs that explain the ideas. Be sure that you understand the ideas.
2. Read through the five parts of the directions: Problem, Aim, Materials, Procedure, and Observations or Conclusions. Be sure that you understand all the scientific words.
3. Study the pictures or

diagrams. Be sure to read the captions and labels.
4. Reread the Problem, Aim, Materials, Procedure, and Observations or Conclusions. Be sure that you understand the procedure before you begin the experiment.

▶ **Word Clues**

Sometimes special terms are explained in a paragraph and also shown in a diagram. When this happens, study both the text and the diagram to understand the terms.

Use **diagram** clues and context clues to find out the meaning of the three underlined terms in the selection.

▶ **Strategy Tip**

After you have read and understood the sections on levers and pulleys in "Work and Machines," study the directions for the experiment on page 140. Use the four steps to help you. Following directions in this way can be very useful to you.

WORK AND MACHINES

People use machines every day. Some machines are complicated and have many moving parts. Others are so simple that most people don't think of them as machines. A **machine** is any invention that makes work easier or faster.

What Is Work?

To a scientist, work has a special meaning. Work means the use of force to move an object through a distance. The object is moved in the direction of the force. This meaning for work can be expressed in an equation.

$$\text{Work} = \text{Force} \times \text{Distance}$$

To move an object, a machine must overcome the force that resists the movement of the object. This force is the **resistance.** The distance through which the machine moves the object is called the **resistance distance.**

How Do Machines Make Work Easier?

When a machine is used, some work goes into making the machine function. The force applied by the user to a machine is called the **effort.** The distance through which the user applies the effort is called the **effort distance.** Some machines make work easier by increasing the amount of force that is applied to them and using it against the resistance force. The amount by which a machine increases a force is called the **mechanical advantage** of the machine.

$$\text{Mechanical Advantage} = \text{Resistance} \div \text{Effort}$$

Figure 1. A lever is a simple machine made up of a rigid arm that pivots on a point called a fulcrum.

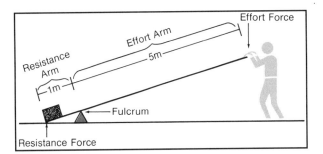

Figure 2. A lever makes moving a heavy object easier by applying force through a greater distance.

Levers

A **lever** is a simple machine that can multiply a small effort force to overcome a large resistance force. A lever is like a seesaw. It has a rigid arm that rocks back and forth on a fixed point called the <u>fulcrum</u>. The woman in Figure 1 is using a simple lever. What is the resistance? How is the effort being applied?

The rigid arm of every lever has two parts. The <u>effort arm</u> is the distance between the fulcrum and the effort force. The <u>resistance arm</u> is the distance between the fulcrum and the resistance force. You can figure out the mechanical advantage of a lever by dividing the length of the effort arm by the length of the resistance arm.

$$\text{Mechanical Advantage} = \\ \text{Effort Arm} \div \text{Resistance Arm}$$

In Figure 2, the resistance arm is 1 meter, and the effort arm is 5 meters. The mechanical advantage of this lever, then, is 5. On a seesaw, the effort arm and the resistance arm are equal. Therefore, the mechanical advantage of a seesaw is 1.

You can figure out how much effort is needed to move an object if you know the mechanical advantage of a machine. To do this, you divide the resistance by the mechanical advantage.

$$\text{Effort} = \text{Resistance} \div \text{Mechanical Advantage}$$

Pulleys

A **pulley,** another highly useful simple machine, is a form of lever. A pulley makes work easier by changing the direction of a

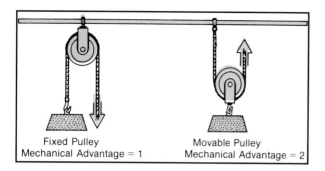

Fixed Pulley
Mechanical Advantage = 1

Movable Pulley
Mechanical Advantage = 2

Figure 3. A fixed pulley, at left, is held in place by a support beam. At right, a movable pulley moves freely on a rope attached to a support beam.

force. A pulley is a grooved wheel over which runs a cord. To lift an object with a pulley, you pull on the cord. Your pull is the effort. The object that is pulled is the resistance.

A pulley attached to a wall, a beam, or any other support frame is called a **fixed pulley**. Window shades and flagpoles often have fixed pulleys. Fixed pulleys do not multiply the effort force put into them. They only change the direction of the force. Often it is easier to pull against a resistance than to lift it.

A greater advantage is gained through using a **movable pulley**. A movable pulley is hung on a rope attached to a support frame. The rope runs through the pulley. The pulley itself moves up the rope as the rope is pulled. A movable pulley makes it easier to lift a heavy weight. You can figure out the mechanical advantage of a pulley by dividing the resistance distance by the effort distance.

Mechanical Advantage =
Resistance Distance ÷ Effort Distance

Experiment

The following experiment will show the advantage of a fixed pulley.

Problem

What mechanical advantage can you obtain by using a pulley?

Aim

In this experiment, you will measure the mechanical advantage of a fixed pulley.

Materials

You will need a support frame, a single lightweight pulley, a length of cord, a kilogram weight, a spring balance, and a meter stick.

Procedure

1. Attach the weight to the spring balance. What is the weight of the load, or the resistance?

2. Remove the weight from the spring balance. Tie the weight to one end of the cord. String the free end of the cord over the pulley. Hang the pulley on the support frame and attach the top of the spring balance to the free end of the cord. Pull slowly on the spring balance. Read the spring balance to determine the value of this effort. How does the effort compare to the resistance? Was it easier to lift the

weight by hand or to lift it with the use of the pulley? Why?

3. Use the meter stick to see how far you must pull down the cord to lift the weight 1 meter. Then compare the two distances. What is the mechanical advantage of a fixed pulley?

Observations or Conclusions

The mechanical advantage of a fixed pulley is 1. Think about what this means. Why is a fixed pulley useful?

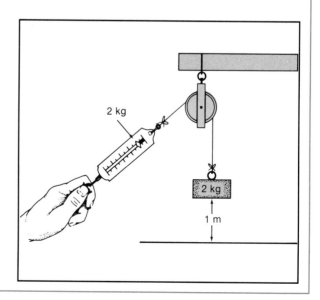

RECALLING FACTS

Recalling details

1. What is a machine? _It is any invention that_ _makes work easier._

Recalling details

2. What is the mechanical advantage of a machine?

It reduces the amount of force necessary.

Reading text with diagrams

3. In Figure 1, what is the fulcrum?

It is a brick.

Using context clues

4. Draw a line to match each term with its explanation.

fulcrum — distance between the fulcrum and the effort force

effort arm — distance between the fulcrum and the resistance force

resistance arm — fixed point over which a lever rocks

INTERPRETING FACTS

Making inferences

1. If a lever has an effort arm of 4 meters and a resistance arm of 2 meters, what is the mechanical advantage of the machine? _2_

Making inferences

2. Which tool is not a lever: a pair of scissors, a nutcracker, a crowbar, an axe?

An axe is not a lever.

Making inferences

3. A pair of scissors is a kind of lever. Where is the fulcrum on a pair of scissors?

The screw joining the blades is the fulcrum.

Making inferences

4. On a pair of scissors, where is the effort applied? What provides the resistance?

handles; object being cut

Making inferences

5. How far must you raise the cord of a movable pulley in order to lift a load 2 meters? _4 meters_

Making inferences

6. How could you make a seesaw work better as a lever?

A seesaw's arms are equal. Making its resistance arm

shorter or its effort arm longer would give it a great

mechanical advantage.

SKILL FOCUS

Write a summary of the experiment on page 140 in your own words. Do not look back. Then check your summary by rereading the experiment. Make any necessary corrections.

Answers may vary. In this experiment, the mechanical advantage of a fixed pulley is determined. First, the load, or

resistance, is measured. Then the load is attached to the fixed pulley and the effort needed to lift the load and the

effort distance are measured. The mechanical advantage of a fixed pulley was 1.

The following experiment should show how much force it would take to lift an object of a certain weight with two different levers. Complete the directions using the experiment on page 140 as a model. Use a ruler or a metric stick for the arm. Use a block of wood for the fulcrum. Use a weight for the resistance. Use other weights to measure the effort needed to lift the resistance. A spring balance will be necessary for this experiment. Be sure to number the steps in the Procedure part. In the box, draw and label a diagram to show what is to be done. The Problem and Aim have been completed for you.

Experiment

Problem

Compare the effort needed to lift an object of a certain weight with two different levers.

Aim

In this experiment, you will compare the effort force needed to lift a resistance of a certain weight with two different levers. The effort arm of one lever should be twice the length of the resistance arm. The effort arm of the other lever should be four times the length of the resistance arm.

Materials

Possible answers include metric stick, block of wood,

weights, and a spring balance.

Procedure

1. Construct lever A by placing a metric stick across

   a block of wood. The effort arm should be twice

   the length of the resistance arm.

2. Weigh the resistance weight on a spring balance.

   Then place it at one end of the lever.

3. Add weights to the effort arm until the resistance is

   lifted. Weigh the effort weights.

4. Construct lever B as in Step 1. The effort arm

   should be four times the length of the resistance

   arm.

5. Place the resistance weight on the end of the

   lever.

6. Repeat Step 3. Compare the results.

Observations and Conclusions

Effort needed to lift an object grows less as effort arm

gets longer.

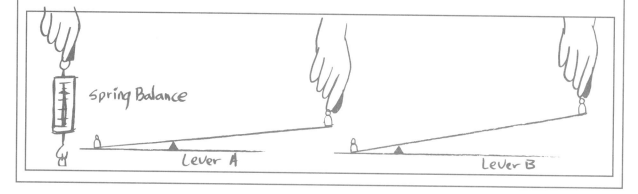

Spring Balance

Lever A   Lever B

▶ **Real Life Connections** Name a kind of pulley and a kind of lever that you use daily.

Circle Graphs

Reading a Mathematics Selection

▶ Background Information

Reading graphs is an important skill to learn. You will find graphs in newspapers and magazines. Graphs often appear in news stories. Facts about an opinion poll on a topic, for example, will often show you the result in a circle graph. This type of graph lets you see at a glance the percentage of people who approve, disapprove, or have no opinion on this topic.

If you are interested in the performance of a team over a period of several months or years, then you may find information about this subject shown in a bar graph. The different heights of the bars enable you to compare the high points and low points in the performance of the team from month to month or from year to year.

When changes over time are smaller and more numerous, a line graph probably will be used to show them. For example. suppose that you want to know the rise and fall of the cost of living week by week over a period of two months. A line graph would show this information. Looking at this graph, you would get a clearer picture of changes in the cost of living during the two-month period.

▶ Skill Focus

Graphs show information very clearly. You can read a graph much more quickly than you can read a paragraph that gives the same information. Graphs also make it easier for you to compare information.

Different graphs are used for different purposes. **Circle graphs** are used for showing parts of a whole. Circle graphs are usually used with percents.

When you look at a circle graph, it may be helpful to think of it as a pizza. The next time you eat a pizza, think about how each slice fits into the whole. For example if the pizza is evenly divided into 8 slices and you eat 2 slices, you have eaten 2/8 of the pie, which is 1/4 of it. As a percent, 1/4 is 25%.

Notice that you are dealing with a percentage or a part of a whole. The pizza, or the circle, represents the whole. The bigger the segment is, the bigger the percentage will be. Circle graphs are easy to understand. If you understand what these graphs are representing, then you will find circle graphs very useful for getting information quickly.

However, before you can understand the facts in a graph, you need to know the purpose of the graph. Be sure to read the paragraphs that come before a graph and the title of the graph. Then you will be able to use the information that the graph presents in a variety of ways.

▶ Word Clues

When you read "Reading Graphs," look for these important words: *data, sectors,* and *label.* They will help you understand more about circle graphs.

▶ Strategy Tip

Be sure to read the title of each graph before you study the graph itself. Also, take the time to understand what the labels stand for. Only by doing these things will you be able to understand details on a graph accurately.

Reading Graphs

Total Medals, 1994 Winter Olympics

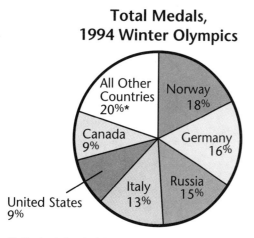

*Switzerland, Austria, S. Korea, Finland

Gold Medals, 1994 Winter Olympics

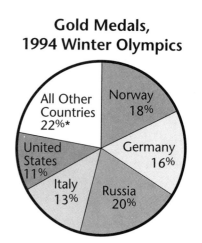

*Canada, Switzerland, Austria, S. Korea, Finland

The graph above is a **circle graph**. The first thing that you should read is the title of the graph. The title tells what kind of information is shown in the graph. The title of this graph is *Total Medals, 1994 Winter Olympics*.

This circle graph is divided into seven sections that show **data,** or information. The sections are called **sectors.** Each sector has a label. The label tells you what the sector stands for. When you read a circle graph, the sectors help you compare data. For example, in this circle graph, the sectors help you compare the total number of medals won by countries in the 1994 Winter Olympics. By looking at the size of the sectors, you can see that Norway won the most medals of the six countries named on the graph. The United States and Canada won the fewest medals. The note below the graph tells you that there were four other countries that won medals—Switzerland, Austria, South Korea, and Finland. The size of the sectors also tells you that four-fifths of the medals were won by Norway, Germany, Russia, Italy, the United States, and Canada. All the other countries won one-fifth of the medals.

There is another circle graph next to the first one. The title tells you that this graph can help you compare gold medals won in the 1994 Winter Olympics. The sectors are labeled with the names of the countries and percents. The graph shows that Russia won the greatest number of gold medals. The United States won the fewest number of gold medals.

When percents are shown on a circle graph,

they should always add up to 100, which stands for the whole circle. The percents make it easier to compare information. In the graph above, you can see that Russia won one-fifth of the gold medals. Because percents are shown, you can also see that Russia won 9 percent more medals than the United States.

The circle graph below can help you

Silver Medals, 1994 Winter Olympics

*Switzerland, Austria, S. Korea, Finland

compare the number of silver medals won in the 1994 Winter Olympics. Each sector in this circle graph is also labeled with a percent. Norway won the most silver medals, with 21 percent. The United States won 10 percent of the medals.

This circle graph shows a great deal of data, but it does not show how many medals were won by each group of countries. You know that the United States won about 10 percent of the silver medals. If the total number of medals were given, you could solve the following numerical sentence:

$$10\% \text{ of } t = m, \text{ or } \frac{10}{100} \times t = m$$

The symbol t stands for the total number of medals won. The symbol m stands for the number of medals won by the United States.

There were a total of 51 silver medals won in the 1994 Winter Olympics. Now you can solve the sentence.

$$\frac{10}{100} \times 51 = m, \text{ or } \frac{10}{100} \times \frac{51}{1} = m$$

$$\frac{510}{100} = m, \text{ or } \frac{510}{100} = 5.1$$

The figure of 5.1 is not an exact number because sometimes percents on circle graphs are rounded off. If you round off the number 5.1, you will find that the United States won five medals in the 1994 Winter Olympics.

When sectors in a circle graph are labeled and the percents are not given, you can still compare the size of the sectors. You can tell which is greatest, which is least, and which are about the same. You can also estimate the amount using fractions.

When the sectors are labeled with percents, you can find how much larger one sector is than another. Also, if the total amount is given as data, you can multiply to find the amount in each sector.

RECALLING FACTS

Recalling details
1. What does the title of a graph tell?
It tells what information is shown in the graph.

Recalling details
2. What use can be made of the total amount when it is given as data?
If percents are also given, you can multiply to find the

actual numbers in each sector.

Reading graphs
3. How many sectors are shown in the last circle graph in the selection?
The last graph shows seven sectors.

Reading graphs
4. In the graph about 1994 Silver Medal Winners, Canada, Norway, and Germany won a total of 47% of the medals. What percent did all the other nations included win?
53%

Reading graphs
5. Using the first circle graph in the selection, what is the percent of medals won by Norway, Germany, Russia, Italy, the United States, and Canada combined, if all the other countries won 20 percent?
80%

INTERPRETING FACTS

Making inferences
1. Why are circle graphs useful for showing percents? They show parts of a whole.
Making inferences
2. What determines the size of a sector in a circle graph? the percent of the whole that it stands for
Inferring cause and effect
3. If the size of one sector of a circle graph were increased, what would happen to the other sectors?

At least one would decrease in size.
Making inferences
4. Put a check mark next to the idea that could best be shown in a circle graph.

_____ increase in attendance at Olympic games from 1896 to 1994

✔ countries winning medals in speed skating in the 1994 Winter Olympics

_____ winning times for women's downhill skiing in the 1994 Winter Olympics

A. Use the graphs in the selection to answer the following questions.

1. Which country won the greatest number of medals overall in the 1994 Winter Olympics?

Norway won the most medals overall.

2. What is the title of the second graph?

The title is "Gold Medals, 1994 Winter Olympics."

3. Which two countries won the same total number of medals in the 1994 Winter Olympics?

The U.S. and Canada won the same number of medals.

4. Which country won 16% of the silver medals in the 1994 Winter Olympics?

Russia won 16%.

B. Use the graph below to answer the questions that follow.

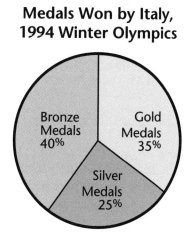

Medals Won by Italy, 1994 Winter Olympics

Total number of medals won in all: 20.

1. What is the title of the graph?

The title is "Medals Won by Italy, 1994 Winter Olympics."

2. How many sectors are shown?

Three sectors are shown.

3. How are the sectors labeled?

They are labeled by types of medals and percents.

4. What is the sum of the percents?

100%

5. What are the three types of medals that Italy won in the 1994 Winter Olympics?

Italy won bronze, gold, and silver medals.

6. Of the three types of medals, which type did Italy win most?

Italy won the most bronze medals.

7. Of the three types of medals, which type did Italy win the fewest of?

Italy won the fewest silver medals.

8. What percent of the medals won by Italy were gold medals?

Thirty-five percent were gold medals.

9. How many gold medals did Italy win?

35% of 20 = 7

10. How many silver medals did Italy win?

25% of 20 = 5

11. How many bronze medals did Italy win?

40% of 20 = 8

▶ **Real Life Connections** Research facts about your community. Put the information into a circle graph.

Multiple Meanings

A word may have a different meaning in literature, social studies, science, mathematics, or music. Some words with multiple meanings follow.

| band | change | crop | legend | pupil | yard |
| cell | cone | front | power | scale | plot |

Read the two definitions for each word below. Choose a word from the list above that fits those two definitions. Write the word on the line above the definitions.

1. _____ yard _____

Mathematics: a measure, 36 inches in length

Social Studies: an open place used for a business or special purpose

2. _____ band _____

Music: a group of musicians playing instruments together

Social Studies: a group of people joined to do something

3. _____ cell _____

Social Studies: a small room in a prison or jail

Science: the basic unit of living matter, usually very small

4. _____ cone _____

Mathematics: a solid object that narrows evenly from a flat circle at one end to a point at the other

Science: the part of evergreen trees that bears seeds

5. _____ change _____

Mathematics: money returned when one has paid more than the amount owed

Social Studies: places or conditions that become different as time passes

6. _____ plot _____

Literature: the action, or series of events, in a story

Social Studies: a secret plan, in politics or during a war, to gain power or harm an enemy, by misleading people, usually by dishonest methods

7. _____ power _____

Science: energy or force that has the ability to do work

Social Studies: a person or group that has authority, right, or control over others

8. _____ pupil _____

Science: the dark opening in the center of the eye

Social Studies: a person being taught by a teacher

9. _____ crop _____

Social Studies: the full amount of produce grown by a farmer in one season

Science: a pouch in a bird's gullet where food is softened for digestion

10. _____ legend _____

Literature: a story handed down through the years and connected with some real events, but probably not true in itself

Social Studies: a title or description under a picture or map

11. _____ front _____

Science: the boundary between two large masses of air

Social Studies: in a war, the part where the fighting is going on

12. _____ scale _____

Music: a series of musical tones arranged in order from lowest to highest or highest to lowest

Science: any of the thin, flat, hard plates that cover and protect certain fish

Lesson 46

Using an Index

The quickest way to find information in a text or reference book is to use the **index.** An index lists all the important subjects included in the book.

On the following page is part of an index from a science textbook. The **topics** are arranged in alphabetical order. Find the topic *Oil.* Below it, three subtopics are listed alphabetically: *pollution from, source,* and *use.* **Subtopics** list the specific kinds of information given in the book about the topic. Notice that some subtopics have such words as *in* and *of* before them. As you can see, these short words don't affect the alphabetical order of the subtopics.

The numbers after each topic or subtopic are the page numbers on which information is found. Numbers separated by dashes indicate that information begins on the page before the dash and ends on the page after the dash. Numbers separated by commas show that information appears on only the pages for which numbers are given.

Study the index on the following page. Then answer the questions on the lines provided.

1. On what page(s) would you find information about mud? _____165_____

2. How many subtopics are listed under the topic *Moon?* _____12_____

3. On what page(s) would you find information about craters on the moon? _____79, 104–105_____

4. How many pages does the book have on nuclear energy? _____3_____

5. On what page(s) would you find information about the moons of Pluto? _____78_____

6. How many pages does the book have on the Milky Way? _____10_____

7. On what page(s) would you find information about nitrogen in the soil? _____324, 469_____

8. What two planets' moons are discussed on the same page? _____Neptune, Uranus_____.

9. If you wanted information on life in the oceans, which page would you *not* read between pages 250 and 256? _____255_____

10. On what page(s) would you find information about nickel in the earth's core? _____192–193_____

11. What five subtopics about the moon are discussed on page 105?

_____craters on, marias, orbit of, phases, revolution of_____

12. What topic comes between nickel and nuclear energy? _____nitrogen_____

13. If the book had information about mold, after which topic would it be listed? _____Mohs scale_____

14. If the book had information about fish farms in the oceans, before which subtopic would it be listed? _____gases in_____

Methane, 475
    in atmosphere, 262
    in outer planets, 75, 77
Milky Way, 25–28, 38–41, 47, 57
Minerals:
    chemical weathering of, 320–324
    conservation of, 473–474
    crystals, 138–140, 161–162
    deposits, 171–172
    gems, 143–145
    identification of, 138, 145–153
    in lithosphere, 29
    in rocks, 158, 161, 168, 323
    soil and, 324–327, 330
    sources of, 141–142, 470–472, 489
Mining, 471–474
Moho, 187, 188
Mohs scale, 148–149
Molecules, behavior of, 122–124, 125
Moon:
    age of, 103, 444–446
    atmosphere of, 104
    axis, rotation of, 102–103
    craters on, 79, 104–105
    eclipses, 108–109
    gravity of, 102
    marias, 103–104, 105
    orbit of, 105
    phases, 105–107, 108
    revolution of, 105
    size, 102
    tides and, 109–111
Moons:
    of Jupiter, 75
    of Mars, 74
    of Neptune, 77
    of Pluto, 78
    of Saturn, 76
    of Uranus, 77
Moraines, 345–346
Mountains, 200–202, 452, 454
    belts, 202
    earth's mantle and, 367–368
    erosion and, 30, 201
    faults and, 372
    folds and, 375, 376
    magma and, 377
    oceanic, 240, 248–250, 404–406
    ores in, 333
    ranges, 201–202, 402–403, 411, 453, 456
    soils, 332–333
    system of, 202
    weathering and, 30
Mud, 165

N

Nebulae, 40
Nekton, 251, 252, 253
Neon:
    in atmosphere, 94
    in meteoroids, 81
Nickel:
    in the earth's core, 192–193
    in meteoroids, 81
Nitrogen:
    in atmosphere, 30, 94, 263–265, 275
    from carbon, 14, 443
    living things and, 264–265, 481–482
    in oceans, 242
    in soil, 324, 469
Nuclear energy, 492–494
Nucleus, 127

O

Oceans:
    basins, topography of, 244–250, 255, 257
    continental margins, 245–246
    depths, 238, 241, 243, 245–246, 250, 251, 252, 253–254
    gases in, 242
    life in, 250–254, 256, 426
    minerals in, 490
    oceanography, 13, 239, 241, 254–257
    salinity, 239–242, 251, 256
    spreading of floor, 404–407, 454
    temperatures and, 241, 242–243, 256, 309
    trenches, 249, 406–407
Oil:
    pollution from, 482–483
    source, 474, 475
    use, 324, 476
Orbit, 24, 69
    of planets, 68–69, 70–76
    of satellites, 87–89
Orbital velocity, 87–89
Ores, 141–142, 143, 333, 470–471
    mining, 471–472
    refining, 472–473
Oxidation, 320–321

Comparing Travel Packages

In planning a vacation, you need to decide on many things—where you will go, how long you will stay, what hotel you will stay at, what you want to see, and how much money you will spend. **Travel packages** are arrangements made by a travel agent or travel company to cover your vacation plans. These arrangements may include any of the following: air travel, hotels, meals, and such extras as sightseeing. Before making a decision on your travel plans, look into several travel packages to compare what they offer.

Carefully read and compare the following travel packages.

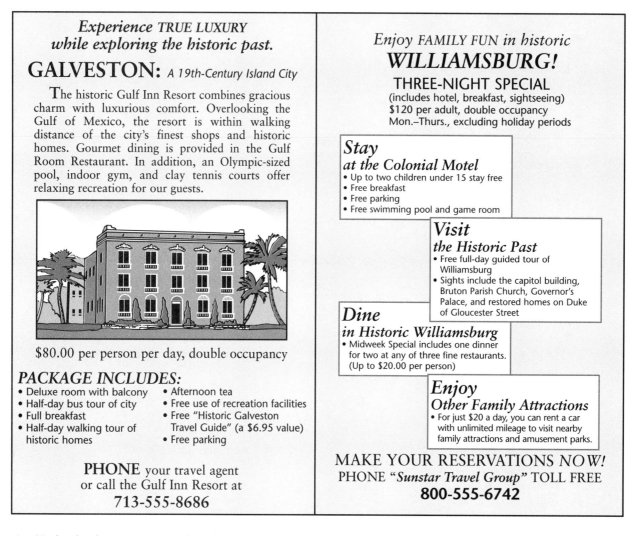

A. Circle the letter next to the phrase that correctly completes each sentence.

1. The Galveston package stresses
    a. family fun.   **b.** sightseeing.   **(c.)** luxury accommodations.

2. The Williamsburg package stresses
    (a.) family fun.   **b.** sightseeing.   **c.** luxury accommodations.

3. The rates for both packages are based on "double occupancy," which means that
  a. the charge is the same for two people in the room as it is for one person.
  (b.) the per-person charge is based on two people in a room, so the price is twice the quoted rate.
  c. the room rate changes with each additional person in the room.

4. If a family wants to save money, it may prefer the Williamsburg package because
  (a.) up to two children can stay free in the motel.
  b. the package offers a free dinner for two.
  c. the package offers use of a pool and game room at the motel.

5. For three nights, the Galveston package costs
  (a.) $240.00 per person.   **b.** $240.00 per room.   **c.** $80.00 per person.

6. Staying in Williamsburg for three nights will cost more than the advertised package price because the package
  a. does not include any sightseeing tours.
  b. does not include any dinners.
  (c.) includes breakfasts and one dinner for two, so additional meals will be extra.

7. Both the Galveston and Williamsburg packages include
  a. a special three-day rate for rooms.
  (b.) a room rate based upon double occupancy.
  c. nightly room rates.

B. Compare the two travel packages by completing the chart below. If no information is given for a particular item, write *no information*. Then answer the questions below the chart.

	GALVESTON	WILLIAMSBURG
price per night per adult	$80.00	$120.00
number of people per room	2	2–4
days available	every day	Mon.–Thurs.; no holidays
children's rates	no information	up to two under 15 free
meals included	breakfast, tea	breakfast, one dinner for 2
free recreation facilities	pool, gym, tennis	pool, game room
number of tours	two half-day tours	one full-day tour
car rental	no information	$20.00/day, unlimited miles
how to reserve	call travel agent or resort	call travel group toll-free

1. Which package is less expensive per night? _____Galveston_____

2. Which package includes more free recreation facilities? _____Galveston_____

3. Which package allows more people in one room? _____Williamsburg_____

4. Which package provides more free meals? _____Williamsburg_____

5. Which package is available on weekends? _____Galveston_____

Point of View

Reading a Literature Selection

▶ **Background Information**

Computers continue to change the way people live, work, and think. This story, in the form of a journal, is about a computer named Dellie, described in the day-to-day journal entries of a student.

▶ **Skill Focus**

Before writing, an author must decide whether the story will be told by one of the characters or by an outsider. The **point of view** determines the kind of information that is given in a story and how it is presented.

When the events of the story are seen through the eyes of a character who participated in the events, the author is using **first-person point of view**. The narrator tells the reader his or her thoughts. The narrator cannot enter the minds of the other characters. Thus, the narrator tells only what he or she actually *sees* others doing.

Read the following paragraph.

Walking home, I heard someone running toward me. I was frightened. A tall man ran by me. He raced to an emergency police phone. He spoke loudly and asked for an ambulance. Feeling relieved, I asked if I could be of any help.

This event is seen through the eyes of a narrator. The reader learns only what the narrator thinks and feels, not how the other character feels or what he or she is thinking.

When you try to determine the point of view, think about the following questions.
1. Is the narrator a participant in the event or an outsider?
2. Do you know what only the narrator is thinking and feeling?
3. Do you know what the other characters are thinking and feeling?

▶ **Word Clues**

When you read a word that you don't know, look for context clues to understand it. Sometimes, however, there may be no context clues. Read the sentence below.

Technicians have been trying to put together the six computer pieces so that our new principal can start functioning properly.

Suppose that you do not know the meaning of the word *technicians*. There are no context clues. You will have to look up the word in a dictionary. You may find it convenient to finish reading first and then look up the word.

Use a **dictionary** to find the meaning of the three underlined words in the selection.

▶ **Strategy Tip**

"The Principal Problem" is written from the first-person point of view. As you read it, notice that the information is limited to the narrator's own thoughts and feelings. Recognizing the point of view will give you a better understanding of a story's characters and plot.

The Principal Problem

September 10 It had to happen, of course. Vacation's come to an end—summer, too, for that matter—and today, I, Carmen Soares, began my last year at Gloria Willis Junior High. I wish it were my last week, though I'm relieved to have Miss James for my homeroom teacher. She's got potential; she just has to be trained right. Seat assignments were handed out, and I'm right in front of Harry Seely. How's that for luck? He asked to borrow a pencil, and I very coolly said, "Keep it, Harry; I've got zillions of them." Definitely a good start!

September 11 A weird thing happened at our first assembly of the year. Mr. Alioto, the assistant principal, announced that Mrs. Uxley would not be returning as principal of Gloria Willis. I guess she's retiring or something. When one of the kids asked about Mrs. Uxley's replacement, Mr. Alioto didn't say anything for a moment, then answered, "Her replacement will be delivered next week."

September 14 I've done nothing for the last three days but wonder about our new principal. How do you "deliver" a principal?

September 19 Well, I got my answer today—you deliver a principal in boxes. Our principal was delivered in six boxes, to be exact. It's a computer—talk about new ideas! It's a good thing that I'm heading for high school after this year. But Luis Garcia says that won't make a bit of difference. He told me that once they get a bad idea in one school, they usually take it around to all the others.

September 23 Technicians have been trying to put together the six computer pieces so that our new principal can start functioning properly. They've been running in and out of the principal's office. Rumors are racing around the school, but no one really knows what's happening. Harry Seely borrowed another pencil. That makes three. What does he do with them?

September 24 Two items of interest! First, they put a suggestion box in each classroom; then they gave everyone, even teachers, a form to complete. In the top part, you had to write your hobbies, your favorite television shows, even the kinds of food that you like best. Also, they wanted you to suggest how life at Gloria Willis could be improved. They also handed out this funny note:

> HELLO:
>   MY NAME IS T12H2679DELTA. CALL ME DELLIE. I AM YOUR NEW PRINCIPAL. ALL NEW DELTA COMPUTERS ARE PROGRAMMED FOR TOP PERFORMANCE IN A SPECIFIC TYPE OF JOB, AND I AM NO EXCEPTION. A SUGGESTION BOX HAS BEEN PLACED IN YOUR CLASSROOM. PLEASE USE IT OFTEN SO THAT YOU CAN HELP ME IN MY JOB. I THINK WE CAN HAVE FUN TOGETHER, DON'T YOU?

September 26 As if things weren't bad enough, I came across a magazine article about my new principal. It said that there were two Delta computers now in use: ours, and one that's working as a town manager out in some small midwestern town. The article talked about how the other Delta has to be a diplomat, which means it has to consider everybody's opinion before it makes any decisions. Our Delta principal, on the other hand, is supposed to act like a dictator. It makes decisions without considering anyone's opinion. I think we're in big, big trouble at Gloria Willis—really gigantic trouble!

September 27 I detest Harry Seely—he's been borrowing Rita Korngold's pencils, too.

September 28 All's well that ends well. Rita Korngold was shipped off to the other side of the room. I don't think it had anything to do with my suggestion, although it was really a very funny <u>coincidence</u>. I dropped another suggestion into the box just to be sure.

September 29 That'll teach me. I thought I was safe telling Milos Kelly, the track star, about the suggestion box, but that just shows how smart I really am! When Miss James said gym was being replaced by <u>aerobics</u>, I knew whose suggestion that was. I just hope she keeps her promise not to tell anyone else.

October 2 Now I know what Milos Kelly's promises are worth! When I walked into class this morning, there was a long line of kids waiting to drop suggestions into the box. To make things worse, when I went to my seat, I found out that Harry Seely was no longer sitting in back of me. He'd been moved to the other side of the room, to a seat next to—Guess Who? They put Ronnie Franks behind me in Harry Seely's place. What a trade that was! Now I'll have to stop wearing my hair in a braid. Ronnie Franks is that kind of neighbor. After I finish writing this, I'm going to spend at least two hours writing suggestions.

October 3 Things are getting weird, to say the least. There's a ten-minute wait at just about every suggestion box in school— at any time of day! Mr. Alioto must have announced six different big changes in school policy over the public address system today. Twice he changed a policy that had been set only yesterday. I wonder who suggested that we be allowed to bring our pets to school.

It seems the people in that town are having a lot of trouble with their computer.

October 5 War was declared in school today, and it's our class against 9C. They started it. Just after we sat down in the auditorium, Mr. Alioto said, "It's been suggested that some of the classes change places at assembly." He said "some of the classes," but he changed only two. Guess which two? What hurt was the way 9C carried on as we walked to the rear of the auditorium.

October 6 Every kid in class suggested that we change assembly places again. Later, during hide and seek, Mr. Alioto announced that there wouldn't be homework anymore. Everybody shouted and clapped, but I felt kind of sad. I wonder what's wrong with me?

October 7 I told my mother that I wanted to move to a new school. When she asked me why, I didn't know what to say. How could I explain that I was tired of seeing movies and playing games all day? She'd take me to a doctor; I'm sure she would.

October 8 I spent most of the day in the nurse's office. Cindy Marshall's snake bit me. Looking over the magazines that they have at the nurse's office now, I came across a story about that Delta computer that's running a town out in the Midwest. It seems the people in that town are having a lot of trouble with their computer. It makes them stand in lines according to their height and gives out demerits when they are late. In a way, I wish that our principal was more like the town manager.

October 13 A quiet day. Our clown phoned in sick, and the movie projector exploded. I dropped six suggestions into the box suggesting that we be allowed to do plain old schoolwork again. No one can ever know about those suggestions! We still didn't get our old seats back in assembly.

October 14 Miss James told us there would be an election in school next month. When we asked her what the election was for, she became very upset. Ronnie Franks tapped me on the shoulder and threatened, "You better vote for me next month or you'll be sorry!" When I asked him what he was running for, he answered, "Homeroom teacher."

October 16 9C was sent down to the basement for a fire drill. They were the only class to go, so you can guess whose idea the whole thing was. They didn't come back until the afternoon relay races. I think I know why we never got our assembly seats back, and why we still haven't been given plain old schoolwork, as I suggested. It's simple mathematics. There are 32 kids in 9C, and 31 kids in our class. We were outnumbered and outsuggested!

October 19 What a day! First, our water balloon fight was called off. Then, at eleven o'clock, people from the board of education broke down the front door and took over the school. At first they thought that our computer principal had <u>malfunctioned</u>. But, as it turns out, we were sent the wrong computer. We should have gotten the one that went out to the Midwest, and they should have gotten ours. *We* got the diplomat, and *they* got the dictator! Nobody would have discovered the mistake if our principal hadn't ordered ten tons of popcorn for the hot lunch program.

November 14 The last three weeks have been great! I love doing math, history, and English again. I feel as if the first month of school was all a bad dream. I'd better save this journal, or else no one will ever believe what happened. Of course, I can always show people the scar where Cindy's snake bit me.

November 16 Something's wrong again. I saw Miss James crying, and she wouldn't tell me why.

November 18 I found out why.

GLORIA WILLIS TEACHERS FIRED

IN A SURPRISE MOVE, THE NEW PRINCIPAL OF THE GLORIA WILLIS JUNIOR HIGH SCHOOL FIRED ALL OF THE SCHOOL'S TEACHERS. WHEN ASKED WHY THE TEACHERS WERE FIRED, T12H2679DELTA ANSWERED, " I HAD TO. ALL THEY DID FOR THE PAST MONTH WAS PLAY GAMES, WATCH MOVIES, EAT COTTON CANDY, AND CAMPAIGN FOR THEIR JOBS." WHEN ASKED IF REPLACEMENTS COULD BE FOUND QUICKLY, T12H2679DELTA ANSWERED, "WITHOUT A DOUBT! MANY OF THEIR REPLACEMENTS HAVE ALREADY BEEN DELIVERED."

RECALLING FACTS

Identifying setting

1. What is the setting of the story?

The setting of the story is September to November, at

Gloria Willis Junior High School.

Identifying cause and effect

2. Why was Gloria Willis Junior High School getting a new principal?

Mrs. Uxley, the present principal, was leaving, probably

to retire.

Recalling details

3. How did the new principal arrive?

The new principal was delivered in six boxes.

Recalling details

4. Where, and how, is the second Delta computer being used?

It is working as a town manager in a small midwestern

town.

Comparing and contrasting

5. Are the two Delta computers alike or different? Explain.

The computers are different: The computer working as

a town manager in a small midwestern town is

supposed to be a diplomat; the computer working as a

principal is supposed to be a dictator.

Using context clues

6. Draw a line to match each word with its meaning.

coincidence — failed to work as programmed

aerobics — events happening at about the same time that seem to be connected but really are not

malfunctioned — physical exercises that improve the circulation of the blood

Making inferences

1. Why was Carmen sorry that she told Milos about the suggestion box?

Milos told others that suggestions put in the box were carried out.

Inferring comparisons and contrasts

2. How did life at Gloria Willis Junior High School change with the delivery of the new principal?

There was a suggestion box for improvements, all of which were carried out regardless of their merit: Gym was

replaced by aerobics classes, seats were changed in classrooms and at assemblies, major policy changes were

made daily, and so on.

Distinguishing fact from opinion

3. Identify the following statements as fact or opinion. Write *F* or *O* on the lines provided.

_O_ Luis Garcia says that once they get a bad idea in one school, they usually take it around to all the others.

_F_ Miss James told us there would be an election in school next month.

_O_ I think we're in big, big trouble at Gloria Willis—really gigantic trouble.

_O_ The last three weeks have been great! I love doing math, history, and English again.

Understanding character

4. a. How did Carmen feel about Dellie when it first arrived?

Carmen was skeptical and not very enthusiastic about having a computer principal.

b. How did Carmen feel about Dellie a few weeks later?

Carmen missed the old ways so much that on October 7 she told her mother that she wanted to move to a new

school—a school without a computer principal.

c. How did Carmen feel when the board of education discovered that the wrong computer had been delivered to the school?

Carmen was happy doing math, history, and English again. She felt as though the first month of school was a bad

dream.

Making inferences

5. Why was Miss James fired?

Miss James, like the other teachers, was fired because, for the past month, she did not teach her students. Instead

she allowed them to play games and watch movies.

Drawing conclusions

6. Do you think a computer could be a good assistant to a principal? Explain.

Answers will vary. Students should consider tasks that a computer could do more efficiently than a principal, as well

as tasks that involve judgment.

In a story told from the first-person point of view, the reader is limited to the narrator's thoughts and feelings about an event. You may go back to the story to answer the questions below.

1. Who is the narrator of the story? Carmen Soares, a student at Gloria Willis Junior High School, is the narrator.

2. Is the narrator a participant in the story's events or an outsider? Explain.
   Carmen is a participant, a student at the school where the principal is a computer.

3. Why is first-person a good point of view from which to tell this story?
   The narrator was there at the school when Dellie, the wrong computer, arrived and while the computer ran the school. She has firsthand knowledge of the events.

4. In the journal entries, the narrator reveals thoughts and feelings about what is going on at Gloria Willis. List two or three of the narrator's thoughts about having a computer principal.
   Answers may vary. "It's a good thing I'm heading for high school after this year"; "As if things weren't bad enough—"; "I think we're in big, big trouble at Gloria Willis—really gigantic trouble"; "Things are getting weird, to say the least"; "In a way, I wish that our principal was more like the town manager."

5. Why does the reader not know how the other students felt, or what they thought, about the computer?
   Because the story is written from the first-person point of view, the narrator cannot enter the minds of the other characters. Carmen, the narrator, can reveal only what she sees others doing.

6. Why is it not possible for Carmen to tell in her journal entry how Miss James felt?
   A first-person narrator can only tell what he or she personally thinks or feels.

▶ Real Life Connections Write your opinion on having the teachers in your school replaced by computers. Use the first-person point of view.

Making Generalizations

___ **Reading a Social Studies Selection** _____

▶ **Background Information**

The ideas of many scientists led to the development of today's computer. The use of computers in education, government, industry, medicine, and at home is constantly increasing.

Before reading the selection, preview it. Read the headings and study the pictures. As you read, pay attention to the facts. They are important in understanding the development of the computer. However, in order to understand fully the computer's origin and development, you will have to **make generalizations** as you read.

▶ **Skill Focus**

Facts are an important part of history, but facts alone cannot provide you with a complete understanding of historical developments. You must be able to draw a principle from a limited sampling of facts or ideas. A principle is a main idea statement that covers all the facts or ideas in the sampling. This principle is called a generalization. The process is called **making generalizations.**

Examine the following facts.

- Many schools use personal computers.
- Robots are used instead of people to produce some parts of automobiles.
- Banks communicate information about accounts using network computers.
- Video games are a popular form of entertainment.

The generalization below can be made based on these four facts:

> The computer is changing the way people learn, work, communicate, and play.

▶ **Word Clues**

Sometimes you may read selections that have a specialized vocabulary. If there are no context clues to help you understand the specialized words, there may be a glossary.

Read the sentence below.

> The Computer Revolution, well underway for some time, has brought about changes more far-reaching than those of the Industrial Revolution.

Suppose you do not know the meaning of the word *computer*. There are no context clues in the sentence to help you. You will need to turn to the glossary for help. The glossary defines the technical words in a selection. A glossary entry for *computer* tells you what a computer is.

> **computer** electronic device used to calculate, store and select data, and perform operations using stored instructions and data

If no glossary is provided, you will have to look up the words in a dictionary.

Use the **glossary** following the selection to find the meaning of the underlined words in the selection. Using the glossary is like using a special, short dictionary.

▶ **Strategy Tip**

Use the glossary following "From the Abacus to the Microcomputer" to help you with the specialized vocabulary in this lesson. However, you should try first to figure out the meaning of the new word by looking at the words around it.

From the Abacus to the Microcomputer

The Computer Revolution, well underway for some time, has brought about changes more far-reaching than those of the Industrial Revolution. What makes this revolution so astonishing is that the computer did not exist 60 years ago.

Many say that the computer is a modern invention. However, many of the ideas used in computer design date back several hundred years. There has always been a need for efficient and accurate counting. Originally, people used their fingers for counting. But as their needs became more complex, this method was replaced by more sophisticated devices.

Abacus

At least 2,500 years ago, the Chinese discovered that they could handle large numbers more easily by sliding little beads on strings. Their invention, the abacus, is still in use. This early mechanical <u>calculator</u> consists of a hand-held rectangular frame. In the frame are several fixed rods strung with movable beads. Numbers are recorded by moving the beads. A skilled abacus operator can easily keep pace with a person using an office calculating machine.

The abacus has been in use since ancient times.

Machine Arithmétique

In 1647, the French mathematician Blaise Pascal invented the world's first calculating machine that could add and subtract. The machine, which he called *Machine Arithmétique,* was based on gear-driven counterwheels. Its operation was similar to that of the odometer, or speedometer, in today's automobile. Similar gear-driven counterwheels were employed in mechanical

Pascal's *Machine Arithmétique* (1647) was the world's first calculating machine.

calculators that were developed over the next 300 years.

Analytical Engine

Charles P. Babbage, an English mathematician born in 1791, was the first to move toward a machine that could go beyond addition and subtraction. In 1833, he tried to construct the first <u>digital</u> computer. He called this machine the Analytical Engine. It had all the features of a modern general-purpose computer, including memory, control, and <u>input/output</u> capabilities. In one minute, it could do 60 additions or subtractions. Most important of all, its operating procedures could be changed at will—the Analytical Engine was programmable!

Unfortunately, Babbage was unable to get the necessary support to continue his project. He died in 1871, frustrated and unhappy. However, his foresight won him recognition that he never lived to see.

Punched Cards and the Tabulating Machine

Development of punched cards and tabulating machines to process them was stimulated by the needs of the United States Census Bureau. In 1880, the census was taken as required every ten years by the Constitution. By 1885, the Census Bureau was still struggling to tabulate the collected facts of the 1880 census. It was soon apparent that this process would take longer than the ten-year span between censuses. A faster way of performing the task was needed.

Herman Hollerith, a statistician with the Census Bureau, devised a method of recording the census <u>data</u> on a strip of paper. His method was quite simple. Information was coded on a strip of paper by means of a series of punched holes in a planned pattern, with each hole having a specific meaning.

This coding system quickly proved to be an efficient method of recording information. The paper strips were soon replaced by three-by-five-inch cards, each containing the entire record of an individual or a family. These cards were the forerunners of punch cards and were called punched cards. To process these coded cards, Hollerith devised a tabulating machine capable of processing approximately 65 cards per minute.

The use of the punched card and tabulating machine saved so much money and time that Hollerith adapted his census tabulator to commercial work. To this end, he organized the Tabulating Machine Company, which later merged with other companies to become the International Business Machines Corporation (IBM).

The First Computers

In 1944, Harvard physicist Howard H. Aiken, with the aid of IBM, constructed a computing device. It performed arithmetic operations on data input using Hollerith punched cards. This machine, MARK I, was an early form of today's digital computer.

✔ By 1947, the University of Pennsylvania had built ENIAC (Electronic Numerical Integrator and Computer). ENIAC filled a space as large as a two-car garage, gobbled up 140,000 watts of electricity, and had

Hollerith's punched card tabulating machine was first used for the 1880 census.

18,000 vacuum tubes. These tubes were large and costly and produced a lot of heat. While ENIAC worked 1,000 times faster than MARK I, it had one major weakness. To perform different operations, it had to be manually rewired—a task that could take several days.

Hungarian-born John Von Neumann suggested feeding data into the computer through a keyboard. The first commercial computer to have this input device was UNIVAC I (Universal Automatic Computer). In 1951, UNIVAC I became the first mass-produced, commercially available computer.

✘ The most important contributions to the development of computers were made by John Von Neumann. His work resulted in improvements in areas from the computer's design to its electronic circuitry. With others, he developed the ideas of the <u>stored program</u> and the <u>binary number system</u>. These concepts are used in the most modern computers.

Modern Computer Generations

In recent years, computer developments have been far-reaching and numerous. Because of this rapid progress, computers have been categorized by generations, each generation featuring a significant advance over the previous generation.

First Generation (1942–1959) These computers used vacuum tubes for the storage of data. The vacuum tube was bulky, caused tremendous overheating problems, and was unreliable. These "maxi" or <u>mainframe computers</u> were large and expensive.

Second Generation (1959–1965) These computers replaced the vacuum tube with the transistor. A transistor is an electronic device made up of semiconducting materials, mostly crystals of germanium or silicon, that control the flow of electric currents. Second-generation computers were small and worked fast. They could perform a single operation in one-tenth the time it took computers that used vacuum tubes. With the second generation of computers, manufacturers began producing business-oriented computers with more efficient storage and faster input/output capabilities. These minicomputers were smaller, more reliable, and less costly than earlier models.

Computers have advanced quickly from the large mainframe computers that took up entire rooms to small desk-sized and laptop computers to multi-media systems.

Third Generation (1965–1970) These computers had microminiaturized integrated circuits on a chip, or plate, as small as a dime and as thin as paper. The components on the chip were so small that they were hardly visible to the naked eye. In addition, new input/output devices were able to communicate with computers over great distances via telephone lines, display pictures on a televisionlike screen, and accept voice input and respond in the same manner. These <u>microcomputers</u> also had tremendous memory capacities. They could work so fast that their operation was measured in <u>nanoseconds</u>.

Fourth Generation (1970–present) These computers brought the <u>microprocessor</u> into use. Essential to the microprocessor is the chip that contains the integrated circuits and the whole <u>central processing unit</u> (CPU) of a simple computer.

The Future Is Now

Microelectronics has moved from the 1940s garage-size computers to the 1990s portable and home computers, complete with <u>CD-ROM</u> drives and <u>modems</u>. People with no technical background can use computers to do a variety of tasks—from performing complex calculations to tracking a personal budget. The home computer can be linked to the <u>Internet</u>, and a fellow computer user anywhere is only a click or a keystroke away. Soon communication by computer will be as common as conversations over the telephone.

Glossary

binary having a two-number system consisting of digits 0 and 1

calculator machine that rapidly adds, subtracts, multiplies, and divides, often by electronic means

CD-ROM (Compact Disc-Read Only Memory) an optical disk containing text and multimedia data that can be retrieved by a laser beam

central processing unit control center for an entire computer system

computer electronic device used to calculate, store, and select data

data information or instructions that a computer can interpret

digital having data in number form

input data inserted or fed into a computer

Internet a worldwide computer network of networks with millions of subscribers

mainframe computer largest and most powerful of the early computers

microprocessor a chip having the capabilities of a simple computer

modem a device for sending data, usually over telephone lines, between computers

nanosecond one-billionth of a second

output information that has been processed through a computer

stored program series of commands that directs what the computer does

---

RECALLING FACTS

Recognizing sequence of events

1. Sequence the following events in the order in which they occurred.

  3 construction of Babbage's Analytical Engine

  1 invention of the abacus

  5 creation of ENIAC

  2 invention of Pascal's *Machine Arithmétique*

  6 production of UNIVAC I

  4 development of Hollerith's punched cards

Recalling details

2. How have the stages in the development of computer technology been labeled?

They have been labeled "generations."

Identifying the main idea and supporting details

3. Reread the paragraph marked with an X. Underline its main idea. Then circle two details that support the main idea.

Comparing and contrasting

4. How were first-generation computers different from the second-generation?

First-generation computers were large and inefficient

and used bulky vacuum tubes for storage.

Using context clues

5. Write three sentences, each using one or more of the specialized vocabulary words listed below.

  calculator   computer   binary

  data   digital   nanosecond

Answers will vary.

  a. A calculator makes doing arithmetic very easy.

  b. The digital computer uses the binary number system.

  c. Doctors, engineers, and lawyers can feed specialized data into a personal computer.

INTERPRETING FACTS

Inferring comparisons and contrasts

1. The ancient Chinese had a need for efficient and accurate counting. Their need resulted in the invention of the abacus. Compare their need with present-day needs.

Answers may vary. Because of the quantity of information available today, people have an even greater need for

faster and more efficient and accurate counting.

2. Reread the paragraph with a check mark next to it. Then circle the letter of the statement that best states the main idea of the paragraph.

   a. ENIAC worked faster than the earlier MARK I.

   (b.) The first fully electronic digital computer worked much faster than earlier types but was large and difficult to program.

   c. The early electronic computers contained thousands of vacuum tubes.

SKILL FOCUS

Following the box below are three groups of facts. Read each group of facts carefully. Then from the generalizations listed in the box, choose the statement that is the most appropriate generalization for each group and write the letter of the statement on the line provided. You may go back to the selection if necessary.

> a. Computers have become smaller, more efficient, and more available.
>
> b. The computer's influence is evident in business, medicine, and education.
>
> c. The limitless potential of the computer will continue to change our future.
>
> d. A standard memory chip can store about 300 pages of text.
>
> e. Many features of today's computers are the result of discoveries made many years ago.

1. **Facts** Computers are used to store employee payroll data, such as weekly salary, taxes, and benefits contributions.
   Computers are used to diagnose medical problems and to monitor patients' progress.
   Computer-assisted instruction is found in some elementary and secondary schools.

   Generalization ___b___

2. **Facts** The abacus was the first mechanical calculator.
   Babbage's Analytical Engine was programmable.
   Hollerith's punched cards and tabulating machine were used to compile information for the 1880 census.

   Generalization ___e___

3. **Facts** Transistors reduced the size of the computer and increased its working speed.
   Integrated circuitry and the microchip made communication possible over great distances via telephone lines.
   The microprocessor led to the development of portable and home computers.

   Generalization ___a___

4. **Facts** The typewriter is being replaced by the word processor.
   Information once found in books and libraries is being stored on tapes and disks.
   Two-way teleconference screens eliminate the need for traveling to meetings.
   Telecommunications provide the homebound with the means of earning a livelihood.

   Generalization ___c___

▶ Real Life Connections How can using a computer help you learn?

Inferences

Reading a Science Selection

▶ **Background Information**

As you read the following selection about computers, pay close attention to the facts. Use the facts to infer information that is not directly stated in the selection.

▶ **Skill Focus**

Sometimes you can **infer**, or figure out, information that is not stated directly in a selection. Read the following paragraphs. Try to infer what the term *computer age* means.

John was feeling sorry for himself. Two of his best friends had just gotten computer games. John really wanted one, but his parents wouldn't agree to buy it.

"I keep hearing that this is the <u>computer age</u>," said John. "If it is, I'm sure not living in it."

"You're surrounded by computers," said his mother.

John looked surprised. "What do you mean?"

"Think about it," replied his mother. "You have a digital clock radio. What controls it? Think about the heater in our car. Remember what the salesclerk said about it? And what about the thermostat on our furnace? What controls that? You are more a part of the computer age than you think."

The following clues can help you infer the meaning of the term *computer age*. John's best friends have computer games. John does not. John believes his friends are part of the computer age while he is not. You can infer that *computer age* means "a time when many people have and use computers."

You could infer other things from these paragraphs. You could infer that many common things are controlled by computers. The following clue could help you figure this out: John's mother hinted that computers were part of their digital clock radio, car, and furnace.

In your reading, you will find it easier to infer information if you go through the following steps.

1. Read carefully.

2. Think about what you've read. Be sure you understand the information that is stated.

3. Read again and look for clues to information not stated.

4. Put together information stated with information that you already know. Use clues to help you make inferences.

▶ **Word Clues**

Sometimes special terms are explained in a paragraph and also shown in a diagram. When this happens, study both the text and the diagram to help you understand the special terms.

Use **diagram** clues as well as **context** clues to find out the meaning of the three underlined terms in Figure 1 on page 166.

▶ **Strategy Tip**

Before you read "What is a Computer?" preview the boldfaced words and the labels in the diagrams. These words are an important part of computer language. Knowing such words will help you live in "the computer age!"

WHAT IS A COMPUTER?

1. A computer is an electronic machine that can store and handle information and solve problems. You could think of a computer as a file cabinet, information organizer, and problem-solver all rolled into one.

2. Computers are sometimes called electronic brains because of the kinds of work they do. A computer can do many of the things that the human brain can do. However, a computer cannot truly understand ideas. It cannot create, or make things up. Unlike human beings, a computer has no imagination. The information that goes into a computer comes from people or from machines controlled by people. The problems computers work out also come from people. Even the methods for working out the problems come from people. Computers can do only what people have built them to do.

The first computers could only compute, or mathematically work out, number problems.

3. A computer has certain advantages over the human brain. In some ways, a computer is much faster and more efficient than the human brain. The fastest computers can solve millions of problems in a few seconds. Also, computers do not make many mistakes. They can handle one dull problem after another without getting tired or bored. They are not distracted by noise or other interruptions.

4. The first computers could do only one kind of job. They could **compute**, or mathematically work out, number problems. Today's computers can do much, much more. They can store company records and make out company payrolls. They can be used as teaching aids. They can help pilots fly. They can help weather forecasters predict weather. They can ring up a bill at the supermarket. They can help the grocer keep track of stock. They can deal with words as well as numbers. If a number or word problem can be worked out in a series of fixed steps, a computer can do it.

Types of Computers

5. Not all computers are the same. They don't all work in the same way. They aren't all used for the same purposes.

Digital Computers

6. The most common computers are **digital** computers. The word *digital* comes from the word *digit*, which means "number." Before information goes into the computer, it is changed into a code in which groups of digits stand for letters, symbols, and numbers. The coded information goes into the machine as electronic signals. The computer works by reading, or counting, these signals. Most digital computers are general-purpose machines. They can do many kinds of work. For instance, a computer might store information about the people in a company. It might also process paychecks.

Analog Computers

7. **Analog** computers work by measuring physical happenings. They might measure the flow of gas and air in an engine. They might measure the speed and direction of an airplane. They change these measurements into electronic signals for the computer to process. Most analog computers are special-purpose machines. They are built to do one kind of job.

Hybrid Computers

8. Some computers both measure and count. These computers are called **hybrid** computers.

Components of Computers

9. Each digital computer has three basic components, or parts. The basic components are made up of many complex parts. These basic mechanical parts of a computer are called its **hardware**.

Central Processing Unit (CPU)

10. The main component of any computer is its **central processing unit**, or **CPU**. It is in the CPU that information and instructions are stored and processed. The CPU has a memory, or storage, unit. This unit stores information and instructions. It holds information and instructions until they are

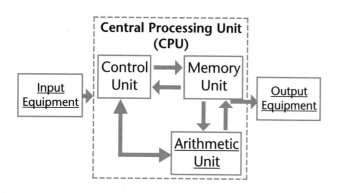

Figure 1. The three basic components of a digital computer are the CPU, the input equipment, and the output equipment.

needed. In some computers, the memory is a group of magnetic cores, or doughnut-shaped rings. In others, it is a magnetic tape, disk, or drum. Information appears on tapes and disks as magnetic spots. In the smallest computers, the memory, or even the whole CPU, may be on a tiny piece of equipment called a **chip**.

11. The CPU also has an arithmetic, or logic, unit. This is the working part of the computer. It sorts information and computes —adds, subtracts, and so on.

12. The control unit of the CPU controls the work of the computer. It is the "captain" of the computer. It gets instructions from the memory. Then it tells the memory what information to send to the arithmetic unit. Finally, it tells the arithmetic unit how to process the information.

Input Equipment

13. **Input** means information that is fed into a computer. Before a computer can do any work, information and instructions must go into it. Such information and instruction for a computer is called **software**. The input equipment takes information and instruction from the outside world. Then it puts it into code for the computer to use. Special keyboards serve as input equipment on most home computers.

Output Equipment

14. **Output** means information delivered from a computer according to coded instruction. Information can come out of a computer in many forms. It can show up on a

display screen, or it can be turned out on paper by a printer.

15. Often input and output equipment is attached to the CPU. However, input and output equipment can also be far away from the CPU. Then they are connected by cables, wires, or remote-control equipment. Remote-control is the ability to control the operation of a machine by means of radio waves.

16. The mechanical components of a computer are called hardware. The instructions and information that go into or come out of a computer are called software.

Computer Codes

17. Information and instructions enter the computer in the form of electronic signals. The computer knows only two signals. In many, these are *on* and *off*. Therefore, all information going into the machine must be put into an "on/off" code.

18. In one computer code, the digit *0* stands for *off*; the digit *1* stands for *on*. Each letter, symbol, and number that goes into the computer has its own code of eight *0*s and *1*s. Figure 2 shows that 00000010 is the code for the number *2*. This passes into the computer as *off, off, off, off, off, off, on, off*. All the *on*s show up in the memory as magnetic spots. All the *off*s show up as blank spaces.

19. Each digit in the computer code is called a **bit**. A group of eight bits is called a **byte**. You can tell if a computer has a large or small memory by the number of bytes it can hold. A kilobyte is 1000 bytes. A typical personal computer might have anywhere from 1 to 16 megabytes. A megabyte is 1 million bytes.

1 = 00000001	A = 01000001
2 = 00000010	B = 01000010
3 = 00000011	C = 01000011
4 = 00000100	(–) = 00101101
5 = 00000101	(+) = 00101011

Figure 2. These are some examples of an eight-bit computer code. Each number, letter, or symbol has a code of eight digits.

RECALLING FACTS

Recalling details
1. What is a computer?

A computer is an electronic machine that can store

and handle information and solve problems.

Recalling details
2. What are the three main components of a computer?

The three main components are the CPU, input

equipment, and output equipment.

Recalling details
3. What is hardware? software?

Hardware is the computer's mechanical parts; software

is its information and instruction.

Recalling details
4. What does each component do?

The CPU stores and processes information and

instructions; input puts information and instructions into

the machine; output delivers decoded information.

Recalling details
5. Circle the letter next to each of the following that a computer can do.
   a. think   **c.** create
   b. solve problems   **d.** understand

Recalling details
6. What is a byte?

A byte is a part of a computer's code—a group of

eight bits.

Classifying
7. Name three kinds of computers.

Three kinds of computers are digital, analog, and

hybrid.

Using context clues
8. Draw a line to match each term with its explanation.

output equipment   computer component that sorts information and solves problems

input equipment   computer component that delivers information

arithmetic unit   computer component that receives information and instructions

INTERPRETING FACTS

Making inferences
1. What kind of computer would be used to keep track of air temperature and humidity?

An analog computer would be used to keep track of air temperature and humidity.

Circle the letter next to the correct answer.

Making inferences
2. In the future, computers will probably be
   a. larger and able to do more.
   b. the same size and able to do less.
   c. smaller and able to do more.

Making inferences
3. In the future, computers will probably replace people who
   a. do large projects keeping track of things.
   b. solve problems that require inventing mathematical theories.
   c. create new ideas for designing things.

Decide which statements can be inferred from the numbered paragraph or paragraphs listed below. Put a check mark next to the statement or statements. On the lines that follow, write the phrase or sentence from the paragraph or paragraphs that helped you decide. Then explain how you inferred the information.

Paragraph 2 (check two)

a. _____ A computer cannot store as much information as the human brain.

b. _✔_ A computer is like the human brain in some ways but not in others.

c. _✔_ The human brain can think, understand, create, and process information.

Clue A computer can do many of the things that the human brain can do. However, a computer cannot truly understand ideas. It cannot create. . .

Explanation A computer cannot think, understand, or create. The human brain can. A computer can, however, work problems given to it by people.

Paragraph 3 (check two)

a. _____ Some human beings have difficulty keeping facts in their heads.

b. _✔_ Human beings get tired and bored from handling dull problems.

c. _✔_ Human beings sometimes make mistakes when they handle dull problems.

Clue Also, computers do not make many mistakes. They can handle one dull problem after another without getting tired or bored.

Explanation Among the advantages a computer has over the human brain is that it does not get tired or bored and it does not make many mistakes when handling one dull problem after another. Therefore, it must be that human beings do get tired and bored and will make mistakes in the same situation.

Paragraphs 17 and 18 (check one)

a. _____ Computer codes are all the same.

b. _____ Computer codes can be read by anyone.

c. _✔_ Computer codes stand for different things depending on the spacing of the *off*s.

Clue *0* stands for *off* . . . *1* stands for *on*. Each letter, symbol, and number that goes into the computer has its own code of eight *0*s and *1*s. All the *off*s show up as blank spaces.

Explanation The spacing of the *off*s changes the pattern of the codes.

▶ **Real Life Connections** Make a prediction: What size computer will you use ten years from today?

Computer Language

Reading a Mathematics Selection

▶ Background Information

In the 1960s, the National Aeronautics Space Administration, or NASA, used computers during their many space flights. These computers helped make landing on the moon a reality. However, these computers were bulky and expensive. As a matter of fact, they took up entire rooms.

Today there are **laptop** computers (computers designed to fit on a person's lap) that have the same capabilities as a room full of computers and are relatively inexpensive.

How is all this possible? The keyboard of a computer looks like the keyboard of a typewriter. However, the similarities stop there. A computer can do much more than a typewriter. It can make calculations in a matter of seconds that would take a person hours, or even days, to complete.

Computers are programmed to do many different things. This is done by typing in certain phrases. These phrases tell the computer what to do. A computer language is a group of these phrases. In

"Understanding Computer Language," you will learn about the computer language called **BASIC**.

▶ Skill Focus

In order for a computer to perform, it must be programmed, or instructed, through its input devices. In other words, you "talk" to a computer using its input devices. This talking is done in a special language that the computer understands. By giving instructions in a computer language, you could ask a computer to solve a problem. The computer would present the solution to the problem through its output devices.

There are many types of computers. Programmers are people who "talk" with computers in different languages. Although different languages are used to program computers, all computers process information the same way. Computers use binary numbers. The word *binary* means "a number system that has 2 as its base." This number system uses only two digits, 0 and 1. The binary number system is used as the basis for computing

because the digits 0 and 1 can be represented by electric current that is either turned on (1) or turned off (0).

▶ Word Clues

When reading "Understanding Computer Language," look for these important words: *input devices, output devices, central processing unit, BASIC, PRINT, LET, END, RUN, GOTO,* and *compiler.* They will help you to understand more about computers.

▶ Strategy Tip

As you read the selection, keep in mind that learning a computer language is something like learning a foreign language. The words may be familiar to you, but you need to learn their meanings as they apply to computers.

Understanding Computer Language

Computers are used because they can solve problems more quickly than people can. A computer gets its instructions from various **input devices,** such as a **keyboard,** a **mouse,** a **light scanner,** and a **light pen.** The instructions present a problem to the computer. The computer presents the solution on a monitor. The solution can also be delivered by a printer or a modem. These viewing mechanisms are called output devices. The instructions are carried out in the **central processing unit,** or **CPU.**

A programmer needs to be able to communicate with the computer in a language that it understands. Some computer languages, such as COBOL, FORTRAN, C, and C++, are used for business. Others, such as LISP and PROLOG, are used in artificial intelligence. BASIC (Beginners All-purpose Symbolic Instruction Code), is the simplest to learn and easiest to use.

Learning BASIC is like learning a foreign language. Commands in BASIC have very precise meanings. The computer understands commands only if they are written in a certain way.

Each line of a program has a number. The lines are read by the computer in the order in which they are numbered. After the program has been put in, the programmer types *RUN.* Then the program is interpreted by the CPU, and the output is shown.

For example, *PRINT* tells the computer to write whatever follows. The programmer might input this statement.

10 PRINT "I AM A COMPUTER"

The output would be I AM A COMPUTER.

The programmer might input these lines.
10 LET X = 32
20 PRINT X
30 END

The output would be 32.

Line 10 puts the number 32 into the memory of the computer. The memory labels that number as *X.* Line 20 tells the computer to output whatever is in memory *X.*

The last line of a program is always *END.* It tells the CPU that the program is over.

The programmer could input this program.
10 PRINT "I AM A"
20 PRINT "COMPUTER"
30 GOTO 20
40 END

The command *GOTO* tells the computer to go back to line 20. The computer would read line 10, line 20, and line 30 and then go back to line 20, on to line 30, back to line 20, on to line 30, and so on. This is called a **loop** because the computer makes a circle as it reads the lines. The program would never end unless the programmer stopped it by pressing a key on the keyboard. The output would look like this:

I AM A
COMPUTER
COMPUTER
COMPUTER (and so on)

When a program is put into the computer, the instructions are translated into a language that the machine understands. This is called a machine language. The **compiler** translates the numbers and letters of machine language into **binary numbers.** *Zero* can be represented as a broken circuit—an electric current that is turned off. *One* can be represented as a completed circuit—an electric current that is turned on. All the numbers and letters of a language can be changed into current turned off and current turned on.

RECALLING FACTS

Recalling details
1. Name three input devices. Three input devices are the keyboard, mouse, and light scanner.

Recalling details
2. Explain the following commands.

a. PRINT tells the computer to print something or to display it on a monitor.

b. END tells the computer the input is finished.

c. GOTO tells the computer to go to a certain line.

Inferring cause and effect

1. What do the quotation marks do in this line? 10 PRINT "HOW ARE YOU?"

They tell the computer where to start and stop

printing.

Drawing conclusions

2. What would the computer print if you gave the command PRINT X? PRINT "X"?

It would print the value of x; x

SKILL FOCUS

A. Write the letter of the output on the line next to the input.

Input

_d_ **1.** 10 PRINT "HELLO"
20 PRINT "GOODBYE"
30 END

_c_ **2.** 10 LET X = 7
20 LET Y = 2
30 PRINT X + Y
40 END

_b_ **3.** 10 LET X = 7
20 LET Y = 2
30 PRINT "X + Y ="
40 PRINT X + Y
50 END

_e_ **4.** 10 LET X = 9
20 PRINT "THE ANSWER IS"; X
30 END

_a_ **5.** 10 PRINT "HELLO"
20 LET X = 5
30 PRINT X
40 PRINT "GOODBYE"
50 END

Output

a. HELLO
5
GOODBYE

b. X + Y =
9

c. 9

d. HELLO
GOODBYE

e. THE ANSWER IS 9

B. Complete the following programs so that they will have the output shown.

1. Output: A COMPUTER MAKES YOUR LIFE EASIER.
Program: 10 PRINT "A COMPUTER MAKES YOUR LIFE EASIER."
20 END

2. Output: I AM
YOUR
FRIEND
Program: 10 PRINT "I AM"
20 PRINT "YOUR"
30 PRINT "FRIEND"
40 END

3. Output: HELLO
GOODBYE
HELLO
GOODBYE
(and so on)
Program: 10 PRINT "HELLO"
20 PRINT "GOODBYE"
30 GOTO 10
40 END

▶ **Real Life Connections** What computer languages are used on the computers in your school or local library?

Reference Books

You use **reference book**s to find all kinds of information about a subject that you are studying or want to know more about. You need to know the kind of information contained in each reference book so that you can select the one you need. By using the right reference books, you can locate the kind of information you need.

Suppose that some friends of yours are discussing a gibbon and you don't know what a gibbon is. You can find the word *gibbon* in the **dictionary**. You already know that a dictionary defines words. It also shows how words are spelled, pronounced, and divided into syllables, and what parts of speech they are. Because many people do not know what a gibbon looks like, some dictionaries include an illustration with the entry.

Gibbon is the smallest of the apes. It also ranges over a wider area than the other members of the ape family— the chimpanzee, gorilla, and orangutan. The gibbon lives in the forests of the Indian state of Assam, and in Burma, Thailand, Malaysia, Indonesia, and elsewhere in Southeast Asia. There are several species of gibbons. All have long arms and legs, but no tail. A gibbon weighs about 15 pounds (7 kilograms) and stands about 3 feet (91 centimeters) high. It ranges from black to pale brown.

Gibbons live in the tops of trees and rarely come to the ground. They eat fruits and leaves. Gibbons use their arms to swing from branch to branch. They also walk on top of tree branches using only their legs. This way of walking is similar to that of human beings. Gibbons live in family groups that usually consist of a male, a female, and one or two of their young. A gibbon family claims an area called a *territory* and uses loud calls and songs to warn other families to stay away.

From the *World Book Encyclopedia.* © 1996 World Book, Inc. By permission of the publisher.

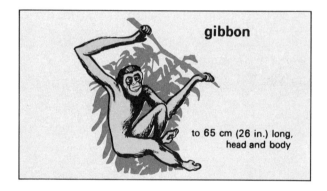

gib•bon (gib′ ən) *n.* a small ape of southeastern Asia, with very long arms.

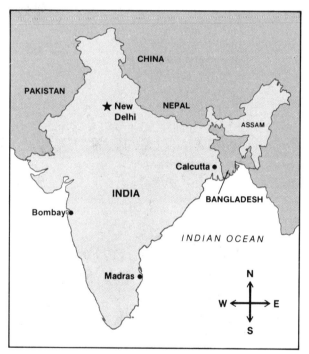

After you learn what the word *gibbon* means, you may want to find out more about the animal. You may become curious about how small an ape it is, exactly what part of southeastern Asia it is from, or if it can be found at a zoo. The next reference book that you would use is an **encyclopedia** because it contains articles on many different subjects. An encyclopedia would provide an explanation of a gibbon that is more detailed than a dictionary definition.

After you have read the encyclopedia article for *gibbon,* you may become curious about Assam, one of the places where the gibbon lives. You may want to look at a map to see the location of Assam in India. The best reference book to check is an atlas. An **atlas** contains different kinds of maps.

Once you learn where Assam is, you may want some specific information about India and its size and population. To locate this kind of information, you would use an almanac. An **almanac** is a book with the most up-to-date information on many different subjects. Although an encyclopedia may provide some of the same information, it may not be as current. The information in an **almanac** is more current than information found in other references because it is published every year. An almanac contains weather reports, statistics, and facts about the United States and other countries, current events, sports facts, world records, and other interesting information.

Area and Population by Country
Mid-1993 Estimates

Country	Area[1]	Population	Country	Area[1]	Population
Afghanistan	250,000	17,400,000	Hungary	35,920	10,300,000
Albania	11,100	3,300,000	Iceland	39,770	300,000
Algeria	919,590	27,300,000	India	1,269,340	897,400,000
Angola	481,350	9,500,000	Indonesia	741,100	187,600,000
Antigua and Barbuda	170	100,000	Iran	636,290	62,800,000
Argentina	1,068,300	33,500,000	Iraq	167,920	19,200,000

Complete each sentence by underlining the name of the correct reference book. More than one answer may be correct.

1. If you want to know how to spell the word *cantaloupe,* you should use the _____.

    atlas   <u>dictionary</u>   almanac

2. If you want to find out what kinds of crops are grown in South America,

    you should use the _____ or the _____.

    almanac   <u>atlas</u>   <u>encyclopedia</u>

3. If you want to know how many people were married in the United States

    in 1982, you should use the _____.

    atlas   encyclopedia   <u>almanac</u>

4. If you want to find out how to pronounce the word *kayak,* you should use the _____.

    encyclopedia   almanac   <u>dictionary</u>

5. If you want to learn which types of birds live in cold climates, you should use the _____.

    dictionary   <u>encyclopedia</u>   almanac

6. If you want to find out how many miles (kilometers) it is from Quincy,

    Massachusetts, to Newport, Rhode Island, you should use the _____.

    <u>atlas</u>   dictionary   encyclopedia

7. If you want to know what kind of boat a schooner is, you should

    use the _____ or the _____.

    <u>encyclopedia</u>   almanac   <u>dictionary</u>

8. If you want to see how to divide the word *molecule* into syllables, use the _____.

    atlas   <u>dictionary</u>   almanac

9. If you want to compare the population of Iceland in 1970 to that of last year, you should

    use the _____.

    dictionary   <u>almanac</u>   atlas

Reading a Job Application

When you apply for a job, many companies will require you to fill out a job application. A **job application** is a written form that asks for information about your work experience, your education, and your interests.

Study the sample job application below.

CAL COMPUTER COMPANY	**APPLICATION FOR EMPLOYMENT**			(Type or print in ink)

PERSONAL

Name	Last: LORENZ	First: DALE	Middle/Maiden: SARAH	Telephone: 555-7431
Address	Number: 1154	Street: 23rd Street	City: SANTA MONICA,	State: CA	Zip: 90404	Social Security No.: 219-68-8429

EDUCATION

	Name and Location	Dates Attended From	To	Diploma Received
High School	SCOTTSDALE HIGH SCHOOL SCOTTSDALE, AZ	9/85	6/88	HIGH SCHOOL DIPLOMA
College	ROLLINS COLLEGE SCOTTSDALE, AZ	9/88	6/92	B.S.
Other	COMPUTER TRAINING INSTITUTE SANTA MONICA, CA	9/94	1/95	COMPUTER CERTIFICATE

Hobbies and Interest SWIMMING, PLAYING THE PIANO, SPEAKING SPANISH

EMPLOYMENT RECORD (Start with last job)

Name and Location of Employer	Dates From	To	Job Title	Name of Supervisor
LINDSEY AND STERLING ACCOUNTANTS SANTA MONICA, CA	1/95	7/95	BOOKKEEPER	BERT GOLDBERG
DAILY NEWS SCOTTSDALE, AZ	7/92	8/94	WORD PROCESSOR	ROSA ALVAREZ

REFERENCES (Not former employers)

	Name	Address	Telephone
1.	MS. DIANE BARTON	90 WILSHIRE BLVD. LOS ANGELES, CA	555-4418
2.	DR. LOUIS GRAYSON	880 W. CAMELBACK SCOTTSDALE, AZ	602-555-3099

EMPLOYMENT DESIRED

Position COMPUTER PROGRAMMER   Date you can start 8/17/95   (Check one) Full-time ✔ Part-time ___

Today's Date 8/10/95   Signature Dale S. Lorenz

Most job applications begin with a section for personal information. The first space is for your first, middle, and last names. Sometimes a married woman writes her maiden name, or her last name before she was married, in the space for the middle name. Spaces are provided for your address and telephone number and your social security number. Everyone needs a social security number to get a job.

Most job applications have sections to fill out about your education or training. Certain jobs require a particular type of education or training.

Job applications also have a section on the jobs that you have held in the past. This section may be labeled "Work Experience" or "Employment Record."

Applications often require you to provide references. References are people who know you well enough to give information about you and how you might perform on a job. Family members and friends should not be listed as references. Possible references might include a teacher; a family doctor; or a pastor, priest, or rabbi. You should ask these people if you can use them as references before you do so.

Applications may ask for other information, such as your interests and hobbies—for example, playing tennis or speaking French.

A section labeled "Employment Desired" may provide a space for the name of the job that you want and the date that you can begin. You usually sign your name at the end of the application.

Print in ink or type your answers on the application. A neat application with complete answers will make a good impression on an employer.

Correct grammar and spelling and clear expression will also make a good impression.

A. Circle the letter next to the phrase that correctly completes each sentence.

1. The debating club, the swim team, and cheerleading are examples of
   a. extracurricular activities.　b. references.　c. hobbies.

2. An employer is a
   a. person hired by another person or company.
   b. person or company that hires people.
   c. person who can give information about your education.

3. A supervisor is a
   a. person who oversees your work.
   b. place where you have a job.
   c. family member who can give information about you.

4. An example of a good reference to use on a job application might be
   a. an employer you did not get along with.
   b. your best friend.
   c. your English teacher.

5. An application may ask for the name of your supervisor at a previous job so that this person
   a. will be informed if you get another job.
   b. may be offered the job that you applied for.
   c. may be called to confirm information about you.

6. This application does not ask for the applicant's
   a. address.　b. date of birth.　c. phone number.

7. After the applicant graduated from college, she
   a. went to the Computer Training Institute.
   b. worked for Lindsey and Sterling as a keypunch operator.
   c. worked for the *Daily News* as a word processor.

8. You can tell that the applicant does not have a job now because
   a. the ending date of her last job is before the date of the application.
   b. she said she could not start working until she left her current job.
   c. she had time to apply for another job.

B. Use the information on the application to answer each question.

1. Who filled out the application? <u>Dale Lorenz</u>

2. What job is she applying for? <u>computer programmer</u>

3. What was her last job? <u>bookkeeper</u>

4. How long did she work at her last job? <u>6 months</u>

5. In what place did she probably live for many years? <u>Scottsdale, Arizona</u>

   How do you know? <u>She attended high school and college there and worked at the Scottsdale Daily News.</u>

6. How soon can she begin a new job? <u>8/17/95</u>

7. According to this application, who is the employer? <u>Cal Computer Company</u>

Context Clue Words

The following words are treated as context clue words in the lessons indicated. Lessons that provide instruction in a particular context clue type include an activity requiring students to use context clues to derive word meanings. Context clue words appear in the literature, social studies, and science selections and are underlined or footnoted for ease of location.

Word	Lesson
adept	11
advocated	35
aerobics	48
Apollo	1
arithmetic unit	50
aspired	20
avalanche	34
blockaded	12
butterfly	41
calculator	49
catastrophe	33
CD-ROM	49
central processing unit	49
chlorine	41
clamber	41
coincidence	48
comet	3
computer	49
coordinates	13
cove	20
Crete	1
cultivation	22
data	49
decathlon	42
demonstrations	12
detention camps	21
digital	49
dismantling	12
donned	2
dubious	35
ebbing	20
effort arm	43
eke	34
endeavor	2
fatigue	41
fulcrum	43
gradually	35
grappling	33
hemispheres	13
innovations	22
input	49
input equipment	50
internal	13
Internet	49
involuntary	13
labyrinth	1
mainframe computers	49
malfunctioned	48
man-of-war	21
marine	22
microcomputers	49
microprocessor	49
modems	49
moderate	34
moored	22
moors	33
nanoseconds	49
orbit	3
origin	42
output	49
output equipment	50
outspoken	11
pentathlon	42
priority	41
proportion	11
public opinion	21
reconstruct	12
reflects	3
reparations	12
resistance arm	43
revive	42
revolve	3
rifts	35
rotates	3
serene	11
sheer	33
Sicily	1
spectator	2
technicians	48
tenders	21
upheaval	34
vastness	2
winch	20

Concept Words

In lessons that feature social studies, science, or mathematics selections, words that are unique to the content and whose meanings are essential to the selection are treated as concept words. Many of these words appear in boldface type and are often followed by a phonetic respelling and a definition.

Word	Lesson
all together	23
analog	50
aquaculture	22
asteroid belt	3
asteroids	3
asthenosphere	35
autonomic nervous system	13
average	23
axon	13
Barringer Meteorite	3
BASIC	51
binary numbers	51
bit	50
byte	50
central nervous system	13
central processing unit	50
cerebellum	13
cerebrum	13
change	36
chip	50
circle graphs	44
coma	3
comets	3
compiler	51
compute	50
connecting nerves	13
continental drift	35
data	44
decimal	36
dendrites	13
digital	50
divided	23
Earth	3
effort	43
effort distance	43
fixed pulley	43
fraction	36
Halley's Comet	3
hardware	50
hybrid	50
inner planets	3
input	50
input devices	51
intersect	4
Jupiter	3
keyboard	51
krill	22
label	44
larvae	22
lever	43
light pen	51
light scanner	51
line	4
lithosphere	35
loop	51
machine	43
Mars	3
mechanical advantage	43
medulla	13
Mercury	3
meteor	3
meteorite	3
meteoroids	3
mil	14
motor nerves	13
mouse	51
movable pulley	43
Neptune	3
neuron	13
ocean-floor spreading	35
outer planets	3
output	50
Pangaea	35
parallel	4
parasympathetic system	13
per	23
percent	36
peripheral nervous system	13
perpendicular	4
plane	4
planets	3
plankton	22
plate tectonics	35
Pluto	3
point	4
pulley	43
reflex action	13
resistance	43
resistance distance	43
Saturn	3
sectors	44
sensory nerves	13
software	50
sympathetic system	13
theory	35
twice as much	23
Uranus	3
Venus	3

Read the following selection. Then choose the best answer for each question. Mark your answer on the answer sheet.

O Mighty Sea

1. The research submarine *Alvin* sank beneath the sunlit surface of the Caribbean Sea. On the surface, the sub had pitched and rolled. But now the sub was sinking peacefully through the fading sunlight.

2. I glanced around the sphere, the sub's interior, and then looked at Jim Ballard, the pilot. "This is like being inside a Swiss watch," I said.

3. He grinned. "You'll get used to it, Anne," he said.

4. The sphere was only 80 inches in diameter. In this very tight space, the three of us—Jim, Ted Moskey, and I—would have to work for the next six hours. Each of us had specific assignments to do. Luckily, our tasks didn't require movement within the sphere.

5. A voice startled me. It was Emory Kirshen, the surface controller on board the ship *Jasper*.

6. "*Alvin*, this is *Jasper*," Kirshen said. "What are your readings?"

7. Jim looked at the depth meter. "We're nearing 1,200 feet," he said, "and we're descending at 90 feet a minute."

8. As we continued our descent, the *Alvin's* interior became darker and darker. Soon we were in total darkness. To save power, the sub's outside lights were kept off. Our only illumination came from three small lights inside the sphere.

9. Hanging over Jim's instrument panel was a small silver medallion. I looked more closely at it. There were words engraved on the medallion: "Be kind to us, O mighty Sea."

10. I smiled to myself. The sea is neither kind nor cruel, I thought. It's only a force of nature, which is being conquered by technology.

11. I looked over at Ted. Like me, he was a geologist. He had made dives before in the *Alvin*; this was my first dive. Our mission was to bring up photographs and rock samples from the sea bed.

12. I glanced at the depth meter. The sub was nearing 8,000 feet. We were within 200 feet of the bottom. Jim turned on the sub's outside lights and cameras.

13. Outside my view port, time seemed to stand still. Fish glided by in the unusual brightness. I felt relaxed in the quiet undersea world.

14. "We're at 40 feet," Jim reported to Emory. "We have visual." A moment later, we touched bottom. "*Jasper*, we've landed. We will begin sampling at Station One. We'll call back when we've finished. Over."

15. "Roger, *Alvin*. Good luck," came Emory's voice.

16. Through my view port, I could make out the sea bed, a rough terrain of deep cracks and giant boulders.

17. "It's time to begin," I said to Ted. "Let's try to get a rock sample every hundred meters."

18. Jim began to operate the sub's mechanical claw. Technology had certainly made our work easier. All Jim had to do was to guide the mechanical claw, and we could collect a number of rock samples without ever getting wet.

19. After about twenty minutes of work, we had picked up five rock samples. The sub's claw dropped each sample into a numbered section of a tray mounted at the front of the sub.

20. We continued cruising about six feet above the bottom. While Jim was busy collecting rock samples, Ted and I recorded our observations on a small tape recorder. Mounted outside the sub were two cameras that automatically took pictures of the sea floor every ten seconds. Through his view port, Jim took more photos with a hand-held camera.

21. As we cruised along the sea floor, we spotted a broad crack across a lava flow. Jim brought the sub down into the wide fissure.

22. "Let's sample the lava while we're here," Ted said.

23. For the next ten minutes, we collected volcanic rock samples. Then we started to rise

out of the fissure. The sub shuddered to a standstill.

24. "What's wrong?" asked Ted.

25. "We've gone too far into the fissure. I think the walls are holding us in," Jim said. "I'll have to back it out."

26. Jim put the sub into reverse. It shuddered and held fast.

27. "Hang on. I'll just jockey it back and forth a bit," said Jim.

28. The sub careened forward, then pitched back. "Come on," Jim said, softly. Slowly, he edged the sub forward, then back.

29. "It's getting free," Jim said. He looked at me and grinned. "It's like trying to back a large car out of a parking space for a compact."

30. The sub edged back out of the fissure. "That's it," Jim said. The *Alvin* shuddered. "Just a little more and—"

31. Suddenly, an ear-splitting roar cut through the sphere. The interior lights went out. Something hit my hand. Then it was deadly still.

32. I clicked on the emergency power switch. The sphere remained in darkness.

33. "Jim! Ted!" I called.

34. "Anne." It was Ted.

35. "You all right, Ted."

36. "I'm bleeding—forehead. Where's Jim?"

37. "I don't know." I groped around in the dark. Jim was slumped over his instrument panel. I felt his pulse. "Jim's unconscious," I said. "But his pulse is all right." I found an emergency flashlight, then reached for the first-aid kit. "What happened, Ted?"

38. "I'm not sure. A boulder must have shaken loose above us and slammed into the sub."

39. As I placed a bandage on Ted's forehead, I saw that my left hand was bruised. Ted's face was streaked with blood. It was getting difficult to breathe. The boulder, or whatever had slammed into the *Alvin*, had damaged the life support and emergency breathing systems. We had also lost phone contact with the surface ship.

40. For a moment, fear took hold of me. What if the sub wouldn't rise? What if the ballast release had also been damaged?

41. I reached for the release lever with my uninjured hand and pulled it. Usually the sub would edge up as the steel ballast dropped from the *Alvin*. I waited. The sub remained motionless. The ballast had not dropped from the sub. I bit my lip, then pulled the lever again.

42. Suddenly, the sub lifted. We were drifting up!

43. The ascent was like a dream. I must have blacked out as the sub went up.

44. The pitching and rolling of the sub brought me to. Water slid off the view port. I could see the *Jasper* resting on the sunlit surface.

45. I turned away from the view port. Above the instrument panel, the silver medallion swayed from side to side. Sunlight struck the medallion, making it glow.

1. The main character's conflict is with

　a. himself or herself.

　b. another character.

　c. an outside force.

2. Which sentence best describes this conflict?

　a. The main character is afraid that the sub will be unable to rise.

　b. The main character thinks that he or she can solve any problem.

　c. The main character tries to revive Jim.

3. The main character faces this conflict when the sub

　a. is damaged.

　b. reaches the sea floor.

　c. begins its dive.

4. How is the conflict resolved?

　a. Ted releases the ballast, and the sub rises to the surface.

　b. Anne pulls the release lever, the ballast drops, and the sub rises.

　c. Jim takes over command of the *Alvin* and manages to save the sub.

5. The first important event that leads to the climax occurs when
   a. the sub enters the fissure.
   b. the sub begins its descent.
   c. the sub reaches the ocean floor.

6. Which event causes Anne to become involved in resolving the conflict?
   a. *The Jasper* orders the sub crew to surface.
   b. Ted and Jim are both injured.
   c. The sub develops a power failure.

7. The most exciting part of the story occurs when
   a. Anne tries to release the ballast.
   b. the sub enters the fissure.
   c. Jim jockeys the sub out of the fissure.

8. The story ends with
   a. the *Jasper* sending a rescue team.
   b. Jim regaining consciousness.
   c. the *Alvin* reaching the surface.

9. When does the story take place?
   a. in the present
   b. about fifty years ago
   c. about a hundred years ago

10. Where does the main action of the story take place?
    a. the surface ship
    b. the Caribbean Sea
    c. the interior of a sub

11. What is Anne's first reaction to the setting?
    a. She thinks the sub is too cramped.
    b. She is confused by all the instruments.
    c. She enjoys looking out the view port.

12. What unusual feature in this setting does Anne notice?
    a. the steel ballast
    b. the silver medallion
    c. the mechanical claw

13. What is the author's message?
    a. Despite technology, the sea is still a mysterious and dangerous force.
    b. During undersea explorations, one must always be on guard.
    c. Working in a research submarine can be a dangerous but rewarding experience.

14. At the beginning of the story, Anne is
    a. amused by the silver medallion.
    b. upset about the silver medallion.
    c. impressed by the silver medallion.

15. By the end of the story, Anne has learned to
    a. get along well with others.
    b. respect the sea.
    c. handle a research submarine.

16. Which of the following titles would also be appropriate for this story?
    a. "The *Alvin* Dives"
    b. "Dangers of the Caribbean Sea"
    c. "The Still Unconquered Sea"

17. What is the unstated main idea of paragraph 4?
    a. The sub's sphere was small.
    b. The sub had a three-person crew.
    c. The sub's working space was cramped.

18. What is the unstated main idea of paragraph 20?
    a. The sub cruised along the ocean floor.
    b. As the *Alvin* cruised, the sub and crew recorded data.
    c. Cameras were an important part of the mission.

19. What is the unstated main idea of the last paragraph in the selection?
    a. the *Alvin* had successfully returned to the surface.
    b. The sea had spared them.
    c. Anne was happy to be alive.

20. Who is the narrator of the story?
    a. Jim
    b. Ted
    c. Anne

21. Why is first-person point of view a good way of telling this story?
    a. The narrator took part in the story's events.
    b. The narrator reports only the facts and not his or her feelings.
    c. The narrator tells what each character thinks and feels about the event.

22. A disadvantage of this point of view is that the narrator cannot
  a. describe his or her feelings.
  b. enter the minds of the other characters.
  c. make judgments about the story's events.

23. Which of these events did the narrator not witness?
  a. Jim taking photos through the view port
  b. the reaction of the crew on board the *Jasper* when the *Alvin* surfaced
  c. a large boulder coming loose and falling toward the *Alvin*

24. Choose the correct definition of the word *port* as it is used in paragraph 13.
  a. place where boats can anchor
  b. the left side of a ship
  c. shortened form of *porthole*

25. The word *illumination* in paragraph 8 means
  a. "light inside a sub."
  b. "to decorate with lights."
  c. "supply of light."

26. The word *fissure* in paragraph 21 means
  a. "lava."
  b. "crack."
  c. "cliff."

Read the following selection. Then choose the best answer for each question. Mark your answer on the answer sheet.

The Panama Canal

1. Until this century, there was only one way for a ship traveling east to reach the Atlantic Ocean from the Pacific Ocean. That was the long route around Cape Horn, the southernmost tip of South America. Ship crews and passengers dreaded "rounding the Horn." The currents of the Atlantic and Pacific oceans meet at Cape Horn, causing sudden, terrible storms. In addition, thick fogs often blanket the area, and dangerous reefs lie just below the water's surface. Many ships sailing around Cape Horn have been wrecked on the reefs or have sunk in the storms.

2. Because the route around Cape Horn was long and dangerous, a shortcut—a passage between the two oceans—was needed. The best location for creating such a shortcut had been known for many years. In 1502, on his fourth and last voyage to the New World, Christopher Columbus was told by natives of Central America about a "narrow land between two seas." Columbus found this narrow land, the Isthmus of Panama, but he did not explore it. In 1513, the isthmus was crossed by Vasco Núñez de Balboa (bal BOH ə), a Spanish explorer. Balboa was the first European to see the Pacific Ocean from the Americas.

The First Attempt

3. Many years passed before an attempt was made to build a canal across the Isthmus of Panama. In the 1860s, France built the Suez Canal to link the Mediterranean and Red Seas. French government leaders decided to follow this achievement with another engineering feat—the building of the Panama Canal. The job was entrusted to Ferdinand de Lesseps (de LES əps). He was given responsibility for the project because his company had built the Suez Canal.

4. De Lesseps and his workers soon learned that building a canal in Panama was much more difficult than at Suez. The Suez

Canal had been dug through flat desert sands. In contrast, Panama had steep mountains, thick jungles, and wild rivers. Worse still, Panama was one of the most disease-ridden parts of the world. Workers soon began to die from yellow fever and malaria. Digging progressed slowly, interrupted by landslides that destroyed months of backbreaking work. Huge sums of money were spent on the project. Finally, in 1889, the company ran out of money, and the French had to give up the effort. They left behind tons of earth-moving equipment, miles of shallow ditches, and cemeteries where thousands of workers lay buried.

America Enters the Picture

5. For many years, the United States had expressed interest in building a canal across the Isthmus of Panama, but it was not until the Spanish-American War in 1898 that Americans became convinced of the need for a canal.

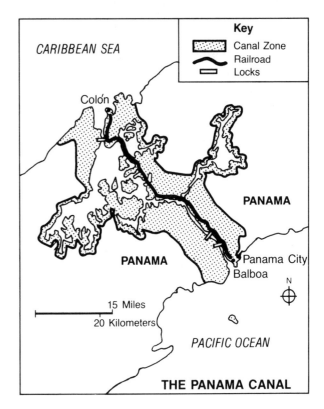

THE PANAMA CANAL

During the war, the battleship *Oregon,* sailing in the Pacific, was ordered to join the American fleet in the Atlantic Ocean. It took the *Oregon* three months to reach the fighting in Cuba. The battleship had to sail around South America, a trip of nearly 13,000 miles (20,800 kilometers). If there had been a canal across Panama, the trip would have been about 4,500 miles (7,200 kilometers).

6. Determined to build a canal across the isthmus, the U.S. government began negotiations with Colombia to buy land for the canal. The talks broke down, however, when the Colombian government refused to accept the price offered and asked for more money. An angry President Theodore Roosevelt decided to arrange terms with Panama instead.

7. Panama was part of Colombia, but for years it had tried to become independent. On November 2, 1903, the United States Navy ship *Nashville* sailed into the port of Colón in Panama. The next day, Panamanians revolted, and U.S. marines blocked the advance of Colombian troops. Panama declared its freedom from Colombia. Two weeks later, Panama and the United States signed a treaty that granted the United States a 10-mile-wide canal zone across Panama.

Digging the Big Ditch

8. When the French had tried to build a canal twenty years before, the causes of malaria and yellow fever were still a mystery. Now the cause of both diseases was known. Under the direction of William C. Gorgas of the U.S. Army Medical Corps, plans were carried out to destroy certain kinds of mosquitoes that caused malaria and yellow fever. Ditches were sprayed with oil. Swamps were drained. Catch basins used for drinking water were removed. Fresh running water was piped through the canal zone. Houses were disinfected and windows were screened. In just a few years, yellow fever was wiped out, and malaria was greatly reduced. Panama was no longer the "pesthole of the world."

9. The Panama Canal was a tremendous engineering achievement, and problems in building the canal were likewise tremendous. A huge dam, one of the largest in the world, had to be built across the wild Chagres River. A deep cut nine miles long (14.4 kilometers) had to be made through a range of mountains. Workers were plagued by hundreds of landslides; many were killed by the slides. Because the Pacific Ocean is a higher body of water than the Atlantic Ocean, locks had to be built. These water-filled chambers with gates at either end were needed to raise and lower ships from one water level to another.

10. In charge of building the canal was Colonel George W. Goethals (GOH thəlz), an army engineer. His labor force—totaling 43,400 workers—came from many parts of the world, including the United States, the West Indies, Italy, and Spain. To carry the earth and rocks away, they used 105 steam shovels, 161 locomotives, and 1,700 railroad cars. After seven years of work, the Panama Canal was completed in 1914. At a cost of thousands of lives and $400 million, the shortcut between the Atlantic and Pacific oceans was finally achieved.

27. Choose the main idea of paragraph 2.

   a. Because the route around Cape Horn was long and dangerous, a shortcut—a passage between the two oceans—was needed.

   b. The best location for a shortcut route had been known for many years.

   c. Balboa was the first European to see the Pacific Ocean from the Americas.

28. Choose the main idea of paragraph 4.

   a. De Lesseps and his workers soon learned that building a canal was much more difficult in Panama than at Suez.

   b. Digging progressed slowly, interrupted by landslides that destroyed months of backbreaking work.

   c. Finally, in 1889, the company ran out of money, and the French had to give up the effort.

29. Choose the main idea of paragraph 9.
    a. The Panama Canal was a tremendous engineering achievement, and the problems in building the canal were likewise tremendous.
    b. A deep cut nine miles long (14.4 kilometers) had to be made through a range of mountains.
    c. Because the Pacific Ocean is a higher body of water than the Atlantic Ocean, locks had to be built.

30. What is the unstated main idea of paragraph 1?
    a. The route around Cape Horn was long and very dangerous.
    b. People were afraid of sailing around Cape Horn.
    c. Many ships never returned from trips around South America.

31. What is the unstated main idea of paragraph 3?
    a. France was a great engineering country.
    b. France wanted to be the first nation to build a canal across Panama.
    c. France was the first nation to attempt building the Panama Canal.

32. What is the unstated main idea of paragraph 10?
    a. Building the Panama Canal took many years of hard work.
    b. The dream of Columbus had finally come true.
    c. In both lives and dollars, the cost of building the canal was high.

33. The main idea of paragraph 5 is that Americans became convinced of the need for a canal during the Spanish-American War. Which detail supports this main idea?
    a. The battleship *Oregon* was ordered to reinforce the American fleet in the Atlantic Ocean.
    b. It took the battleship *Oregon* three months to reach the fighting in Cuba.
    c. The United States had long been interested in building a canal in Panama.

34. Find the main idea of paragraph 8. Then choose the detail that supports the main idea.
    a. Fresh running water was piped through the canal zone.
    b. Now the cause of these diseases was known.
    c. Panama was no longer the "pesthole of the world."

35. The reason the French gave up their effort to build the canal was that
    a. too many workers died.
    b. they ran out of money.
    c. the problems were too difficult.

36. Because certain kinds of mosquitoes were destroyed, Panama
    a. became a healthier place to live and work.
    b. was free of mosquitoes in certain areas of the country.
    c. had fresh drinking water for all its people.

37. Locks are necessary in the Panama Canal because
    a. there are many bandits and few police officers in the area.
    b. ships need different water levels.
    c. the Pacific is a higher body of water than the Atlantic.

38. In contrast to the Suez Canal, the Panama Canal had to be dug
    a. with fewer people and equipment.
    b. through mountains, jungles, and rivers.
    c. through flat desert sands.

39. Unlike the French who had worked on the canal, the Americans
    a. spent huge sums of money.
    b. knew what caused yellow fever and malaria.
    c. used thousands of workers.

40. In both the French and American efforts to build the canal, workers were
    a. plagued by landslides.
    b. without fresh running water.
    c. subjected to cruel treatment.

41. The French should have been able to build the Panama Canal because
    a. The French had built the Suez Canal.
    b. France was a rich nation.
    c. The French were determined to build the Panama Canal.

42. "The French would have succeeded in building the canal if they had been able to control yellow fever and malaria." Which detail supports this idea?
    a. Panama was one of the most disease-ridden areas in the world.
    b. At the time, the French did not know what caused yellow fever and malaria.
    c. Thousands of workers died from yellow fever and malaria.

43. In contrast to the French, the Americans had a better chance of building the canal because
    a. The Americans were better builders than the French.
    b. The Americans, unlike the French, knew the cause of malaria and yellow fever.
    c. The French, unlike the Americans, ran out of money.

44. In Panama's revolt against Colombia, the United States played
    a. a minor role.
    b. an important role.
    c. no role.

45. Other European countries were not as interested in building a canal connecting the Atlantic and Pacific oceans as France was because
    a. they had neither enough money nor workers.
    b. they were not interested in trade.
    c. they had no experience building canals.

46. Spain did not propose the construction of a canal after the Spanish-American War because
    a. it was not at war with Colombia.
    b. its naval fleet was not in the Pacific.
    c. it had signed a treaty with Panama.

47. Ditches were sprayed with oil and swamps were drained because
    a. they were in the way of the canal.
    b. workers often stumbled into them.
    c. mosquitoes bred in them.

48. Choose the correct definition of the word *catch* as it is used in paragraph 8.
    a. that which holds
    b. act of catching
    c. to grasp or seize

49. Choose the correct definition of the word *plague* as it is used in paragraph 9.
    a. troubled
    b. infested
    c. diseased

50. The word *entrusted* in paragraph 3 means
    a. "a job assigned."
    b. "given trust of."
    c. "given responsibility for."

51. The word *negotiations* in paragraph 6 means
    a. "dealings."
    b. "talks."
    c. "planning."

52. The word *locks* in paragraph 9 means
    a. "parts of a firearm."
    b. "mechanical devices."
    c. "water-filled chambers."

Use the map on page AT5 to answer questions 53 through 56.

53. In which direction does the canal go across Panama?
    a. from the northwest to southeast
    b. from the northeast to southwest
    c. from the southwest to northeast

54. Coming into the canal from the Caribbean Sea, a ship passes the city of
    a. Balboa.
    b. Panama City.
    c. Colón.

55. How many locks does the canal have?
    a. 2
    b. 3
    c. 4

56. What is the approximate length of the Panama Canal?
    a. 40 kilometers
    b. 60 kilometers
    c. 80 kilometers

Read the following selection. Then choose the best answer for each question. Mark your answer on the answer sheet.

Another Energy Source for Life

1. For many years, scientists believed that sunlight was the main source of energy for life. Now scientists know that deep in the ocean there is life that uses heat from Earth, rather than the sun, for energy. This major discovery was made while scientists were exploring the Midocean Ridge.

The Midocean Ridge

2. The longest mountain range in the world is at the bottom of the sea. Called the Midocean Ridge, it curves around Earth like the seam of a baseball. The Midocean Ridge extends for 80,000 kilometers.

3. The Midocean Ridge has been mapped by a system called sonar (SOH nar), which stands for <u>so</u>und <u>n</u>avigation <u>a</u>nd <u>r</u>anging. A sound wave, or signal, is sent from a ship. When the sound wave hits an undersea object, it is reflected back. The distance to the object is determined by how long it takes the signal to make the round trip.

4. Although scientists have been able to map the entire length of the Midocean Ridge, they have actually seen only a very small part of it. Descending in tiny submarines, scientists have seen only 64 kilometers of the ridge. Yet, it was along those few kilometers that scientists discovered animals unlike any they had seen before.

Warm-Water Vents

5. The crust of the earth is made up of major sections, called plates. The plates move apart a few centimeters each year, forming valleys, called rifts, that run along the whole Midocean Ridge. While studying rifts in the Pacific Ocean, scientists saw fountains of black material billowing from the ocean floor like smoke coming from a chimney. These were warm-water vents.

Strange Creatures

6. Along the rifts, seawater seeps down through porous rocks, becomes heated, and comes up through the vents. The vent water registers up to 13°C, which is much warmer than the usual deep-sea chill of 2°C. Yet, heat is not the main reason that a multitude of animals gather at these hot springs. As the water rises to the ocean floor, it brings up minerals from inside the earth. The minerals set off a chemical change in bacteria that causes them to multiply rapidly. The great numbers of bacteria nourish larger forms of life. Animals gather at the vents because of the large food supply available there.

7. Many of the animals living near the vents are strange in appearance. Among the strangest are giant worms, some of them 36 centimeters long. The worm is surrounded at one end by a forest of white, tubelike projections. The worm's bright red color is caused by a red blood pigment called hemoglobin (HEE mə gloh bin).

Sound waves are used to map the ocean floor and locate undersea objects.

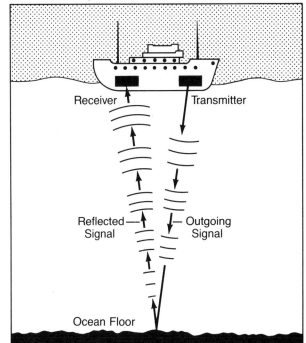

8. The worm is strange in yet another way. It has no eyes, mouth, or stomach. Food and oxygen from the water are absorbed through its more than 300,000 tiny tentacles. Blood carries this nourishment throughout the worm's body.

9. Another strange animal found near the vents belongs to the jellyfish family. Using a threadlike stem, the creature fastens itself to rocks. Attached to the stem is a gas-filled bag that allows the animal to float. Around the bag are hundreds of petal-like projections that have different tasks—some capture food, others ingest it, and still others carry on reproduction.

10. Giant, smooth-shelled clams are also found living near the vents. The clams are about 30 centimeters long. Unlike most clams, which are gray in color, the fleshy inside of these clams is red. The color is caused by hemoglobin.

11. Crabs also live near the vents. Although they look like crabs found in shallow water, they are blind. They belong to a crustacean (krus TAY shən) family not known before. In addition, new species of barnacles (BAR nə klz), leeches, and mussels live near the vents.

New Chain of Life

12. The food chain for animals living near the vents is based on energy from inside the earth, rather than energy from the sun. In the total darkness of the deep sea, 2.5 kilometers below the surface, another source of energy for life has been found.

57. Choose the main idea of paragraph 2.
    a. The longest mountain range in the world is at the bottom of the sea.
    b. Called the Midocean Ridge, it curves around the earth like the seam of a baseball.
    c. The Midocean Ridge extends for 80,000 kilometers.

58. Choose the main idea of paragraph 6.
    a. Yet, heat is not the main reason animals gather at the hot springs.
    b. The minerals set off a chemical change in bacteria that causes them to multiply.
    c. Animals gather at the vents because of the large food supply available there.

59. The main idea of paragraph 8 is that the worm is strange in yet another way. Which detail best supports this main idea?
    a. The worm has more than 300,000 tentacles.
    b. It has no eyes, mouth, or stomach.
    c. Blood carries nourishment throughout its body.

60. Find the main idea of paragraph 10.
    a. The fleshy inside of the clams is red.
    b. The color is caused by hemoglobin.
    c. Also found living near the vents are giant, smooth-shelled clams.

61. When the sound wave in sonar hits an undersea object, the signal is
    a. reflected back.
    b. timed.
    c. charted on a map.

62. The giant worms are red in color because of the presence of
    a. hemoglobin.
    b. hot water.
    c. oxygen.

63. The main reason animals gather at the vents is the
    a. higher temperature.
    b. chemical change.
    c. food supply.

64. Unlike most clams, the fleshy inside of the clams found near the vents is
    a. white.
    b. red.
    c. tasty.

65. In contrast to the usual temperature of deep-sea water, the temperature of vent water is
    a. lower.
    b. higher.
    c. about the same.

66. Why does the animal described in paragraph 9 belong to the jellyfish family?

    a. It captures food through petal-like projections.

    b. It uses a stem to attach itself to rocks.

    c. It looks like a jellyfish.

67. The vent crab is a new species of

    a. crustacean.

    b. barnacle.

    c. hemoglobin.

68. What do vent crabs and shallow-water crabs have in common?

    a. They both live in shallow water.

    b. Their meat is a bright red.

    c. They look alike.

69. In what way are crabs found near vents different from shallow-water crabs?

    a. These crabs are blind.

    b. These crabs have extra claws.

    c. These crabs are about a foot long.

70. In their undersea explorations, scientists

    a. purposely looked for another source of energy for life.

    b. accidentally discovered another source of energy for life.

    c. confidently expected to find another source of energy for life.

71. In further explorations of the Midocean Ridge, scientists are likely to find

    a. more undersea objects.

    b. more warm-water vents.

    c. more sources of energy for life.

72. Choose the correct definition of the word *registers* as it is used in paragraph 6.

    a. keeps a record of

    b. makes an impression

    c. shows on a scale

73. Choose the correct definition of the word *multiply* as it is used in paragraph 6.

    a. grow in number

    b. spread

    c. perform multiplication

74. What is the meaning of the word *wave* in paragraph 3?

    a. signal

    b. section

    c. rifts

75. What is the meaning of the word *multitude* in paragraph 6?

    a. small number

    b. large number

    c. average number

Use the diagram on page AT9 to answer questions 76 through 79.

76. The two basic parts of a ship's sonar unit are the

    a. reflected signal and outgoing signal.

    b. ship and ocean floor.

    c. transmitter and receiver.

77. The outgoing signal is sent by the

    a. ship.

    b. receiver.

    c. transmitter.

78. The outgoing signal is reflected off the

    a. transmitter.

    b. ocean floor.

    c. receiver.

79. The reflected signal is picked up by the

    a. receiver.

    b. transmitter.

    c. ocean floor.

Questions 80 through 83 are word problems. Use the space below each one for your calculations.

80. The battleship *Oregon* had to sail around South America, taking 104 days to complete the trip. If there had been a canal across Panama, the trip would have been about 7,200 kilometers. Assume that the *Oregon* could travel 200 kilometers a day. How much time would the ship have saved if it had gone through the canal?

   a. 14 days

   b. 68 days

   c. Not enough information is given to solve the problem.

81. At point A, a ship sends out a sonar signal showing that the ocean depth is 9,186 meters. At point B, the signal takes 8 seconds to return. The signal travels at 1,531 meters per second. How much deeper is the ocean floor at point B than at point A?

   a. 3,062 meters

   b. 7,346 meters

   c. Not enough information is given to solve the problem.

82. The average temperature of the water near the surface of the Atlantic Ocean is 27°C. The following two temperature readings are taken: 23°C and 30.5°C. Which is closer to the average?

   a. 23°C

   b. 30.5°C

   c. Not enough information is given to solve the problem.

83. The average depth of the Atlantic Ocean is 4,270 meters, and the lowest depth is 8,648 meters. The lowest depth in the Pacific Ocean is 11,033 meters. Which ocean has a greater range between its average depth and its lowest depth?

   a. Atlantic Ocean

   b. Pacific Ocean

   c. Not enough information is given to solve the problem.

Use the following dictionary entry to answer questions 84 through 88.

Use the following index from a science book to answer questions 89 through 94.

fa·vor (fā′vər) *n.* **1** a helpful and kind action [I did my sick friend the *favor* of shopping for her.] **2** liking or approval [The waiter tried to win our *favor*.] **3** a small gift or souvenir [Every guest at the party received a pen as a *favor*.] ◆*v.* **1** to like or approve of [We *favor* any plan for lower taxes.] **2** to help or aid [The dark night *favored* his escape.] **3** to prefer or help in an unfair way [The umpire seemed to *favor* the other team.] **4** to look like [The baby *favors* her mother.] **5** to use gently so as to keep from hurting [He *favors* his injured leg.] —**in favor of,** **1** supporting or approving. **2** to the advantage of. —**in one's favor,** to one's advantage.

Comets, 79–80
Compounds, 125–126, 131–132
Conservation
    air, 483
    fossil fuels, 477
    land, 468–470
    minerals, 473–474
    water, 480–481, 490
Continental drift
    fossils as proof of, 427, 453
    ocean-floor spreading, 404–407, 454
    plate movements, 410–411
    theory, 400–404, 405
Continents, 28–29, 185–186, 199–206
    formation of, 404, 450–452
    margins, shelves, 244–245, 249
Copper
    sources, 141, 333, 470, 471
    uses, 141–142, 470, 472
Core, of earth, 29, 192–193

84. How many noun meanings of the entry word are given?

  a. 5
  b. 2
  c. 3

85. How many verb meanings of the entry word are given?

  a. 3
  b. 5
  c. 2

86. Which of the following is the respelling of the entry word?

  a. fā′vər
  b. —in favor of
  c. [I did my sick friend the *favor* of shopping for her.]

87. Which of the following is a verb meaning of the entry word?

  a. to look like
  b. supporting or approving
  c. a helpful and kind action

88. The second idiom given in the entry is

  a. —liking or approval.
  b. —to the advantage of.
  c. —in one's favor.

89. On what page(s) would you find information on water conservation?

  a. 483
  b. 480–481, 490
  c. 404–407, 545

90. In how many separate parts of the book would you find information on the sources of copper?

  a. 4
  b. 141–147
  c. 2

91. How many subtopics are listed under the topic *Continents*?

  a. 5
  b. 4
  c. 2

92. If the book had information about constellations, after which topic would it be listed?

    a. Compounds
    b. Continental drift
    c. Conservation

93. If the book had information about computers, before which topic would it be listed?

    a. Compounds
    b. Comets
    c. Conservation

94. How many pages does the book have on the uses of copper?

    a. 4
    b. 6
    c. 8

95. To change the meaning of *freezing* to "below freezing," you would add the prefix

    a. *non-*.
    b. *semi-*.
    c. *sub-*.

96. To change the meaning of *danger* to "having danger," you would add the suffix

    a. *-ly*.
    b. *-ous*.
    c. *-ity*.

97. Choose the correct way to divide the word *member* into syllables.

    a. mem ber
    b. memb er
    c. me mber

98. Choose the correct way to divide the word *margin* into syllables.

    a. mar gin
    b. marg in
    c. ma rgin

99. Which of the following shows the accent mark correctly placed?

    a. hon est ly´
    b. hon est´ ly
    c. hon´est ly

100. Which word shows the schwa sound correctly circled?

    a. l(e) gal
    b. hon (e)st
    c. h(u)n der

Name _____

Student Answer Sheet

Test 1	Test 2	Test 3	Test 4
a b c	a b c	a b c	a b c
1 ○ ○ ○	27 ○ ○ ○	57 ○ ○ ○	84 ○ ○ ○
2 ○ ○ ○	28 ○ ○ ○	58 ○ ○ ○	85 ○ ○ ○
3 ○ ○ ○	29 ○ ○ ○	59 ○ ○ ○	86 ○ ○ ○
4 ○ ○ ○	30 ○ ○ ○	60 ○ ○ ○	87 ○ ○ ○
5 ○ ○ ○	31 ○ ○ ○	61 ○ ○ ○	88 ○ ○ ○
6 ○ ○ ○	32 ○ ○ ○	62 ○ ○ ○	89 ○ ○ ○
7 ○ ○ ○	33 ○ ○ ○	63 ○ ○ ○	90 ○ ○ ○
8 ○ ○ ○	34 ○ ○ ○	64 ○ ○ ○	91 ○ ○ ○
9 ○ ○ ○	35 ○ ○ ○	65 ○ ○ ○	92 ○ ○ ○
10 ○ ○ ○	36 ○ ○ ○	66 ○ ○ ○	93 ○ ○ ○
11 ○ ○ ○	37 ○ ○ ○	67 ○ ○ ○	94 ○ ○ ○
12 ○ ○ ○	38 ○ ○ ○	68 ○ ○ ○	95 ○ ○ ○
13 ○ ○ ○	39 ○ ○ ○	69 ○ ○ ○	96 ○ ○ ○
14 ○ ○ ○	40 ○ ○ ○	70 ○ ○ ○	97 ○ ○ ○
15 ○ ○ ○	41 ○ ○ ○	71 ○ ○ ○	98 ○ ○ ○
16 ○ ○ ○	42 ○ ○ ○	72 ○ ○ ○	99 ○ ○ ○
17 ○ ○ ○	43 ○ ○ ○	73 ○ ○ ○	100 ○ ○ ○
18 ○ ○ ○	44 ○ ○ ○	74 ○ ○ ○	
19 ○ ○ ○	45 ○ ○ ○	75 ○ ○ ○	
20 ○ ○ ○	46 ○ ○ ○	76 ○ ○ ○	
21 ○ ○ ○	47 ○ ○ ○	77 ○ ○ ○	
22 ○ ○ ○	48 ○ ○ ○	78 ○ ○ ○	
23 ○ ○ ○	49 ○ ○ ○	79 ○ ○ ○	
24 ○ ○ ○	50 ○ ○ ○	80 ○ ○ ○	
25 ○ ○ ○	51 ○ ○ ○	81 ○ ○ ○	
26 ○ ○ ○	52 ○ ○ ○	82 ○ ○ ○	
	53 ○ ○ ○	83 ○ ○ ○	
	54 ○ ○ ○		
	55 ○ ○ ○		
	56 ○ ○ ○		

	Test 1	Test 2	Test 3	Test 4		
Number Possible	26	30	27	17	Total	100
Number Incorrect	____	____	____	____	Total	____
Score	____	____	____	____	Total	____

AT15

Class Record–Keeping Chart

Name

Test Item	Skill										
1–4	Identifying conflict and resolution										
5–8	Identifying plot										
9–12	Identifying setting										
13–16	Inferring theme										
17–19, 30–32	Inferring the unstated main idea										
20–23	Indentifying point of view										
24, 48–49, 72–73	Recognizing multiple meanings of words										
25–26, 50–52, 74–75	Using context clues										
27–29, 57–58	Identifying the main idea										
33–34, 59–60	Identifying the main idea and supporting details										
35–37, 61–63	Identifying cause and effect										
38–40, 64–65	Comparing and contrasting										
42	Distinguishing fact from opinion										
41, 43–47, 70–71	Making inferences										
53–56	Reading a map										
66–69	Classifying										
76–79	Reading text with diagrams										
80–83	Solving word problems										
84–88	Using a dictionary										
89–94	Using an index										
95-100	Recognizing prefixes, suffixes, syllables, accented syllable, and schwa sound										
	Total Incorrect										
	Score (subtract total incorrect from 100)										

AT16